Local Government from Thatcher to Blair

To Ros Wade and Myriam Wilks-Heeg

Local Government from Thatcher to Blair

The Politics of Creative Autonomy

Hugh Atkinson and Stuart Wilks-Heeg

Polity

Copyright © Hugh Atkinson and Stuart Wilks-Heeg 2000

The right of Hugh Atkinson and Stuart Wilks-Heeg to be identified as authors of this work has been asserted in accordance with the Copyright, Designs and Patents Act 1988.

First published in 2000 by Polity Press in association with Blackwell Publishers Ltd

Editorial office:
Polity Press
65 Bridge Street
Cambridge CB2 1UR, UK

Marketing and production:
Blackwell Publishers Ltd
108 Cowley Road
Oxford OX4 1JF, UK

Published in the USA by
Blackwell Publishers Inc.
350 Main Street
Malden, MA 02148, USA

ISBN 0-7456-2203-8
ISBN 0-7456-2204-6 (pbk)

A CIP catalogue record for this book is available from the British Library.

Library of Congress Cataloging-in-Publication Data

Atkinson, Hugh (Hugh Parker)
    Local government from Thatcher to Blair : the politics of creative autonomy / Hugh Atkinson and Stuart Wilks-Heeg.
        p. cm.
    Includes bibliographical references and index.
    ISBN 0-7456-2203-8 (alk. paper) – ISBN 0-7456-2204-6 (pbk. :alk. paper)
    1. Local government – Great Britain. 2. Great Britain – Politics and government – 1979–1997. 3. Great Britain – Politics and government – 1997-
I. Wilks-Heeg, Stuart. II. Title.

JS3111 .A86 2000
320.8′0941′09048 – dc21   00-033612

Typeset in 10 on 12 pt Sabon
by Best-set Typesetter Ltd., Hong Kong
Printed in Great Britain by MPG Books Ltd, Bodmin, Cornwall

This book is printed on acid-free paper.

Contents

List of Figures and Tables   vii
Preface and Acknowledgements   ix
List of Abbreviations   xii

Introduction   1

Part I   The Context of UK Local Government

1   The Evolution of Local Government in the UK   9
2   Theories of Local Government and Local Governance   31
3   British Local Government since 1979
    Two Decades of Change   55

Part II   Local Government from Thatcher to Major
   Three Dimensions of Change

4   The Financing of Local Government   85
5   The Changing Structure and Shape of Local Government   106
6   Local Government and the Private Sector   122

Part III   Local Government Reinvents Itself?

7   Local Elections, Political Realignment and Change in
    Local Authorities   147
8   Getting Their Own Houses in Order
    *New Directions in Local Government Internal
    Organization*   162

Contents

9   Global Problems, Local Solutions
    Local Government and Sustainable Development   183
10 The Europeanization of British Local Government?   203

Part IV   Sub-national Government under New Labour

11 Towards Regional Government?
    The Introduction of Regional Offices, the Moves towards
    Devolution and the Notion of Regionalism   227
12 Local Government under New Labour   252

Conclusion   270

Notes   275
References   276
Index   293

Figures and Tables

Figures

1.1	Local government structure in England and Wales to 1974	14
1.2	Local government structure in London, 1965–86	17
1.3	Local government structure in England and Wales, 1975–86	19
1.4	Scottish local government, 1974–86	23
4.1	Local authority income by source, 1980/1 and 1995/6	87
4.2	Percentage of general and specified central government grant, 1980/1 and 1995/6	89
5.1	The structure of local government in London and metropolitan areas after 1986	108
5.2	The structure of local government in England after 1998	115
5.3	The structure of local government in Wales and Scotland after 1998	116
7.1	Local and European election turnout, 1984–99	158
10.1	The European function in local authorities	205
11.1	Distribution of seats in the Scottish Parliament, 1999	233
11.2	Distribution of seats in the Welsh Assembly, 1999	241

Tables

1.1	Arguments for and against the creation of unitary authorities	20
6.1	Local authority PFI pathfinder projects	132
7.1	The state of the parties in local government, May 1996	148
7.2	Party control in local government, 1999	150

List of Figures and Tables

8.1	The changing role of LEAs, 1988–94	174
8.2	Local government adoption of strategic management principles	177
10.1	Numbers of sub-national offices in Brussels, 1995	208
11.1	Share of the vote in the Scottish Parliament elections, 1999	233
11.2	Share of the vote in the Welsh Assembly elections, 1999	240
11.3	GDP per capita in the English regions, 1996	245

Preface and Acknowledgements

This is a book about local government in the UK. It is an academic text and we anticipate that most of its readers will be students, teachers and researchers in higher education. The book is written particularly with the undergraduate student in mind and seeks to provide a thorough introduction to local government, including recent important changes under the Labour government. However, we also anticipate that the book will be of interest to a broader readership. In particular, we hope that this book generates debate and discussion among all those concerned about the future of local government. To this end, we would welcome both academic and practitioner comment on the central thesis of this volume: that far from being moribund, British local authorities have found a number of ways of pursuing strategies of creative autonomy.

The idea for this book arose in the immediate aftermath of Labour's victory at the May 1997 general election. Labour's victory brought to an end eighteen consecutive years of Conservative rule. During this period, local government had been subject to a barrage of reforms, which have, in the main, been interpreted as a concerted, and largely successful, attempt to weaken local authorities and centralize the British system of government. Like many others concerned with local government, we asked ourselves whether things were about to change under Labour, whether 'things could only get better' for local authorities. Though it perhaps meant little to the layperson, a Labour government promised important changes in relation to a number of key aspects of local government, such as the abolition of compulsory competitive tendering and greater freedom in the use of capital receipts. More fundamentally, with Labour committed to devolution for Scotland and Wales and to the introduction of new regional bodies in England, the British state was about to experience major changes to its long-established unitary structure, possibly with major implications for local authorities. At the very least, it suggested a reversal of almost two decades of efforts to centralize power in Westminster and Whitehall.

However, as we considered the issue in more depth, we began to wonder whether our questioning was built on the right assumptions. We had never assumed that the Blair government was a saviour riding in to save local government. But we did begin to ask whether local government was actually in need of saving. Certainly, local authorities had suffered under Conservative governments. In particular, they had lost functions and were forced to operate under tight financial constraints. Yet, despite the onslaught, it was evident to us that local government not only remained a sizeable part of the British state, it also continued to be the source of important policy innovation. Moreover, while local government's role had certainly been redefined by eighteen years of Conservative rule, this redefinition had not come entirely from the centre – a great deal of fresh thinking had been done by the local government community itself.

These thoughts were compounded by comparative work we were carrying out at the time on British and German regionalism. Although we could not measure it empirically, we got the impression that, despite constitutional protection and a greater degree of financial autonomy, German local authorities were in some ways less creative and less innovative than their British counterparts. Indeed, to our initial surprise, aspects of British local government were held up as potential models for German local authorities. Germans were speaking of the UK's success in bringing about 'public–private partnerships' at the local level. Prominent local politicians in Frankfurt told us that they felt that, despite the evident problems which the abolition of the Greater London Council had created, local government in Greater London appeared to them to have been more successful in responding to the resultant problems of administrative fragmentation than was the case among the large number of authorities that make up 'Greater Frankfurt'. Perhaps most surprisingly of all, there was praise among German policy-makers for the success of British local authorities in developing local environmental policies.

Looking at British local government from this perspective, we began to realize that, despite the pervasive attempts at centralization, there were a whole host of ways in which local authorities in the UK had sought to defend their independent policy-making role. It was also apparent, however, that this aspect of local government had received scant attention in the academic literature on the subject. It is in this light that we present this work, which we see as providing a corrective to some of the more pessimistic recent analyses of local government.

Preface and Acknowledgements

If local government has undergone a transformation over the past two decades, so too has the nature of scholarship. In an age of information technology, we certainly have fewer people to thank than would have been the case in the late 1970s. We have no secretaries to thank, as we typed the manuscript ourselves. Similarly, since most of the official documentation cited in this work was found on the Internet, we have not found it necessary to pester local government officials, civil servants or librarians with requests for such material. However, there are important functions which computers cannot yet replace, most particularly the task of providing supportive but critical advice to a book's authors. Consequently, we would like to extend our thanks to Alan Harding, Derek Long, Michael Parkinson, Norman Flynn and Tim Field, all of whom provided valuable comments on various parts of the manuscript. We hope that we have been able to respond to at least some of the issues that they raised and would wish to add that they bear no responsibility for what appears under our names. The text also benefited at a later stage from the insightful views of Polity's two anonymous referees. We are also grateful to Rebecca Harkin, our commissioning editor at Polity, who has been supportive of this project since the idea was first mooted in summer 1996.

Particular thanks are also due to our respective partners, Ros Wade and Myriam Wilks-Heeg, for their support and tolerance during the months in which writing this book dominated our lives. Finally, thanks to Martin Theis, Sandy Watson and Shaun McInerney for 'el duende', without which half of this book may never have been written.

The authors and publishers would like to thank the following for permission to reproduce figures and tables:

Blackwell Publishers for tables 8.1 and 8.2 taken from K. Young, 'Reinventing local government? Some evidence assessed', *Public Administration*, vol. 74, no. 3 (1996), pp. 354 and 359 respectively;

Her Majesty's Stationery Office for figures 4.1 and 4.2 taken from *Local Government Financial Statistics*, 1980/81 and 1995/96, Crown copyright is reproduced with the permission of the Controller of Her Majesty's Stationery Office;

Local Government Chronicle for table 6.1 and figure 7.1 taken from *Local Government Chronicle*, special supplement on partnerships, 29 May 1998, p. 14, and *Local Government Chronicle*, 11 June 1999, p. 15, respectively;

Local Government Information Unit for table 7.2 taken from their website http://www.lgiu.gov.uk

Abbreviations

ACC	Association of County Councils
ADC	Association of District Councils
ALA	Association of London Authorities
ALG	Association of London Government
AM	Assembly Member (Wales)
AMA	Association of Metropolitan Authorities
BOOM	Business Opportunities on Merseyside
CAR	Co-operation between Automobile Regions
CCC	Coalfield Communities Campaign
CCLGF	Consultative Council on Local Government Finance
CCT	compulsory competitive tendering
CLD	Commission for Local Democracy
CoSLA	Convention of Scottish Local Authorities
CTC	city technology college
DETR	Department of the Environment, Transport and the Regions
DLO	direct labour organization
DOE	Department of the Environment
DSO	direct service organization
EAGGF	European Agriculture Guarantee and Guidance Fund
EC	European Community
EEC	European Economic Community
ERDF	European Regional Development Fund
ESF	European Social Fund
EU	European Union
EURACOM	European Action for Mining Communities
FPTP	first past the post

GLA	Greater London Authority
GLC	Greater London Council
GMS	grant maintained school
GORs	Government Offices for the Regions
GREA	grant-related expenditure assessment
HAT	housing action trust
IGC	intergovernmental commission
ILEA	Inner London Education Authority
IMF	International Monetary Fund
LBA	London Boroughs Association
LCC	London County Council
LDDC	London Docklands Development Corporation
LEA	local education authority
LFCDA	London Fire and Civil Defence Authority
LGA	Local Government Association
LGIB	Local Government International Bureau
LGMB	Local Government Management Board
LIT	local income tax
LMS	local management of schools
LRT	London Regional Transport
LSVT	large-scale voluntary transfer
MILAN	Motor Industry Local Area Network
MSP	Member of the Scottish Parliament
NCR	New Commitment to Regeneration
NDC	Northern Development Company
NHS	National Health Service
NNDR	national non-domestic rate
PFI	Private Finance Initiative
PRG	Project Review Group
RDA	regional development agency
RDO	regional development organization
RECITE	Regions and Cities in the New Europe
RSG	revenue support grant
SNP	Scottish National Party
SPD	Single Programming Document
SRB	single regeneration budget
SSA	standard spending assessment
STV	single transferable vote
SWS	Schumpeterian workfare state
TEC	training and enterprise council
UDC	urban development corporation
UNCED	United Nations Conference on Environment and Development

Introduction

It is a truism that a great deal has changed in the world of British local government over the past twenty years and that much of this change has been the subject of intense political and media debate. Consequently, even readers who have never previously opened a book on the subject will doubtless be aware of some of the key issues in the recent history of local government in the UK. The huge political fall-out created by the poll tax suggests that memories of the events of a decade ago are likely to linger for some time to come. During 1999, the debate about whether 'Red' Ken Livingstone should be allowed to put himself forward as Labour's candidate for mayor of London revived discussion about the last days of the Greater London Council, abolished some thirteen years previously. Moreover, high-profile changes in local government were not restricted to the 1980s; the debate about the role of local government continues to hit the front pages of the newspapers. When Tony Blair, the Prime Minister, aired public criticisms of public sector employees during the summer of 1999, the Deputy Prime Minister, John Prescott, responded the very next day by saying that 'councils have a long and proud record. It has been local councils and the public sector which have forged a modern society.' And behind the headlines, important changes are taking place. By the time this book is published, Londoners will have voted for the capital's first elected mayor. It is also possible that by the year 2000, at least one other major British city will have opted to introduce similar arrangements.

It is also safe to say that those events in local government which make the headlines are generally just the tip of the iceberg. Since the early 1980s a far greater number of equally significant, if less dramatic, changes have been taking place. In particular, the changes introduced under the Conservative governments of 1979–97 have, in the eyes of many observers, been interpreted as a direct attack on the very notion of local government. Moreover, for those who have experienced the events of the past two decades first hand, working at the 'sharp end' of local government, this interpretation may well appear to be an accurate one. Local authorities have lost important functions over the past ten years, have experienced dramatic reductions in government grants, particularly for capital expenditure, and have been left with little, if any, capacity to raise extra revenues through local taxes. Furthermore, having to deal with constant, and at times contradictory, change emanating from the centre has, without doubt, frustrated local authorities' efforts to deal with specifically local problems. Some in local government today might well suggest that this latter tendency has only been heightened by the recent election of a Labour government, which has launched a series of new local initiatives since coming to power.

This book attempts to grapple with the full range of changes that have taken place in local government over the past two decades. In doing so, it calls into question some of the conventional wisdom that has grown up in academic analyses of local government over the same period. Put simply, we reject the notion that local government under the Conservatives became the defenceless victim of an all-powerful central government for two main reasons. First, many of the government's attempts at centralization were achieved only as a result of persistent legislation over a number of years, others were to fail to achieve their objectives, while some backfired spectacularly. Second, while local authorities have been forced to concede important sources of autonomy, they have also found a variety of ways of protecting and expanding their independent policy-making capacity in other areas. They have done so by forging relationships with actors and institutions, both locally and internationally, which operate outside of the direct control of central government. In other words, local authorities in the UK have pursued a policy of 'creative autonomy'.

The notion of creative autonomy is arguably of particular importance in a British context because, compared to their counterparts elsewhere, local authorities in the UK lack a power of general competence. As we shall see in chapter 1, this means that there are significant legal constraints to what activities local authorities are able to undertake if they have not already been permitted to do so. Although there have been regular attempts by local authorities in the past to pursue independent initiatives, these have received only limited attention in the literature on local government. Moreover, over the past two decades, despite the centralizing policies of the Thatcher and Major governments, such attempts at creative autonomy have been encouraged by wider changes to the context in which local government operates. These changes are multi-farious but include the concern of the European Union to promote subsidiarity in the process of European integration, the international recognition of the importance of local authorities in promoting sustainable development and the growing consensus that economic globalization is enhancing the importance of local policy intervention. The changes, which operate externally to the system of central–local relations, have seen local authorities take on important new roles that are almost certain to expand in future decades.

Given these concerns, this book presents an analysis of the politics of local government rather than a study of the detailed issues of management and service delivery. It focuses particularly on assessing the dynamic tension between attempts at central control and local efforts to realize creative autonomy. In part I of the book we begin by approaching this question both historically and theoretically. Thus, chapter 1 provides an historical overview of the evolution of local government in the UK up to 1979. In this chapter we show how local government's role has expanded, particularly in the second half of the twentieth century as a result of the growth of the welfare state. We also note the way in which local government has been the subject of significant political dispute and draw out a number of examples of ways in which local government has pursued creative autonomy in the past. Our attention then turns in chapter 2 to theoretical approaches to the subject. Here we review a range of theoretical approaches with a particular eye on their value in explaining recent change in local government and the extent to which they may support the creative autonomy thesis. In chapter 3 we provide a detailed overview of policy towards local government during the period of Conservative rule from 1979 to 1997. This chapter questions the extent to which centralization was achieved by the Thatcher and Major governments and outlines the creative autonomy thesis in more depth.

In part II of the book we provide a more detailed assessment of three particular dimensions of change that have impacted significantly on local government in recent years. The first of these, local government finance, constituted the cornerstone of the Conservatives' attempts to centralize power and is explored in chapter 4. We chart the difficulties that the centre experienced in achieving its objectives and again identify a number of examples of creative autonomy on the part of local authorities. The chapter also discusses the failure of the poll tax, which represented the Thatcher government's most far-reaching attempt to control local expenditure. We also note, however, that its subsequent replacement with the council tax did effectively signal the end of significant local financial autonomy. In chapter 5, the focus is on the structure and shape of local government. In the first part of the chapter we assess the major changes to the overall structure of local government introduced under the Conservatives: the abolition of the GLC and the metropolitan counties in 1986 and the appointment of the Local Government Commission in 1992. The second part of the chapter looks at the changing nature of local governance, particularly the rise of non-elected local government and the significance of these developments for local authorities. We suggest that, although such changes were instigated by governments intent on curtailing local authorities' policy-making role, they have in fact enabled councils to emerge as the lead strategic agencies within complex networks of local governance.

The theme of the changing nature of local governance is continued in chapter 6, where we discuss the significance of local authority relationships with the private sector. Three particular types of relationship are highlighted: compulsory competitive tendering (CCT), the Private Finance Initiative (PFI) and public–private partnerships. We show that, despite concerted central government attempts to enhance the private sector's role in service delivery, CCT has not led to the widespread contracting-out of local government services that was originally envisaged. Likewise, the PFI, which was introduced in 1992 with the intention of encouraging private sector funding of public sector capital projects, has also experienced a number of problems in relation to its original objectives. Indeed, local government PFI projects have only emerged since a number of changes were introduced by the Labour government following its election in 1997. We also show how significant changes have been brought about at a local level through the growth of public–private partnerships, many of which were instigated by Labour local authorities, independently of central government. We highlight the significance of such initiatives and suggest that partnership formation has been an important source of creative autonomy for cash-strapped local councils.

Such examples of the means by which local government has found ways of reinventing itself are explored in more depth in part III of the book. This discussion begins in chapter 7 with an analysis of recent political change in local authorities. We discuss recent electoral trends in local government and point to the worrying decline in turnout. However, we also show how the virtual elimination of the Conservatives from local government in the mid-1990s proved to be an important catalyst for change in local government, leading to greater levels of cross-party co-operation. The focus shifts in chapter 8 to local authority internal organization. In this chapter we chart the long-run concern to reform the 'traditional' model of local authority organization and note the highly political nature of the debate. Particular attention is given to showing how the notion of the 'enabling authority', initially inspired by a new-right vision of the future of local government, has been adopted by local authorities in the radically redefined form of community governance. We suggest that the organizational models which have had lasting influence are those developed by local authorities rather than those imposed by the centre.

The focus in chapter 9 is on the role of local authorities in promoting sustainable development. The chapter charts the way in which local government has become increasingly involved in this policy area and notes that this development has had relatively little to do with central government policy. Using the example of Agenda 21, we show how a number of local authorities have used the sustainable development agenda as a basis for independent policy development at the local level. While this trend is far from universal, its significance should not be denied. Much the same conclusion is reached in the discussion of the Europeanization of local government in chapter 10. Here, we demonstrate that there are a number of ways in which local authorities have become engaged in the process of European integration, many of which occur beyond the reach of central government. While our analysis suggests that claims about the hollowing-out of the nation-state may have been exaggerated, we propose that the European Union has presented local government with a significant source of creative autonomy.

Part IV of the book deals with recent changes to local government introduced by the Labour government and, consequently, is most speculative of all. In chapter 11 we look at the rise of the regional agenda in the UK and chart the steps taken by Labour in introducing devolution to Scotland and Wales and new regional institutions in England. We discuss the rationale for these reforms and assess their significance for local authorities. Finally, chapter 12 considers the government's intentions to modernize local government through a number of reforms, ranging from the creation of the Greater London Authority through to the introduction of Best Value. We suggest that, while many of the proposed reforms will be welcomed in the local government community, they fall far short of reversing the trend towards centralization in recent years. In particular, local authorities will not be returned any significant degree of financial freedom for the foreseeable future.

Although it remains unclear as to what the future may bring for local government, the developments charted in this book suggest that this is not a prospect which local authorities should reflect on gloomily. Indeed, the evidence that local authorities enjoyed at least some success in defending their autonomy under eighteen years of centralizing Conservative rule should make them relatively sanguine about their prospects under the current administration. While there will be no return under Labour to the days of local authorities as providers of extensive public services in an expanding welfare state, every opportunity exists for local government to re-establish itself at the heart of British political life.

Part I
The Context of UK Local Government

1

The Evolution of Local Government in the UK

Introduction

This chapter provides a broad-brush overview of the development of British local government over the past 150 years. This period has seen an expanding role for local government, with a growing recognition that it has a key role to play in the delivery of public services. At the same time, however, there have been important limits in the extent to which local authorities have been able to define this role themselves. Of particular significance is the fact that local government in the UK has, since its inception, operated under the broad constitutional principle of *ultra vires* (Chandler, 1996; Loughlin, 1997). Put simply, it has been permitted to act only in those areas where it is allowed to do so by virtue of Acts of Parliament. Consequently, there have been recurring tensions arising from the growing importance of local government in service delivery and the rather circumscribed role that local government is formally accorded. These tensions are reflected in, among other things, persistent central attempts to restructure local government and regular efforts among local authorities to assert a more independent role.

The chapter is divided into six sections. First, it begins with a discussion of the purpose of local government. Second, it charts the development of local government in the nineteenth century and assesses a number of reforms to its structure and organization. In the third section, developments in the structure and role of local government in the twentieth century in the period up to 1979 are discussed. Fourth, the chapter then turns to analyse some of the various factors which have driven the process of local government reform. Fifth, the causes and consequences

9

of increasing politicization of local government from the latter part of the twentieth century are assessed. The final section notes the growing role of local government in the period after the Second World War, and outlines the broad cross-party consensus about its key role in the development of the welfare state, a consensus that began to unravel in the mid-1970s.

Why Local Government?

Before we look at the historical development of local government in the UK, it is important that we analyse the rationale behind it. The case for local government can be analysed in terms of the two interconnected themes of democracy and effectiveness.

Democracy

A number of democratic arguments have been put forward to advance the case for local government. First, local government is closer to local people than central government and is consequently more accountable. Second, it creates multiple centres of power that act as an important brake on an overweening central state (Jones and Stewart, 1985). Thus, local government encourages pluralism. The Widdicombe Report in 1986 noted that 'the case for pluralism is that power should not be concentrated in one organisation of state, but should be dispersed, thereby providing political checks and balances, and a restraint on arbitrary government and absolutism' (Widdicombe, 1986, p. 48). Third, elected local government buttresses democracy by encouraging and facilitating the participation of the electorate, (Wilson and Game, 1998). Sharpe (1970, p. 160) speaks of the 'democratic primacy' of local government over central government 'because it does enable more people to participate in their own government'. This participation may take the form of being an elected councillor, being active in a local pressure group, or simply voting in local elections.

However, the democratic value of local government is open to challenge. Voter turnout at the local level is relatively low: under 40 per cent in local elections recently (Wilson and Game, 1998, p. 205). In some cities, such as Liverpool, it has fallen as low as 25 per cent. This reflects a fair degree of voter apathy and suggests a weakness in local democracy. In addition, voters are increasingly using local elections as referenda on central government policies, rather than passing judgement on the acceptability or otherwise of local services, a trend encouraged, if not fostered, by national government and the main political parties. Such developments serve to undermine the notion of local accountability.

Goldsmith (1986, p. 2) has spoken of the role of local government 'as the advocate of a locality'. Indeed, the local government reforms of the current Labour government lay some stress on this. However, Goldsmith goes on to concede that, given the highly centralized nature of the British state, a situation exacerbated by the reforms of successive Conservative governments from 1979 to 1997, the voice of localities often goes unheard. The notion of locality is also undermined, it has been argued, by the fact that the UK 'has larger, less community based local authorities than almost any other liberal democracy' (Chandler, 1996, p. 12).

Effectiveness

The second key element in the case for local government are arguments about its effectiveness as a form of state intervention. These arguments are, to a significant degree, based on the supposed advantages of the much-vaunted concept of subsidiarity. While remaining a problematic concept, its broad thrust is one of decentralization, in that it advocates that public policy decisions should be made at the most appropriate level and as close to the local level as practicably possible. A number of arguments flow from this principle. First, local government is in the best position to provide the most appropriate local response to a particular issue, given its local knowledge. Second, it allows for diversity and flexibility. Local services can be matched to local needs, which vary from 'locality to locality' (Jones and Stewart, 1985, p. 5). As Wilson and Game (1998, p. 35) note, 'local councils on the spot ought to be able to identify better and faster than central government the most appropriate response to any local situation'. This responsiveness is based on local knowledge and the availability of specialist staff. Third, local government, by virtue of the fact that it is local, is more accessible to the local community than is the centre. It is therefore more responsive to complaints about service quality. This has a beneficial impact on service delivery.

Fourth, local government can act as a test bed for new and innovative approaches to policy delivery (Jones and Stewart, 1985). This aids creativity at the local level, and provides important pointers for local authorities and government in general. Under the previous Conservative government, a number of local authorities, among them Norfolk, were used to test a nursery school vouchers scheme. Under the current Labour government, a number of local authorities have bid to take part in a pilot project for road pricing and workplace car levies. Initiatives also come from local authorities themselves. Oxford, for example, has introduced a licensed rickshaw taxi service with the aim of easing inner city congestion and reducing pollution. The London borough of Croydon, in conjunction with the private sector, reintroduced trams to Croydon in 1999, again with the objective of tackling the traffic problems and helping the environment. The first door-to-door recycling scheme was introduced in Milton Keynes. Best practice arising from such policy experimentation is shared and disseminated through bodies such as the Audit Commission, the Local Government Management Board (LGMB) and, more recently, the Local Democracy Network. Finally, and on a practical level, it simply is not possible or desirable to run a country the size of the UK and with a population of over 50 million people from the centre. The result would be communication overload.

However, there are problems in relation to local government effectiveness. First, there is the question of diversity in service response. This could well result in inconsistencies. Why should services be available in one local authority but not in another? One might argue, of course, that local people can express any dissatisfaction with service delivery through the ballot box. However, elections tend to be unsatisfactory instruments for passing comment on specific issues. Rather voters are presented with a package of policies by political parties. Second, local authorities, as large bureaucratic organizations, can become insulated from the electorate, particularly in areas where a single party has a large 'natural' majority or where local electoral turnout is very low. Clearly, in such cases responsiveness is likely to be undermined.

The Origins of Local Government

The UK has a long and well-established local government system that has played an important role in directing and shaping major aspects of public policy. The earliest origins of local government in Britain can be traced back to medieval times when a number of local boroughs were governed by Royal Charter. As one example, Kingston-upon-Hull was granted a charter in 1299 by Edward I. Throughout the following centuries local government continued to grow, albeit in a rather *ad hoc* and piecemeal fashion in response to particular issues and problems.

Local government reform in the nineteenth century

The most significant developments in the growth of local government have their genesis in the process of industrialization that gathered momentum from the middle of the nineteenth century onwards. This process brought with it a complex pattern of social and economic problems. The exigencies of industrialization produced large movements of population from rural to urban areas. There developed an increasing realization among policy-makers that the state had to make provision for the increasing numbers of industrialized workers and their families in areas such as education, housing, public health and sanitation. The situation required a more interventionist stand by government than had hitherto been the case.

The initial outcome was the setting-up of a series of single-purpose and *ad hoc* bodies charged with the responsibility of meeting the needs of the new industrialized age. Local boroughs, many dating back to medieval times and largely controlled by landowning interests, continued to operate alongside such bodies. The result was a complex myriad of bodies providing a wide range of services that failed to match the needs of an increasingly urbanized and complex society. There were increasing calls for change. The 1835 Municipal Corporations Act was the outcome.

The philosophy underpinning the Act was a growing recognition of the importance of the rapidly expanding towns and cities. It set up 178 elected municipal councils in the largest towns and cities with a variety of powers and introduced democratic procedures for the election of borough councillors. The Act represented the early emergence of the modern system of local government as we understand it today. The mid to late nineteenth century was a pioneering time for local government. Some 120 years ago, the city of Birmingham, under the leadership of Joseph Chamberlain, pioneered a form of municipal enterprise. Concerned by slums in the city centre, Chamberlain decided that the city council (then known as the corporation) should buy the land, demolish the slums and lease everything to private developers. A new city began to emerge in 1878. The council also municipalized electricity, gas and transport services. It used the profits from such enterprises to keep down local taxes.

However, the overall local government system was far from coherent. Essentially it was a patchwork quilt of appointed and elected bodies, both single and multi-purpose. It was to be fifty-three years, moreover, before the next important change to the structure of local government took place. As the end of the nineteenth century approached, there was a growing recognition that the local government system was out of kilter with the requirements of a developing industrialized society. The 1888 Local Government Act was intended to address this problem. It created sixty-two county councils, largely though not exclusively in rural areas, and sixty-one all-purpose bodies, known as county boroughs, principally in the urban areas across England and Wales. The picture in the sixty-

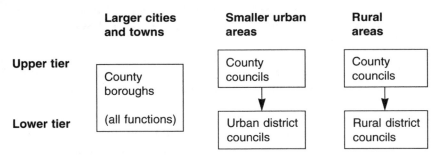

Figure 1.1 Local government structure in England and Wales to 1974

two county councils was complicated by the 1894 Local Government Act, which introduced district councils, both urban and rural (see figure 1.1). The 1899 Local Government Act brought reform to London with the setting-up of a two-tier system comprising the London County Council (LCC) and the borough councils. Territory was taken from the counties of Kent, Middlesex and Surrey. All the authorities created in these reforms were directly elected: that is, with the exception of the aldermen. Aldermen tended to be 'senior and experienced councillors who were appointed by elected councillors to bolster their numbers by up to an additional third, and to add expertise and continuity' (Wilson and Game, 1998, p. 219). The aldermen, and their Scottish equivalents, bailies, survived until their abolition in the local government reforms of the early 1970s.

The original rationale for these reforms had been to create a two-tier system of local government for the bulk of England and Wales. However, a growing lobby developed in the urban areas, with many towns and cities concerned about what they perceived as a loss of autonomy to the county councils. The success of this lobby meant that the new county boroughs were to become responsible for a wide range of services in their respective areas. Though they were abolished in the local government reforms of 1972, the whole question of unitary local authorities was to be a central feature of the deliberations of the Local Government Commission in the 1990s (see chapter 5).

The county councils were originally given responsibility for only a limited number of services. However, their role was to expand considerably into the twentieth country, especially with the development of the welfare state, as they took on responsibility in areas such as education and social welfare. As a second tier, the district councils were charged with relatively few services, the counties being the key service providers. Such a limited role was a source of periodic resentment in some district councils, which were irritated by what they perceived as the dominance of the counties. This issue again came to the fore in the deliberations of the Local Government Commission in the 1990s.

Reform in the Twentieth Century

Following the reforms of the late nineteenth century, the structure of local government remained largely unchanged for over sixty years. However, the debate about local government structures still continued with doubts raised about the appropriateness of existing arrangements. For example, in the Second World War, experience demonstrated that the established local government institutions did not meet with the requirements of local administration in a time of total war (Alexander, 1982). As a consequence, Administrative Regions were set up under the direction of an appointed Regional Commissioner. Such reforms were driven to a large extent by 'the demands of the emergency and the fear of invasion or of the destruction of a government centralised in London' (Alexander, 1982, p. 11). However, it also revealed, as Robson (1948, p. 39) has noted, a 'serious lacuna which local authorities should not have overlooked'. In 1940, a government-commissioned report identified large shifts in population to the major urban conurbations, which had to a large extent overtaken the boundaries established at the end of the nineteenth century (Barlow, 1940). It argued that the structure of local government taken from the previous century was established 'in conditions vastly different from those of today. With but rare exceptions the important industrial towns have long outgrown their boundaries as local government units' (para. 151). The report was also critical of the detrimental effects on services such as housing and areas such as planning due to the number of overlapping authorities.

In 1945, the government produced a White Paper on local government in England and Wales (HMSO, 1945), which, in turn, led to the establishment of the Local Government Boundary Commission. Crucially, however, issues such as the most appropriate type and size of local government unit for particular services were excluded from the Commission's brief. The Commission was critical of its lack of jurisdiction over functions (Alexander, 1982). It did, in fact, make recommendations to alter the distribution of functions between the tiers of local government, proposing a new type of local government unit: 'an all purpose urban county council for each of twenty large towns and conurbations' (p. 14). However, the proposal was not implemented by the Labour government for two principal reasons. First, it would have harmed the local electoral prospects of the Labour Party (Elcock, 1982). Second, the minister responsible for local government, Aneurin Bevan, did not view it as a policy priority. For him, the key focus was on the other part of his policy brief, health, and in particular the establishment of the National Health Service (NHS).

There were few developments for the next decade until the Conservatives, who had been elected to government in 1951, set up a Royal Commission on the Local Government of Greater London in 1957. This was followed a year later by another Local Government Royal Commission, this time for England and Wales. The 1958 Royal Commission produced little substantive change. Alexander (1982, p. 17) identifies two particular reasons for this. First, the workings of the Commission were effectively skewed in favour of the status quo. For example, the county boroughs had to make a special case for any extension of their boundaries. Second, the final decision on the Commission's recommendations rested with the minister in charge. Perhaps inevitably, he fell prey to political pressures, particularly from those lobbying to maintain civic pride. A recommendation to merge Rutland, the smallest county in England, with neighbouring Leicestershire was rejected by the minister, Keith Joseph, after strong lobbying by various groups in Rutland, including the local Conservative Party which controlled the local council. For example, Joseph, together with his Labour successor, Richard Crossman, 'delayed, watered down, and rejected recommendations made by the Commission' (Alexander, 1982, p. 18).

Local government reform in Greater London

In contrast to the rest of England and Wales, the late 1950s and early 1960s witnessed significant developments in the structure and shape of London's local government structures. Changes were long overdue. Indeed, the structure of London local government had remained largely unchanged since the end of the nineteenth century. However, it was becoming increasingly apparent that the boundaries of the LCC had simply been outgrown by the expanding conurbation that was London. The economic and social reality of London was thus out of kilter with its local government structures. Factors such as population drift, which had been identified by the Barlow Report in 1940, had if anything intensified. Indeed, Barlow had recommended changes to London local government. The Herbert Commission, set up in 1957, was charged with reviewing London local government (Herbert, 1960). It was the first truly comprehensive review of local government in London since an earlier Royal Commission in 1923 had delivered a divided report. Its delibera-

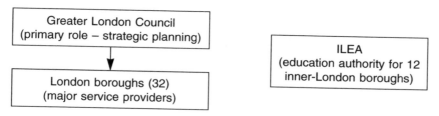

Figure 1.2 Local government structure in London, 1965–86

tions culminated in the 1963 London Government Act. The LCC was replaced by a much larger Greater London Council (GLC) together with thirty-two London boroughs. The ancient City of London Corporation remained untouched and independent from the GLC. In addition, the Inner London Education Authority (ILEA) was set up, charged with responsibility for the education service within the boundaries of the former LCC (see figure 1.2).

Alexander (1982, p. 22) argues that the work of the Herbert Commission highlighted the inadequacies of the 1958 Local Government Commission, which had been shackled 'by the need to stay within the confines of the existing county and county borough pattern'. By contrast, the report of the Herbert Commission was 'independent, authoritative, radical, and unanimous' (p. 21). However, the findings of Herbert were still the subject of significant opposition. The Conservatives lobbied with some success for some parts of Surrey to be excluded from the proposed GLC. The Labour Party in London, which controlled the LCC, was concerned about the electoral implications of the proposed reforms, although its attempt to block them failed. The Conservative government of the time did, however, make concessions, such as establishing ILEA to serve the twelve new boroughs in the old LCC area. Alexander is critical of this decision, arguing that 'the creation of ILEA as a single-purpose indirectly elected local authority . . . clearly ran counter to the historic trend towards all-purpose or multi-purpose authorities' (p. 22). However, the policy can be justified on two grounds. First, the creation of ILEA meant that the education service in inner London did not have to be broken up, thus avoiding disruption. Second, handing the education service to the individual twelve inner London boroughs would have resulted in some of the smallest education authorities in Europe, presenting problems in terms of economies of scale and the delivery of specialist services.

Alexander argues that the result of the bargaining and concessions that took place was a less rational outcome than that originally proposed by the Herbert Commission. Yet, while there may be a degree of truth in this view, it also neglects a key point. The whole issue of local reform and structure is not merely a technical issue, requiring rational solutions, whatever they may be. Rather, as this book will seek to demonstrate, it is a highly contentious and subjective area shot through with ideology and politics. The experience of the Herbert Commission demonstrated that local authorities cannot simply be forced into actions: they will fight to defend their interests.

The new London local government structure, which came into effect in 1965, was a two-tier one. The top-tier GLC was seen as having broad responsibility in the areas of strategic planning and co-ordination. Responsibility for direct service delivery fell, in the main, to the thirty-two boroughs. The GLC did, however, have some functional responsibilities. These included housing (the boroughs also had responsibility here), the London Ambulance Service, fire and civil defence, and refuse disposal. However, the GLC was the subject of criticism almost from its inception. In particular, it was argued that it had failed to deliver on its strategic mission. Tensions surfaced between the two tiers of local government in London. This was particularly the case in the relationship between some of the outer London boroughs and the GLC. Such tensions were often, but not exclusively, based on ideological differences. For example, the Conservative-controlled London borough of Bromley actually took the Labour-controlled GLC to the High Court in 1981 over the latter's 'Fares Fair' policy (Lansley, Goss and Wolmar, 1989; Atkinson, 1996). In addition, the 1980s saw a series of high-profile clashes between the GLC and the Conservative government, culminating in the decision to abolish the GLC in 1986 (see chapter 5).

Local government reform in the 1970s: the case of England and Wales

Changes to the local government structure outside London were introduced in 1974. A number of factors drove the process of change. It was becoming increasingly evident, as in the case of London, that a system of local government designed at the end of the nineteenth century did not meet the requirements of the last third of the twentieth century. There was, in effect, a mismatch between institutional arrangements at the local level and the reality of economic and social life. Significant shifts in population had occurred, especially in the period since the end of the Second World War, and local structures had not been adjusted accordingly.

There was significant divergence in the size of local authorities. For example, Lancashire county council had a huge population of some 2.2 million. This contrasted with Rutland County Council, where the population was a mere 27,000. This led to disparities in the resources avail-

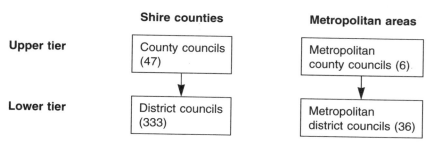

Figure 1.3 Local government structure in England and Wales, 1975–86

able to local authorities and had an impact on the services they provided. The system had also resulted in fragmentation. As an illustration of this, the system of county boroughs and county councils, each with its own policy responsibilities, had resulted in a number of tensions, and was a barrier to effective strategic co-ordination in areas such as planning and transport.

Following the 1972 Local Government Act, a two-tier system of local government was introduced in England and Wales (see figure 1.3). The upper tier consisted of thirty-nine English and eight Welsh county councils, and six metropolitan county councils. The metropolitan county councils were established in the large conurbations of Greater Manchester, Merseyside, South Yorkshire, Tyne and Wear, the West Midlands and West Yorkshire. The intended role of these authorities, like that of the GLC created some ten years earlier, was to provide strategic co-ordination and oversight in areas such as transport and planning. The bottom tier of metropolitan districts was responsible for the delivery of the bulk of services. By contrast, in the non-metropolitan areas, the top-tier county councils were responsible for the majority of high-profile services.

The original impetus for reform came from the deliberations of the Redcliffe-Maud Royal Commission, which was set up by the then Labour Government in 1966 to review the structure, workings and functions of local government in England (Redcliffe-Maud, 1969). There was no Royal Commission for Wales. Instead, a White Paper was published by the Secretary of State for Wales, setting out various proposals and recommendations. The final recommendations of Redcliffe-Maud and the reactions of central government towards them cast an interesting light on the continuing debate about the respective merits of a unitary as opposed to a two-tier system of local government. As noted above, the reforms implemented in 1974 created a two-tier system of local government for the whole of England and Wales. The Redcliffe-Maud

Table 1.1 Arguments for and against the creation of unitary authorities

For	Against
Efficiency	
The two-tier system means that decision making is often slowed down and delayed because of the overlapping and duplication of functions between the tiers.	The problems of overlap and duplication are very limited. Counties and districts have clearly distinctive tasks and share competence only in areas such as land-use planning.
Economy	
The two-tier system is costly and uneconomic. Unitary authorities reduce administrative costs by decreasing the total number of local authorities.	The creation of smaller authorities means the loss of economies of scale achieved by providing services to a larger population and across a wider area.
Effectiveness	
Granting the full set of local government functions to single authorities enables them to integrate services more efficiently and tackle problems more comprehensively: unitary authorities would improve the quality of local services.	The creation of smaller, unitary authorities means the loss of essential strategic functions. Co-ordination of services such as transport and land-use planning becomes more difficult and creates tensions between authorities. Some services, such as specialist education, need to be provided on a larger scale to be viable.
Democracy	
Voters find the division between district and county councils confusing and are unsure which services are provided by which tier. Creating all-purpose authorities removes this confusion and improves the democratic process. Unitary authorities promote local democracy because councils are 'closer' to the populations which they serve.	Voters are perfectly able to distinguish between the two-tiers and may have different preferences for district and county level government. The need for unitary authorities to create forums such as joint boards to replace the broader strategic functions of county councils means that certain policy decisions are made outside of the formal democratic process. The creation of unitary authorities removes the existence of smaller, more accountable district councils.

Commission came to some very different conclusions. However, before we look at Redcliffe-Maud in more detail, we need to set it in context by looking at the question of local government reform in general terms.

Pressure for change in local government structures emanates from a variety of factors. One key factor is where 'social and economic change' takes place 'without concomitant change in administrative structures' (Pycroft, 1995, p. 51). It has been argued that, while we have witnessed rapid changes in the urban environment over the last fifty years, 'administrative reform has suffered from inertia' (p. 51). While this overstates the case somewhat, it is certainly true that local government administrative units do not always fit with the geographic region with which people identify (Bennett, 1993; Cochrane, 1991). Specifically, Pycroft highlights two dysfunctions of local government structure: under-bounding and over-bounding. Under-bounding occurs where 'people's activity spaces cross over the administrative spaces creating spill-over effects, confusing the lines of representation and finance' (Pycroft, 1995, p. 51). The local authority is simply too small. In the case of over-bounding, 'the local authority is too large, containing within its boundaries multiple activity spaces and diluting the sense of common identity' (p. 51).

For Redcliffe-Maude, the problem was one of under-bounding. It recommended major changes to the historical boundaries of English local government. Its recommendations had two strands. First, in the large urban conurbations of Birmingham, Liverpool and Manchester, a two-tier system of metropolitan government, similar to that of London, was proposed. Second, for the rest of England, the proposal was for the creation of fifty-eight unitary authorities. However, it is worth noting that one of the Commission's members, Derek Senior, issued a minority report proposing a two-tier system for the whole of England with more metropolitan areas. The remainder of the country was to be divided into regions and districts. The rejection of the Commission's majority findings by the Conservative government of Edward Heath, and its decision to go for a two-tier structure, provoked a number of criticisms. It was claimed that the reforms had failed to address the problems of poor bounding and that many local government structures still remained confusing, unaccountable, inefficient and remote (Byrne, 1994). Such criticisms have a great deal of validity. Of equal significance, however, is how these two differing conclusions reflect the very subjective and problematic nature of local government structures and the question of unitary versus two-tier local government. This debate, which has continued until the pre-sent day, revolves around the relative advantages and disadvantages of unitary and two-tier local government structures (see table 1.1). The issue was revisited most recently in the deliberations of the Local Government Commission in 1992 (see chapter 5).

As far as Wales is concerned, in 1967 the Secretary of State for Wales had issued proposals for local government reform which included the creation of new and larger county and district councils. The new system was to be a two-tier one except in the south, where the county boroughs of Swansea, Cardiff and Newport were to be retained as all-purpose authorities. However, these proposals were changed after Redcliffe-Maude published its recommendations in 1969. The eventual outcome for Wales was a two-tier system for the whole of the Principality, comprising eight non-metropolitan councils, and below them thirty-seven non-metropolitan district councils.

A number of other reforms took place in the 1970s that affected local government in England and Wales. First, responsibility for the provision of water supplies, sewerage and drainage was switched to the newly created regional water authorities under the 1973 Water Act. Second, local authorities lost a number of health functions as part of the 1974 reorganization of the NHS. Third, the metropolitan counties and the GLC became responsible for public transport, excluding British Rail services, in the areas they served.

Local government reform in Scotland

By the end of the nineteenth century, local government structures in Scotland were more complex than those of England and Wales. Elected county councils were set up in the local government reforms of 1889. At the same time, Scotland's four largest cities – Glasgow, Edinburgh, Aberdeen and Dundee – were given a status comparable to that of the English county boroughs. The system set up at this time remained broadly the same until the reforms of the mid-1970s. In April 1975, a two-tier system was established, consisting of nine regional councils and fifty-three district councils. In addition, three island councils were set up as all-purpose unitary authorities (see figure 1.4). The new arrangements drew heavily on the recommendations of the Royal Commission, chaired by Lord Wheatley, which had been created to look at the whole question of reform (Wheatley, 1969).

The new system came in for a number of criticisms (Chandler, 1996). Some of the larger regional councils were criticized for being inaccessible and remote. Strathclyde, for example, had a population of some 2.5 million. There was considerable divergence in the size of local government units. Strathclyde's population compared to 100,000 in the Borders regional council. The populations in the three island councils ranged from 20,000 to 30,000. Tensions developed between the two tiers of local government where responsibility for services was shared.

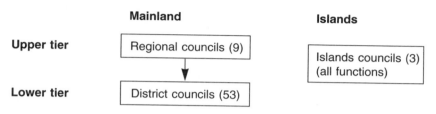

Figure 1.4 Scottish local government, 1974–86

Community and parish councils – the third tier of British local government

Reference has already been made to the two-tier system of local government introduced in the UK in 1974. However, such a description does not do full justice to the nature of local politics. In fact, for a very long time, there has been another tier of local government comprised of parish councils in England and community councils in Scotland and Wales. For some commentators, they survived the reorganization of the early 1970s not only largely intact but with their 'powers in some respect enhanced' (Elcock, 1982, p. 35). They are located predominantly in rural areas and have responsibility for basic services such as the maintenance of footpaths and street lighting and amenities such as village halls and playing fields. They provide an important channel of communication between local people and the other tiers of local government and indeed other public agencies, acting as a pressure group on behalf of local people. Though both their functions and resources are limited, community and parish councils play their part in the workings of local democracy.

Northern Ireland

The current system of local government in Northern Ireland has it basis in the 1970 Macrory Report (Macrory, 1970). The report arose from pressures and demands in the 1960s for modernization of the system of local government in Northern Ireland, paralleling demands for reform in England, Wales and Scotland. The principal organizational problem was the large number of small local authorities (seventy-three councils for a population of 1.5 million) with a small rate base and therefore limited finances. There was also an important political imperative shaping the reform process with 'grievances expressed by the minority (nationalist) community over religious discrimination by some local authorities in employment and housing' (Knox, 1998, p. 3). The Macrory Report divided services into regional services (requiring large spatial areas) and district services (suitable for small areas). The devolved parliament of Northern Ireland, Stormont, was to take responsibility for regional services, with twenty-six local councils responsible for district services. However, the Macrory Report was overtaken by the onset of the so-called 'troubles' in Northern Ireland and the abolition of Stormont in 1972, direct rule being introduced from London in its place. Key services such as education, housing, personal social services, roads, water and sewerage became the responsibility of Northern Ireland-wide public agencies. The functions of the twenty-six local district councils were limited to such things as leisure services, refuse collection, street cleaning and licensing.

As a result, it has been noted that local government in Northern Ireland has a smaller scope of activity than its counterparts elsewhere (Meehan, 1999). For example, in 1997/8, net spending for local authorities in the province amounted to a figure in the region of £230 million. This represents less than 3 per cent of total Northern Ireland public expenditure (Department of the Environment for Northern Ireland, 1997). However, other commentators strike a more optimistic tone. Knox (1998, p. 2) argues that, despite their limited budgets, locally elected councillors remain the 'most accessible source for constituents with concerns about centrally provided services'. Furthermore, since 1992 local councils have been permitted to spend rates of up to five pence in the pound on economic development. This amounted to some £9 million in the financial year 1995/6 (Department of the Environment for Northern Ireland, 1997). Though the figure is small compared to the budgets of central government agencies, councils have been energetic in their use of the funds available to them (Knox, 1998, p. 6). They have in effect achieved some degree of creative autonomy. This has involved establishing networks with local businesses and the setting-up of arm's-length economic development bodies. Some councils have 'used their limited resources as seed-corn finance or matching grants to tap into larger EC funding sources' (p. 6). One study has highlighted the key role played by local authorities as mediators and co-ordinators between local communities and regional agencies. It also highlighted their potential for attracting substantial funds (Scott and Hoye, 1996, p. 231).

The Factors Involved in the Structure and Reform of Local Government

The nature of local government structure, organization and reorganization is complex and problematic. There are no off-the-shelf solutions.

There is no holy grail. Indeed, the history of local government reform in the UK is one of controversy and argument. There are many questions to be answered. For example, what is the most appropriate size of local government units for particular services? Is a two-tier system of local government preferable to a unitary one? In a very real sense, reorganization can be endless. We can, however, identify a number of explanations and reasons for local government structural reform.

First, it is argued that larger spatial areas provide greater equalization in service provision. This was one element in the 1974 local government reorganization. Mention has already been made of the difference in the size of county councils before 1974. This can lead to disparity in resources and a consequent variation in quality and level of service. In addition, some services, such as special education, can only be provided in larger spatial areas, since they require a critical mass of recipients to make them viable. Second, some contend that larger local government units are more efficient. The Herbert Commission on London local government made such an assumption, albeit without empirical data to back it up. Furthermore, the Scottish local government regions, which were set up in 1974 and were among the largest local government units in Europe, came in for considerable criticism for their inefficiency and lack of effectiveness. In determining size, there is also a balance to be struck between efficiency and effectiveness on the one hand and democracy and accountability on the other. Conversely, one can argue that the two go hand in hand. Larger units may or may not lead to efficiency gains. On the other hand, there is the 'small is beautiful' argument. Smaller units may lend themselves to a greater sense of political identity among people, improving the accountability of local government and hence the quality of local services.

Third, from a rational administrative perspective, it is argued that some policy areas are better handled in larger spatial areas: for example, land use planning and transport. This was part of the rationale for the creation of the GLC and the metropolitan counties. However, the fact that the GLC took until 1976 to produce its first strategic plan might be said to undermine this argument. Fourth, reform can be viewed from the so-called city-region perspective: that is, the situation whereby the socio-economic development of a particular area does not fit with the formal institutional arrangements. This view underpinned reform in London with the creation of the GLC in 1965. In effect, the economic and social reality that was London had outgrown the boundaries of the old LCC. Such a view also informed the Redcliffe-Maud Commission in its recommendation for metropolitan counties in the major urban conurbations of England.

25

Fifth, technical reasons also sometimes come into play. An illustration of this is the 1973 Water Act where the boundaries of the newly created water authorities were defined to coincide with the major watersheds. Sixth, we have also seen the pivotal role of politics and ideology in the area of local government reform. Whether it be local political parties lobbying to protect their interests or national politicians looking at the electoral implications, local government reform cannot be divorced from subjective values and judgements. It is a theme we shall return to in chapter 5. Finally, sometimes there is a view that policy problems can be solved by merely changing structures. The desire is to achieve a quick policy fix, instead of focusing on more fundamental questions such as the kind of local government we want and the role it should play in the British political system.

The Development of Party Politics in Local Government

The decline of the independent

One significant development in local government has been the decline of the so-called independent councillor and the rise of partisan politics (Alexander, 1982). This trend has increased significantly since the 1974 local government reorganization, which saw the setting-up of larger local government units that helped to undermine the independent councillor. Indeed, reference has been to the 'catalytic impact of reorganisation' (Game and Leach, 1996, p. 127). Larger spatial units tend to require greater organizational resources at the political level. This can put independent councillors at a disadvantage compared to relatively well-resourced political parties. Second, the larger local government units helped to weaken local identity, accelerated the 'nationalization' of local politics and consequently undermined the independent councillor's position (Rao, 1998). Third, many 'independent' councillors, many of whom in reality were Conservatives, were incorporated into the Conservative camp. To do otherwise would have risked facing the opposition of official Conservative candidates (Game and Leach, 1996, p. 127). As evidence of the decline of non-partisanship, Elcock (1982, p. 75) has noted how, since 1974, the large majority of local authorities in the UK have been dominated by political parties. The Maud Committee, which had been set up by central government to look into the management of local government, found that in 1967, 50 per cent of local councils were under the control of political parties (Maud, 1967). Subsequent research found that this figure had increased to 80 per cent by 1985. Independents controlled only 16 per cent of all local authorities, the majority of these in the more rural parts of the UK (Widdicombe, 1986). By 1995, independent councillors were in a majority in only 10 per cent of British local councils (Game and Leach, 1996, p. 132).

Party politics has had long established roots in the modern system of local government. Kingdom (1991, p. 109) notes how, from the 1835 Municipal Corporations Act onwards, there were groups 'contesting municipal leadership' who held a collective view on both the nature and role of local government and how services should be delivered. One of the earliest, and most famous, examples of this phenomenon was in the city of Birmingham. As we noted above, the Birmingham caucus, led by the legendary Joseph Chamberlain, played a pivotal role in the development of the municipal idea. The LCC was dominated by party politics from its creation in 1899. Party politics sometimes led to clashes between local and central government. One of the most famous concerns the borough of Poplar in London. The Labour-controlled council, under the leadership of George Lansbury, clashed on several occasions with central government in 1919 by paying higher wages to its workers and higher rates of poor relief. It also refused 'to collect rate precepts for other local authorities until a more equitable distribution of income had been introduced between rich and poor authorities' (Boddy and Fudge, 1984, p. 86). As a result of their actions, thirty local councillors went to gaol and a number of surcharges were imposed.

Historically, the Labour Party placed less emphasis on local government than it did on central government. In large part, such a downplaying of local government has its roots in the Fabian tradition of paternalistic social welfare provision and central planning. In general terms, it was the central state that was viewed as the key agency for economic and social change (Wilks, 1993). However, it should be pointed out that from 1896 onwards, the early Fabians did place some stress on the role of local government and municipal socialism. Other traditions within the Labour Party, such as 'Guild Socialism', also stressed the importance of local action (Bassett, 1984). Nevertheless, by the mid-1920s, interest in a local road to socialism had started to recede.

Labour's landslide victory in the 1945 general election brought with it some countervailing trends in relation to local government. On one level, the setting-up of a National Health Service in 1946, which resulted in a number of health functions being taken away from local authorities, and nationalization of key sectors of the economy such as gas and electricity to create central public corporations (these areas had been the responsibility of local authorities) seemed to point to the Labour government's preference for the central state as the most appropriate arena for policy action. On the other hand, the fact that many of the key policy areas of the emerging welfare state, such as education, public housing and social services (social security was and remains the responsibility of the centre), were to be delivered and to some extent shaped at the local level pointed to an increase in the role of local government.

In the twentieth century, all three major political parties, Conservative, Labour and Liberal (later emerging as the Liberal Democrats), were active in local government. The rise of the Labour Party in the early part of the century saw the role of the Liberals reduced considerably at the local, and indeed at the national, level. However, the 1970s saw a revival of the fortunes of the Liberal Party at the local level with their brand of community politics that aimed to build support by concentrating on 'bread and butter' issues such as street cleaning and parks maintenance. The Liberal Party gained important footholds in a number of local authorities and the Liberal Democrats continued this trend from the early 1990s onwards (see chapter 7).

Local Government and the Development of the Welfare State

From the middle of the twentieth century, the role of local government was to change fundamentally as part of a wider shift in thinking about the role of the state. This shift was reflected in the so-called post-war consensus, which saw the UK experience similar policies under both Labour and Conservative governments after 1945. While the precise nature of the consensus has been much debated, and in some cases its very existence disputed (Glennerster, 1995), it is generally supposed that there were two key elements of policy agreement. First, much of the consensus was in relation to economic policy. Thus, post-war governments agreed on the importance of Keynesian demand-management policies designed to maintain full employment and on the desirability of a mixed economy in which a number of key industries were in the ownership of the state. There was also a common use of corporatist bargaining arrangements, whereby the peak organizations of capital and labour were involved in aspects of economic policy making. Second, also of fundamental importance to the consensus was a cross-party commitment to the welfare state, embracing a whole series of provisions designed to care for British citizens 'from the cradle to the grave'. Central to these provisions was the NHS, but they also included a range of other services and state benefits, including public housing, education, social security and pensions.

It was the development of the welfare state, in particular, that brought about a rapid growth in the role of local government. Post-1945, local government was given responsibility for the delivery and administration of a wide range of social welfare policies, such as education, housing and social services. There was a rapid increase in the activity of local authorities (Cochrane, 1991). This, together 'with the ever increasing proportion of GNP allocated to the welfare state', itself managed by local government, 'enhanced the power and influence of local government' (Pycroft, 1995, p. 53). The rise of the welfare state therefore furnished local authorities with an important and creative role in British public policy.

This broad, cross-party agreement on public policy was maintained for some thirty years. But by the mid-1970s, cracks had started to appear in this consensus. The world oil crisis of 1973, together with the growing evidence of structural problems within the British economy, led to the challenging of old orthodoxies and the advocacy of new nostrums. As a consequence, there was an increasing spotlight on the role of the public sector and, in particular, the role of local government. In 1976, the IMF agreed with the Labour government to implement a 'rescue package' for the ailing British economy. One of the conditions of the IMF loan was cuts in public expenditure, which fell heavily on local government. The election of a Conservative government in 1979 saw an explicit rejection of Keynesian economic policies, which now gave way to a monetarist philosophy. The new government spoke of the overburdening state and stressed the value of markets and the private sector. Moreover, it was concerned to rein in what it perceived to be a bloated public sector and was deeply suspicious of Labour-controlled local authorities. Evidently, the new governmental agenda posed a considerable threat to local government. We will discuss this in more detail in subsequent chapters.

Conclusion

In this chapter, we have seen how local government in the UK has undergone significant changes in the past 150 years. Industrialization, demographic changes and other pressure led to an expanded and developed local government. Local government became increasingly important, providing innovation in both the formulation and delivery of public policy. The aftermath of the Second World War and the development of the welfare state took this process a stage further.

We have also seen, however, that local government has not been without its controversies. Competing political interpretations of the role and purpose of local government have had important implications for the structure of local government and the functions with which local authorities have been charged. The structure of local government has been particularly contentious and subject to continuous change. This is a reflection of the fact that local government is not only constructed on the basis of scientific and rational criteria, but also strongly influenced by values and ideology. Indeed, we have seen how party politics has come increasingly to dominate the world of local government. This should not be surprising. Modern local government has been involved in the delivery and shaping of public services for over 150 years. The nature of services to be delivered and the way in which they are to be delivered are both highly contentious and the party political nature of local government reflects this reality.

2

Theories of Local Government and Local Governance

Introduction

A variety of theoretical positions have been applied to the study of local government over the past two decades. In addition, both the number and range of theoretical approaches have increased significantly since the mid-1980s, as academics have attempted to theorize the rapidly changing context within which local authorities operate. We are strongly aware that, if recent changes in the world of local government can sometimes appear bewildering, the proliferation of theories that attempt to explain these events often only adds to the sense of confusion experienced by students of, and practitioners in, local government.

This chapter therefore begins with a discussion of the relevance of theory to the student of local government and then moves on to provide a general overview of the issues that these theories address. At this stage, a clear distinction is made between theories of local government and theories of local governance. The former are summarized and discussed in the first half of the chapter, via an introduction to the three main theories of the state that have dominated attempts to theorize local government: pluralism (and its subsequent neo-pluralist variants), elite theory and Marxism. This is very much a context-setting exercise for the subsequent discussion of local governance in the second half of the chapter, where particular attention is paid to those theoretical perspectives that have sought to explain the significant changes in British local government over the past twenty years. Three particular perspectives are examined: the power-dependence model, urban regime theory and regulation theory.

We wish to make no pretence that this chapter provides a comprehensive assessment of competing theories of local government and local governance. While we do consider the major issues raised by the full range of theoretical approaches, our principal concern is the particular significance of those theories which relate closely to the principal theme of this book: local government's search for ways of defending and extending its active policy-making role in the context of ongoing attempts at governmental centralization. Consequently, we are deliberately selective in the range of approaches reviewed here, and we focus particularly on the way in which they portray the implications of change in local government for the scope for local authorities to act autonomously from the central state.

Why Bother?

It is difficult to begin a chapter on theoretical approaches to local government without feeling a need to justify its existence. Among students and practitioners concerned with local government, and many readers of this book will fall into both categories, there may well be a view that abstract theorizing does little to enhance their understanding of the 'real world' of local government. That a degree of scepticism about the value of theoretical approaches should arise is perhaps understandable. For those with little first-hand experience of local government, being asked to judge between competing theoretical perspectives can often seem like being asked to run before you can walk. Conversely, for those with more detailed working knowledge of local government, theoretical perspectives often appear to be too detached from reality and ignorant of the day-to-day concerns that actually determine how a local authority operates, such as the personalities of a council's chief officers and members.

Perhaps mindful of these objections, many recent books on local government have either ignored theoretical questions altogether or relegated consideration of such matters to their penultimate chapter. We are reluctant to follow such precedents, however, and wish to defend our early foray into theory on three main grounds. The first of these is generic to the study of government and politics, and indeed to social science in general, and has frequently been rehearsed elsewhere. It is the argument that even an apparently atheoretical or objective analysis of political or social change will be based on a particular set of assumptions. Indeed, some level of 'theory' is present at all stages of the research process and this will guide the decision of what to research, shape the definition of research questions being posed, tend to bias the researcher towards the use of particular methodologies and influence the way in which they interpret the data collected (Dunleavy, 1980; Hampton, 1991). Where theoretical values are left implicit, such accounts can be deeply problematic, since it is difficult, if not impossible, to assess either the coherence of the account on offer or its possible broader implications (Dunleavy, 1980). Moreover, as the same author adds, failing to make key assumptions explicit may obscure the fact that blatantly ideological criteria lie behind the way in which research and analysis have been carried out. We therefore concur with the view that 'An attempt to make theory explicit provides at least some safeguards against the most common distortions of social science work' (p. 21).

A second justification relates directly to local government. It is generally agreed that, in recent years, local authorities in the UK have undergone significant change, involving a fundamental challenge to the role they had played in the post-war British polity (Cochrane, 1993; Stewart and Stoker, 1995a). The changes involved are so far-reaching that they demand a level of explanation which goes beyond simple description or a narrative of events; we need theories to help us to assess why these changes happened, rather than just to say how and when they occurred. At the same time, while there is agreement that local government is changing, there is uncertainty about the precise nature of its trajectory. While theoretical approaches cannot provide ways for researchers and practitioners to 'surf the chaos' of local government reform, they do at least offer us a variety of ways of perceiving 'the bigger picture'. By outlining change in broad brush strokes rather than in minute detail, theories of local government can thus help both to inform the definition of key areas of research and to guide the day-to-day practice of local government policy making. Thus, while theories may often seem unnecessarily abstract, they are vital if we are to distinguish the key trends that are taking place from those that are largely incidental.

The third and final reason for our concern to engage with contemporary theoretical debates is specific to the nature of this book. Our thesis that, despite concerted attempts at centralization, local authorities have found ways of exercising creative autonomy, challenges the conventional wisdom that has grown up over the past twenty years. While the ultimate test of the thesis rests with the empirical evidence that we provide in subsequent chapters, it is also important to establish the extent to which it can be underpinned by wider theoretical interpretations. Moreover, it is equally important to assess the extent to which the creative autonomy thesis may be challenged or contradicted by recent theories of local government. Hence, the way in which the notion of creative autonomy relates to broader theoretical approaches is central to the development of our thesis (see chapter 3) and informs the analysis of the remainder of the book.

Types of Theory

Since Hunter's pioneering (1953) study of local politics in Atlanta, a vast number of theoretical approaches have been put forward that have some bearing on local government. Space precludes comprehensive analysis of these competing perspectives: even limiting consideration to only the most significant accounts would require us to assess more than a dozen separate theoretical contributions.[1] These theories exhibit considerable diversity, not only in relation to the variety of positions that they advance, but also in the nature of the theoretical assumptions and antecedents that underpin them, in the degree to which they have been, or can be, tested empirically and in the extent to which they attempt to explain empirically observable phenomena rather than making normative prescriptions of how local government should operate.

Given this evident diversity of approaches, it is perhaps useful to map out some of the most important contours of the theoretical exchanges that have taken place. First, theories of local government have tended to address two distinctive sets of issues. A first group of theories has examined the way in which local government operates within the wider context of the local political system. Such studies, which have invariably been undertaken in large towns and cities, stem mainly from the American political science tradition. Originating from Hunter's (1953) study of Atlanta and Dahl's (1961) account of New Haven, such theories have increasingly attempted to broaden their definition of the local political system. This broadening of focus has been characterized, on the one hand, by a growing concern to examine the way in which particular interests – particularly, although not exclusively, businesses – are involved in the local political process (Stone, 1989; Harding, 1991; Peck, 1995) and, on the other hand, by attempts to understand the way in which the local political environment is impacted upon by wider structural economic changes and by globalization (Ronneberger and Keil, 1993; Keil and Lieser, 1989).

A second distinctive set of theories examine the way in which local authorities relate to the wider governmental system. Usually labelled as theories of intergovernmental relations, such accounts have drawn particularly on British experience and have been particularly concerned with the way in which the relationships between central and local government are structured. A core interest of such theories, many of which were motivated by a concern to assess the impact of the Thatcher governments on central–local relations, has been the extent to which localities are able to operate autonomously from the centre (Rhodes, 1981; Duncan and Goodwin, 1988a). However, in more recent years, the focus has broadened beyond central–local relations to include analysis of the significance of new forms of institutional intervention at a variety of spatial scales. Particular attention has been given to the role of the European policy process (Marks, 1993; John, 1996b; Rhodes, 1997). There is also evidence of an increased level of concern, albeit generally empirical rather than theoretical, with the growth of new regional bodies (Atkinson and Wilks-Heeg, 1999), and the impact of single-purpose bodies and initiatives set up by central government, but operating in specific local contexts (Wilks, 1995; Painter, Isaac-Henry and Rouse, 1997).

To some extent, this distinction between accounts of intergovernmental relations and theories of local policy and politics is an artificial one. There are, for instance, a limited number of theoretical perspectives that seek to integrate concern with intergovernmental relations with concern with the specificity of the local policy context. Thus, Duncan and Goodwin (1988b) propose a theoretical framework that aims to explain both geographical variation in local government policy making and ongoing attempts at government centralization. Likewise, authors who have drawn on regulation theory have pointed both to the reconfiguration of institutional arrangements at a local level and to a progressive loss of central government control, which they see as part of a process of 'hollowing out' the nation-state (Jessop, 1994). Moreover, as we have noted, studies of the local policy process have increasingly sought to understand the significance of extra-local institutional linkages. Nonetheless, at the risk of some over-simplification, it is reasonable to suggest that most theories tend to fall primarily into one of the two categories outlined above.

The second significant distinction within the literature is a sharper one and distinguishes between theories of local govern*ment* and theories of local govern*ance*. In more recent years, the very notion of local government has increasingly come into question as the concept of local governance has emerged in its place. This distinction is based on the general recognition that the role of local authorities is in the process of being fundamentally redefined (Stoker, 1998; 1999). It is argued that the key feature of this redefinition has been a shift from councils operating independently and monolithically as sole provider of public services (local government), to one where they act as strategic directors of a complex variety of overlapping local institutional networks involving a range of public, quasi-public, private and voluntary sector organizations (local governance). Despite partially valid criticisms that this portrayal of recent events overstates the idea of a transition from one set of local political arrangements to another (Imrie and Raco, 1999), the notion of local governance has achieved a status of general acceptance among academics and local government practitioners. As such, the distinction between local government and local governance sets down a clear chronological marker in the development of theoretical approaches.

We are of the view that theories of local governance cannot be fully understood without reference to the main theoretical perspectives that preceded them. Some reference to earlier approaches is therefore required in order to understand the theoretical significance of the shift that has been posited from local government to local governance. Moreover, some of the more recent approaches are difficult to classify as theories and are instead best portrayed as concepts that have developed from the insights of these broader theories of the state. Most modern theoretical variants are invariably descendants of previous accounts, albeit occasionally with mixed parentage, and this recognition has, somewhat ironically, led many to revisit the more comprehensive theoretical frameworks advanced by previous accounts. Our review therefore begins with an overview of the three principal theories of the local state.

Theories of Local Government: Pluralism, Elite Theory and Marxism

Pluralism

Virtually all reviews of the principal theories of state institutions begin with pluralism. There is good reason for this convention and we do not wish to challenge it here. Pluralism can largely be regarded as the mother of theories of liberal democracy and has been credited with freeing political science from narrow constitutional assumptions (Hampton, 1991). As Judge (1995) notes, since the emergence of the pluralist paradigm all subsequent theories have either developed it or explicitly contested it. Indeed, for a long period, the battering of pluralism provided the main source of theoretical inspiration in political science. Thus, writing in 1987 Hampton noted that 'the critique of pluralism forms the starting point of much of the recent work on urban politics'. Ironically, in more recent years, pluralism appears to have enjoyed something of a rebirth, to the extent that it may legitimately be asked whether 'we are all pluralist now?' (Judge, 1995, p. 30).

Pluralism may be defined simply as 'the belief that there are, or ought to be, many things' (Dunleavy and O'Leary, 1987, p. 13). Applied to a political context, this principle supposes a scenario where competing

36

political parties put alternative programmes to the electorate in a bid to gain the power to direct a political system characterized by a set of checks and balances that prevent any particular grouping from gaining absolute control. The political system will also be open to a myriad of specialist interest groups, representing virtually every facet of political opinion and drawing their legitimacy from their popular support (as expressed by membership levels), which lobby elected representatives on all key policy issues. In addition, political affairs will be analysed and discussed by independent and diverse media, which offer a broad range of political viewpoints and provide a further check on the exercise of power. Pluralism therefore represents a situation where political power is fragmented and dispersed and where the decision-making process can operate only if underpinned by a broad consensus that encompasses the views of the majority of citizens.

The seminal work presenting a pluralist view of local government is Robert Dahl's (1961) book, *Who Governs?* Dahl examined the political processes associated with three key policy issues in New Haven: urban development, public education and political nominations. On the basis of this analysis he suggested that the local political system was characterized by a set of 'dispersed inequalities', whereby different individuals and groupings possess diverse kinds of resources, the influence of which will vary significantly from one policy area to another. Thus, it is impossible for any single group to dominate local government decision making. Admittedly, it was possible to identify a relatively small number of individuals who were most heavily involved in the political process, but Dahl felt that their direct influence was always tempered by a powerful counterweight, namely that 'most citizens . . . possess a moderate degree of indirect influence' (p. 164). As a result, political outcomes always tend to reflect the views of the majority and are produced via 'complex processes of symbiosis and change that constitute the relations of leaders and citizens in a pluralist democracy' (p. 325).

Clearly, pluralism presents a highly sanguine view of local government. It assumes that the local decision-making system is open and transparent and that it will, despite its complex character, always be responsive to the will of the majority. The pluralist view also implicitly assumes a significant degree of local autonomy, since local government is seen to have the requisite resources and legal capacity to translate local opinions into policy measures. It is unsurprising, therefore, that the pluralist perspective has been subject to extensive criticism from political scientists and sociologists who have pointed to the existence of significant inequalities of power. This critique, which came initially from elite theorists and subsequently from Marxist sources, has led to an increased acceptance among pluralists of the particular influence wielded by business interests. As a result, a distinctive neo-pluralist position has since emerged, which addresses many of the weaker elements of the original pluralist position and has been a key influence behind more recent theoretical advances (Lindblom, 1977). Paradoxically, in the course of this debate, it has been recognized that Dahl was more neo-pluralist than has generally been accepted (Judge, 1995).

Elite theory

Initially, the critique of pluralism came from political scientists who regarded political control as being the preserve of a relatively small elite. This perspective, which came to be known as elite theory, actually predated Dahl's work. It had originated in the work of Hunter, whose (1953) study of local politics in Atlanta, Georgia, suggested that effective power was exercised by a group of no more than forty individuals, among whom business interests played a dominant role. Indeed, Hunter saw business representatives exerting a particularly significant influence over policy outcomes, suggesting that 'within the policy-making groups the economic interests are dominant' (p. 82).

The critique of pluralist accounts of local politics was developed particularly by Bachratz and Baratz (1963, 1970). There were two key elements to their critique. First, they argued that accounts such as Dahl's made no serious attempt to distinguish between 'important' and 'unimportant' issues and that the choice of policy areas studied in New Haven was therefore entirely arbitrary. Second, they proposed that the pluralist approach pioneered by Dahl focused exclusively on those issues that were already on the local political agenda. Bachratz and Baratz suggested that pluralists therefore take it as given that all important issues reach the public arena, when in fact it is likely that only relatively 'safe' decisions are allowed to be subjected to such exposure. Thus, in their application of elite theory to the study of the local politics of air pollution, Bachratz and Baratz (1970) showed how 'difficult' issues are often purposefully kept off the political agenda.

Although central to the study of local politics in the USA, this series of exchanges between pluralists and elite theorists, which became known as the community power debate, made little impression on British studies of local government. Indeed, surveying the literature at the end of the 1970s, Dunleavy (1980) noted that only a sum total of two community power studies had ever been carried out in the UK, both of them doctoral theses. In part the paucity of such studies was a reflection of the fact that the community power debate did not seem to live up to its billing. Harding (1995) notes that, as the 1960s progressed, the protagonists in the community power debate were increasingly talking past each other, rather than engaging in any serious theoretical discourse. However, more importantly, the scant attention to the theoretical insights and methodological innovations stemming from the debate reflected the entrenched conservatism of local government studies in the UK. Indeed, until the 1970s, most academic accounts of local politics in the UK continued to adopt a narrow, institutional focus and were 'insistent in their refrain that power lies where it is supposed to lie, formally or legally' (Dunleavy, 1980, p. 9).

Marxism

During the 1970s the community power debate was eclipsed by the rise of a powerful new body of theories inspired by Marxism, which rapidly came to dominate the way in which local government was theorized. In part, this development was a reflection of the general rise of Marxist theory in social studies and the humanities at that time. A growing number of theorists began to seek to apply Marxist principles to the study of the modern world, and the state became a key focus of their attention. Since then, Marxists have interpreted the state in a variety of ways and there is a range of competing Marxist accounts of the particular nature of the local state (Cockburn, 1977; Castells, 1977; Duncan and Goodwin, 1988b).

There is no scope here to rehearse the central theoretical tenets of Marxism. Instead, it must suffice for us to note that Marx's primary concern was to theorize the workings of the capitalist economic system, which ultimately he felt would collapse under the twin pressures of its own inherent contradictions and the unstoppable surge of working-class uprising. According to Marx, economic forces provided the dynamic of history and he put forward the view that this economic 'base' would lead to the creation of particular sets of social relations, cultural norms and political institutions, which he collectively termed the 'superstructure'. However, beyond this, Marx said relatively little about the role of the state, except for the much-quoted passage in the Communist Manifesto, 'The executive of the modern state is but a committee for managing the common affairs of the entire bourgeoisie' (Marx and Engels, 1983, p. 16). The limited attention that Marx gave to the state is perhaps one reason for the subsequent divergence of views as to what should constitute a Marxist theory of the state.

Fortunately, Marxist theorists have managed to find some common ground. As Pickvance (1995) notes, there is general agreement among Marxists that the state performs two key functions that are critical to the survival of the capitalist system. First, it provides a range of general prerequisites that the market would fail to deliver and that are essential to the functioning of the capitalist system. These include the legal system, the transport and communication infrastructure, and education and training to ensure a suitably qualified workforce. Second, the state maintains social order, mediating the class conflicts produced by the operation of the capitalist economic system. Following O'Connor (1973) these two roles may be termed the 'accumulation function' and the 'legitimation function' of the state.

Beyond this basic level of agreement, however, Marxist theories of the state begin to part company. There is one primary source of disagreement: the issue of the extent to which the state acts autonomously from the dominant ruling class. Based on this division, two distinctive Marxist camps can be identified. The first consists of 'instrumentalist' accounts, which see the state as a unified actor operating always and everywhere in the interests of the capitalist class. Such accounts see the state as nothing more than an instrument of the ruling class, frequently offering a quite literal reformulation of the view expressed in the Communist Manifesto (Cockburn, 1977). The second grouping comprises theorists who take a 'structuralist' view of the state. These authors suggest that, while the state operates in the general, long-term interests of capital, the existence of divisions within the capitalist class requires that state institutions are less unified and operate with a degree of autonomy in order that such conflicting pressures can be reconciled. Moreover, structuralists take the view that the state must not only act as an arbiter between different sections of a divided ruling class, but also respond to the strength of the working-class challenge. As a result, the state becomes a central stage for the class struggle and offers some scope for working-class gains to be made (Poulantzas, 1978).

These differences of perspective gave rise to a number of competing accounts of the local state, some avowedly Marxist (Cockburn, 1977; Castells, 1977; Duncan and Goodwin, 1988b), others less so (Cawson and Saunders, 1983). The earliest accounts did little more than reinforce the somewhat artificial division between instrumentalist and structuralist accounts. Thus, Cockburn (1977) presents a highly instrumentalist account which posits that local government is nothing more than an extension of the central state, designed to ensure the conditions through which capitalism can be reproduced locally. By contrast, Castells (1977) offers a more obviously structuralist account in which the local state is ultimately seen as a means of organizing 'collective consumption', in essence public services such as health, education, housing and public transport, which plays a dual role of ensuring capitalist reproduction and appeasing social conflict.

We do not wish to examine each of these contributions in depth, partly because this has been more than adequately undertaken by others (see Stoker, 1991; Pickvance, 1995) but also because the above accounts receive little credence in contemporary analyses of local government. Instead, two general comments will suffice to explain the general demise of Marxist theories of the local state. First, given their common focus on the essential role of the local state in providing accumulation and/or legitimation functions, all Marxist accounts faced the difficulty of explaining the pattern of local government reform in the 1980s. During this period, a number of services provided by local councils were cut back significantly, apparently without endangering either the process of capital accumulation or the delicate balance of social order. In particular, given that Marxist accounts laid particular stress on the central importance of the local state's provision of welfare services, whether defined as 'collective consumption' or 'social consumption', the rapid contraction of, say, public housing provision was evidently difficult to explain. Moreover, a number of services were also privatized, despite the fact that Marxist accounts postulated that they could not be provided by the market. As Savage and Warde (1993, p. 157) suggest, 'there is a dated ring about arguments concerning the inevitability of state welfare and their functional value for capitalism following a decade of major restructuring and considerable diminution of welfare provision'.

Second, Marxist theories faced a related problem in light of tensions that characterized central–local relations in the UK during the 1980s. On the one hand, the resistance of local councils to a series of central government reforms did not sit easily with the notion that they were merely extensions of the central state. Yet, on the other hand, it would be equally difficult to argue that the heavy-handed way in which the Thatcher governments dealt with local authorities in general was the central state's response to local working-class resistance, since this was at most characteristic of a small number of councils.

Theories of Local Governance

Marxist theories were not the only ones to be left exposed by developments in local government during the 1980s. Indeed, all accounts of local government in the post-war period had, at least implicitly, been concerned with the dynamics of local politics in the context of a relatively long period of continuous economic growth and expanding state intervention. Once these conditions changed, there was little reason to suppose that local government would continue to operate in the same role as it had previously. Likewise, whether or not the institutions of local government were assumed to constitute the foci of local political power, all of the theoretical perspectives discussed above assumed that local authorities were the principal providers of local services. Once again, the fact that this assumption no longer holds is likely to have had significant implications for the way in which the role of local government should be theorized. Consequently, our attention now turns to theoretical approaches that have sought to grapple with the changing context in which local government now operates.

We have already made mention of the notion of a transition from local authorities acting as local government to one where they operate as a lead-player in a system of local governance. We have also noted that many of the theories of local government that typically featured in textbooks such as this in the late 1980s have been fundamentally, if not fatally, undermined by these developments. However, over the past ten years, as the character of local governance has become more clearly defined, local government specialists have sought to respond to these changes with a fresh set of theoretical approaches. Their sources of inspiration have been varied. Some have sought to update theories developed in a British context during the 1980s, while others have turned to the North American urban politics literature or to French neo-Marxist political economy. Yet, all continue within the tradition of the principal theories of the state.

Before turning directly to consider these more recent theoretical contributions, it is first necessary to give greater consideration to the notion of local governance, which is common to all of them. Like many of the ideas discussed in this chapter, there are a vast number of alternative accounts of the governance concept. Jessop (1998) suggests that the literature on governance is disjointed and eclectic. In a similar vein, Rhodes (1997) identifies six distinctive uses of the term, ranging from its association with conceptions of the minimal state through to notions of socio-cybernetic systems. Fortunately, Stoker (1998) has provided a framework that distils much of this literature down to a relatively simple set of propositions about the nature of the changes that are taking place. Specifically, Stoker suggests that there are essentially five key propositions made about governance, namely:

1) Governance refers to a complex set of institutions and actors that are drawn from but also beyond government;
2) Governance identifies the blurring of boundaries and responsibilities for tackling social and economic issues;
3) Governance identifies the power dependence involved in the relationships between institutions involved in collective action;

4) Governance is about autonomous self-governing networks of actors;
5) Governance recognizes the capacity to get things done which does not rest on the power of government to command or use its authority. It sees government as able to use new tools and techniques to steer and guide. (p. 18)

The notion of governance thus points to the formation of networks of mutually dependent actors that operate independently from formal systems of government. Although motivated by a wish to enhance the capacity of those involved to deliver effective policy measures, the rise of complex governance networks also raises concern about confused lines of accountability, the increased likelihood of unintended consequences and the risk of policy failure. It is generally agreed that the concept of governance does not, in itself, constitute a theory (Jessop, 1998; Stoker, 1998). Indeed, the basic assumptions of the governance thesis have been applied by authors writing from a diverse set of theoretical backgrounds. It is to some of these accounts that we now turn.

Power-dependence in central–local relations

The theory of power-dependence has developed alongside the governance concept and shares much in common with it. Associated principally with the work of Rhodes, the power-dependence model began life as an attempt to theorize central–local relations (Rhodes, 1981), was subsequently developed around the concept of policy networks (Rhodes, 1988) and has more recently engaged directly with the notion of governance (Rhodes, 1997). In including Rhodes' work here, we wish to add two important caveats. First, although it began as a way of theorizing central–local relations, the power-dependence model has become progressively less specific in its consideration of local government. Indeed, since it is based on an assumption of the interdependency of governmental actors, the very notion of power-dependence implies that there can be no separate theory of local government or local governance. Second, given the manner in which it has evolved, it might reasonably be asked whether the theory of power-dependence exhibits enough continuity to be classified as a theoretical approach. Yet, despite these reservations, Rhodes' attempts to revise his early model in the light of both academic critique and the reconfiguration of the British state have made it a valuable lens through which to view the changing world of local government.

Originally, Rhodes (1981) proposed a model of intergovernmental relations that portrayed central and local actors as participants in a complex game in which they manoeuvre for advantage. In this game, inter-organizational relationships take a variety of forms ranging from pluralistic bargaining to corporatist arrangements that offer a privileged role to certain interests. Within this context each protagonist seeks to deploy the resources it has to hand to maximize its influence and minimize its dependence on the other players. Although dominant coalitions can form that are able to condition the rules of the game, none of the participating organizations is in full possession of the constitutional, legal, organizational, financial, political and informational resources it requires to achieve its goals. As a result, while individual levels of government may be hierarchically organized, their relationships to other tiers are characterized by interdependencies, and an exchange of resources is therefore the necessary outcome of this mutual dependency.

The theory was criticized on two main grounds (cf. Rhodes, 1997). First, it was suggested that it failed to link the behaviour of individual players in the game of intergovernmental relations to more macro theories of how power and interest are structured in society. Second, the approach was criticized for its vague use of the notion of corporatism, which was used to describe a wide range of situations in which pressure groups gain formal contact with state actors. In light of these criticisms, Rhodes subsequently sought to develop the model by differentiating between three discrete tiers of analysis – macro, meso and micro (Rhodes, 1988). He then paid particular attention to analysing the nature of the meso-level, which he suggested was characterized by a vast array of policy networks. Depending on the policy area concerned, these networks vary from relatively tight-knit and influential policy communities found in sectors such as agriculture, through to the more open and less influential issue networks concerned with policies such as inner-city decline. Because of the importance of these overlapping policy networks, Rhodes portrayed the British system of government as a 'differentiated polity'.

The Rhodes model may be termed neo-pluralist (cf. Dunleavy and O'Leary, 1987). It recognizes that power is likely to be concentrated among certain groups, but by pointing to the way in which the differentiated structures of the state create mutual dependencies, it highlights the fact that such latent power cannot always be mobilized. The implications of this model of intergovernmental relations are that the centre is more constrained than had generally been recognized by earlier accounts of central–local relations. These constraints are both internal and external to the central state. Internally, the state is constrained by its own fragmentation and limited capacity to co-ordinate other organizations. Externally, the centre is constrained by its reliance on other organizations to carry through its policies. As such, central government is unable simply to command other actors or impose its will on sub-national government. Instead, in order to achieve its objectives, central government must seek to work through a range of policy networks, many of which include significant local government representation. Failure to do so, suggests Rhodes, will invariably result in 'a policy mess'. Thus, the importance of policy implementation receives considerable stress in the power-dependence model and it has been argued that policy networks can fundamentally alter the intended objectives of a policy once it is put into practice (Marsh and Rhodes, 1992).

The revised Rhodes model has also been subject to a number of criticisms, with most centring on what are regarded as the pitfalls of attempting to construct a meso-level theory of the state. There have been repeated calls for links to be made to the principal theories of the state (Smith, 1993; Dowding, 1995; Wilks, 1995), which have been justified on three main grounds. First, it has been suggested that the notion of policy networks continues to pay insufficient attention to how the macro-level conditions the way in which institutional power is structured (Cochrane, 1993; Stoker, 1995a). As a result, there is a tendency to suggest that such networks 'exist in a separate system of their own', more or less divorced from external pressures (Cochrane, 1993, p. 25). Second, it has also been argued that, by focusing on the meso-level, the policy network approach is always likely to portray the state as a fragmented set of institutions and will tend seriously to under-estimate both the role of the centre (Atkinson and Coleman, 1992) and its capacity for coher-ent, strategic intervention (Pickvance, 1991). Third, it is proposed that the explanatory power of the policy network concept is extremely limited and that the relationship between networks and policy outcomes has been inadequately explored (Wilks, 1995). While notions such as 'policy community' and 'issue network' describe how policy is made differently in different sectors, 'the labels do not themselves explain the difference' (Dowding, 1995, p. 142).

Despite these criticisms, empirical evidence has been produced to support many of the central tenets of power-dependence theory and the importance of policy networks. The most convincing evidence has been that concerned with the implementation consequences of policy net-works. For instance, Rhodes (1997) has applied his own theoretical principles to a review of trends in local government during the period 1979–95. In this account, Rhodes points to a series of policy failures and unintended consequences, which he sees as the product of central gov-ernment attempting to engineer change without reference to the variety of meso-level structures.

Regime theory

The second approach, which has come to focus more specifically on the emergence of a fragmented system of local governance, is regime theory. Although its origins are in American political science literature concerned with the politics of urban development (Fainstein and Fainstein, 1986; Elkin, 1987), regime theory has since been expanded to include reference to regimes that are not specifically growth orientated (Stone, 1989; 1993). Advancing an essentially neo-pluralist view of local politics, in which the particular influence of business interests is recognized, regime theory has been applied almost exclusively in an urban context. Moreover, with one or two exceptions (Harding, 1999; Dowding et al., 1999), its application to the study of local policy making in the UK has been limited. Nonetheless, it would appear that, with some adaptation, the notion of local regimes has much to commend it and may potentially have value in explaining the rise of local governance.

In keeping with the tradition of the US urban politics literature, regime theory concentrates particularly on the issue of power. However, in contrast to pluralists and elite theorists, authors such as Stone are less concerned with 'who governs' than with the issue of how these actors assemble the capacity to govern. This is an important distinction. Regime theory suggests that urban politics is characterized by diversity and complexity in which relations are conditioned by mutual dependencies rather than simple, hierarchical power relations. The local political system thus exhibits a fragmentation of control, in which power is diffused into complex webs of relationships between governmental and non-governmental actors and where governmental response frequently results in policy spillover and unintended consequences. As a result, a key issue for regime theorists is the extent to which governmental and non-governmental actors are able to co-operate to achieve what are frequently shared economic and social objectives. It may be noted at this point that regime theory thus shares many of the assumptions of Rhodes' model of the British polity, suggesting that the tendencies he points to in intergovernmental relations also encapsulate the nature of the local political process.

Regime theorists are therefore concerned with the issue of how coalitions are formed which enable effective local governance in conditions of complexity, rather than with questions of who dominates those coalitions. Regime theory is thus concerned with the notion of 'power to' rather than that of 'power over'. At the same time, however, regime theorists accept that there are significant inequalities of power. In particular, it is recognized that business interests generally occupy a privileged position in the local political system, since the control of the local economy is effectively in their hands. Since the decisions that business interests make about investment and resource allocation have a funda- mental influence on social welfare, it is suggested that they collectively exercise 'systemic power'. However, while local politicians and public officials are constrained by the socio-economic context in which they operate, they are not powerless. Not only do city governments possess significant resources of their own, they are also charged with the role of protecting the wider public interest. In this context, while a city gov- ernment does not have the capacity to control the local economy or the status of an arbiter between competing social claims, it can become 'more visible as a mobiliser and co-ordinator of resources', (Stone, 1986, p. 87).

Regime theory thus suggests a changing role for local authorities which is very much in line with the notion of a transition from local government to local governance (Stoker, 1995b). In the words of Stone (1986, p. 89), the division of power between governmental and non- governmental forces 'does not lend itself to the establishment of direct and intense control over a large domain in a wide scope of activity'. In this context, networks, rather than hierarchies or markets, are the most significant means of shaping local fortunes. In order to govern effectively, local political actors must therefore recognize the limits to independent action: 'governments must blend their capacities with those of various non-governmental actors' (1993, p. 6). In contrast to some more deter- minist accounts, this suggests that politics continues to matter, although it also contains an implicit recognition that the way in which cities are governed is not necessarily a reflection of a popular mandate and that policy options which would benefit the wider population are not neces- sarily followed. In this sense, regimes imply a trade-off between local democracy and policy effectiveness that is echoed by Stone's definition of a regime as 'an informal yet relatively stable group with access to in- stitutional resources that enable it to have a sustained role in making decisions' (1993, p. 4).

A further important feature of regime theory, which distinguishes it from related concepts such as growth machines, is the suggestion that a variety of regime types can be formed. As such, there is scope for local choice, although this is suggested to be conditioned by the membership of the regime, the nature of the relationships between them and the level of resources that they bring to the table. Consequently, regimes can vary in character over time and across space. Stone suggests a fourfold classification of maintenance regimes, development regimes, middle-class progressive regimes and lower-class opportunity expansion regimes. These four also represent a continuum with each becoming progressively more difficult and more expensive to maintain. Resources are therefore particularly critical, since for a regime to be viable it must be able to mobilize the resources required to fulfil its policy agenda (Stone, 1993).

Whether Stone's classification of regime types has any useful application to British local government is unclear. Although the regime concept has been applied in a British context, this has generally involved a reworking of definitions. In a recent application of the regime concept to six London boroughs, Dowding et al. (1999) put forward an eight-point characterization of regimes which they suggest captures the nature of a regime operating in a metropolitan context. To summarize briefly, they suggest that a regime will involve a distinctive and relatively long-lived policy agenda, which is sustained by coalitions operating within and beyond formal institutional structures and crossing sectoral boundaries. They add that such coalitions are likely to survive changes of leadership, involve the mobilization of external resources, be associated with a particular political vision and be based on partnership forms that bridge the public–private sector divide. Applying these criteria to six London boroughs, the authors suggest that three may be considered as distinctive regime types, while the remainder can only be classified as 'failed regimes'. The authors therefore warn against the universal application of the regime approach, suggesting that 'it is a mistake to search for a regime in every council office' (p. 541). Nonetheless, the authors conclude that the approach has several virtues: in particular, its capacity to capture the diverse forms that local coalitions may take and its scope to explain these differences with reference to factors other than local party control.

However, regime theory has also met with a number of criticisms. First, it has been suggested that, while regime theory is able to describe what is happening in a number of US cities, it lacks the capacity to explain the dynamics of power distribution (Stoker, 1995b). In common with the notions of power-dependence and policy networks put forward by Rhodes, proponents of the regime thesis have therefore had to face up to the criticism that it 'at best describes a model or a concept rather than a theory' (Dowding et al., 1999, p. 516). Second, it has been argued that studies such as Stone's (1989) analysis of politics in Atlanta place too much stress on exploring the local specificity of regimes and tend to downplay 'wider processes of change' (Stoker, 1995b, p. 66). As with the community power studies that went before it, there is a need to place local regimes in their wider political and governmental context (Keating, 1991). Yet, despite these problems, we would echo the conclusion reached by Dowding et al. (1999) that regime theory also has some important attractions. First, its particular focus on the importance of regimes as an attempt to assemble the capacity to act does offer a potential explanation of the causal factors that may be driving the shift from local government to local governance. Second, regime theory recognizes that there are likely to be a variety of local responses to the challenge of bringing about effective governance and demonstrates that there are choices available to local policy-makers.

Regulation theory

A final body of ideas that have received considerable attention in recent years are those derived from neo-Marxist regulation theory. There are at least seven principal strands of regulation theory and a host of associated theoretical positions (see Jessop, 1990; and Amin, 1994 for reviews). Consequently, we shall restrict ourselves here to a brief general summary of the core propositions of the regulationists before turning to a more detailed analysis of how these ideas have been applied to the study of local government.

The regulationist approach was inspired by a concern among Marxist scholars to explain the survival of capitalism, despite the existence of the contradictions and crises that Marx predicted would destroy it. The regulationists suggest that the answer to this apparent paradox is twofold. First and foremost, capitalism has shown the ability to adapt and change in the face of crisis. Regulationists thus identify distinctive periods of capitalist development, each characterized by particular kinds of economic relations, and they describe these as 'regimes of accumulation'. Although prone to crisis, the dynamics of capitalism effectively ensures the system's survival by developing new regimes of accumulation at critical moments. Of particular importance is the distinction that regulationists draw between what they term the 'Fordist' and the 'post-Fordist' regimes of accumulation. The former was seen as characterized by the rise of mass production in the period from the 1930s, which enabled the achievement of large-scale productivity growth and which, in turn, could be translated into real wage increases. As wage levels increased, producers found that they had large markets for their goods and were able to increase production further. This 'virtuous cycle of mass production and mass consumption' (Jessop, 1990) is said to have characterized the capitalist economic system from the late 1930s to the mid-1970s. By way of contrast, the nature of post-Fordism, which is seen to be emerging from the collapse of the Fordist regime of accumulation, is less clear. However, its principal characteristics are suggested to include the growth of more flexible production methods based on new technologies, a diversification of economic activity, the increased importance of the service sector and the emergence of more segmented consumption patterns. It is also suggested that the process of transition from the

Fordist to the post-Fordist era has resulted in a significant degree of economic and social dislocation. Thus, the period since the mid-1970s has borne witness to a number of economic crises associated with the progressive demise of the Fordist regime.

The second reason for capitalism's survival, according to the regulationists, is that it has been able to foster particular political and social arrangements which regulate the system's internal contradictions and the conflicts that it generates. These 'modes of regulation' grow up within the context of particular regimes of accumulation and do not constitute permanent arrangements, since they are themselves prone to periodic crisis and reconfiguration. However, despite this transience, regulationists have identified a set of relatively long-lived regulatory arrangements that they suggest underpinned the Fordist regime of accumulation. In particular, it is generally suggested that the Keynesian welfare state was particularly crucial to the operation of Fordist capitalism (Jessop, 1994). As a mode of regulation, the Keynesian welfare state provided a means of underpinning the virtuous cycle of mass production and mass consumption. On the production side, a range of social policy measures were introduced to ensure the availability of a sufficiently healthy and skilled labour force. At the same time, on the consumption side, Keynesian macro-economic policies and the provision of welfare benefits helped to maintain the overall level of consumer demand.

Since there is no general agreement about how the post-Fordist regime of accumulation should be characterized, there is also some dispute about how it may or may not be being regulated. Indeed, some observers have suggested that the crisis of Fordism has done little more than lead governments into a desperate search for the policy mechanisms with which to manage the new economic order (Peck and Tickell, 1994). The most coherent statement of the changing role of the state under post-Fordism is provided by Jessop (1994), who suggests that two particular tendencies are observable. First, he points to the demise of the Keynesian welfare state and suggests that it is progressively being replaced by what he describes as the Schumpetarian workfare state (SWS). Although there are held to be several possible variants of the SWS, it is generally held to signify a scaling down of welfare commitments and the subordination of social policy concerns to economic policies that lay increased stress on supply-side issues such as competitiveness rather than demand-management. Second, he points to a reconfiguration of the geographical levels at which the state intervenes in social and economic affairs. Specifically, Jessop points towards a 'hollowing-out' of the state, involving the transfer of central state capacities upwards (to transnational bodies such as the EU) and downwards (to new and existing forms of local and regional institutions).

Stoker (1989) was the first to attempt to apply the logic of regulation theory to the specific context of British local government.[2] In this pioneering account, Stoker identified three distinctive roles that local government had played in the UK during the course of the twentieth century, each of which he suggested was linked to a particular phase of capitalist development. Thus, in the early part of the century, local authorities were engaged mainly in the provision and management of infrastructure and utilities required to underpin the functioning of the factory system. However, in the early post-war period, the role of local authorities began to be redefined, a process that Stoker links directly to the rise of Fordism.

> Under Fordism, local authorities increasingly re-focused their activities and spending in order to become key instruments of the welfare state. Local authorities in this country lost responsibility for trading utilities – such as gas, electricity, and later, water – but were given new responsibilities for a range of services associated with the welfare state. They provided key services such as housing and education directly. They planned future provision and established future need. . . . As such local authorities helped to ensure an educated, housed and healthy workforce. (pp. 149–50)

Moreover, having argued that the transition to Fordism had brought about a shift in the role played by local government, Stoker goes on to suggest that the onset of a post-Fordist era may have had similarly far-reaching implications. Reviewing the key changes in local government during the 1980s in light of the main propositions of the regulationist approach, Stoker points to a number of trends that he suggests are indicative of a transition to post-Fordism. First, Stoker suggests that the contracting-out of local government services, the creation of local quangos operating beyond the control of elected local authorities, the enhanced influence of the private sector in local government and the more general challenge to the notion of local authorities as providers of services are all key features of the new order. Likewise, changes in the delivery of public services, such as the emergence of more segmented patterns of public service consumption and attempts to adapt service provision to individual needs through greater 'customer focus', are also seen to portend the role of local government in the post-Fordist era. In addition, the changing management of local government is seen as a further area in which post-Fordist tendencies are apparent, such as in the use of more flexible labour arrangements, a flattening of hierarchical structures and the introduction of New Public Management techniques inspired by management innovation in the private sector.

There are a number of problems with the regulationist account put forward by Stoker. First, it is not clear whether the changing face of local government is seen as the product of a transition to a new form of capitalist accumulation or whether it is rather more simply the result of a particular ideological perspective, i.e. Thatcherism. In Stoker's view, the changes he describes are indicative of the rise of a distinctive neo-liberal response to the prevailing patterns of social and economic change created by the transition from Fordism. He thus suggests that the intention was to create local government structures that are 'compatible with the flexible economic structures, two-tier welfare system and enterprise culture which, in the Thatcher vision, constitute the key to a successful future' (Stoker, 1989, p. 159). However, by proposing that the creation of a post-Fordist local government is a specifically neo-liberal response to the crisis of Fordism, Stoker conflates these two dimensions and fails to demonstrate that the Thatcherite agenda for local government was intended to address specific problems arising in the post-Fordist regime of accumulation.

Second, Stoker also fails to distinguish in his account between the role that local government may play as part of a broader mode of regulation and the principles on which the management of local government is based. Thus, while evidence that local authorities are adopting supply-side economic development measures could be interpreted as part of a wider shift to a post-Fordist mode of regulation, the same clearly cannot be said about the emergence of flatter organizational structures in local government. Recent changes to the way in which services are delivered or local authorities are managed could, perhaps, be interpreted as being characteristic of a post-Fordist system of production (Painter, 1991). But they are probably best seen as a reflection of a longer-run tendency for local government to seek to import models from the private sector – a practice that dates at least as far back as the adoption of corporate management in the early 1970s. Third, even if the transition to customer-focused service delivery and flatter, less hierarchical structures were an indication of the emergence of post-Fordist local government, such an assumption would hold only if local authorities had hitherto been characterized by rigid service-uniformity and strict organizational hierarchy. However, as Cochrane (1993) notes, the central role played by professional groups in local government after 1945 had already served to create less hierarchical structures and encouraged the growth of professional discretion and, by implication, variation in the decision-making process.

Despite the flaws in Stoker's account, it is important not to throw the baby out with the bath water. Other aspects of the regulationist account appear to be less problematic. For example, the notion of the hollowing-out of the nation-state, although often over-stated, may potentially be employed to explain a diverse set of trends in local government, including the increased attention that local authorities have given to local economic development functions, the emergence of sub-regional partnerships and regional bodies, and the growing role played by local authorities in the European policy process. It is this aspect of the regulation theory that we will primarily return to in the remainder of this book.

Conclusion

In this chapter we have seen how theories of local government have increasingly given way to theories of local governance in recognition of far-reaching changes in the local policy process in recent years. Although governance remains a somewhat slippery concept, it is nonetheless valuable as a means of signifying the nature of the shift that has taken place (see chapter 5). However, governance does not, in itself, represent a theory and does not, therefore, provide any significant insight into the factors that lie behind these developments. Consequently, it is important to consider the way in which governance itself has been theorized. To this end, we have assessed the relative merits of three distinctive theoretical contributions: the power-dependence model, regime theory and regulation theory.

We now return to a question that was raised towards the beginning of the chapter: how do these theoretical positions relate to the creative autonomy thesis? Though none of the theories considered deals directly with issues of local autonomy, a number of insights can be drawn from them that are developed subsequently in this book. First, the conclusions drawn from the power-dependence and policy networks approaches are important for the stress that they place on the degree to which the centre is limited in its capacity to direct local government. In chapter 3 we shall see how power-dependencies in the British state were to impose important restrictions on the capacity of central government to achieve its objectives in relation to local government during the 1980s. Second, regime theory also has value in that it suggests that local government can, with the support of other actors at the local level, assemble a capacity to govern that is not dependent on the central state. This conclusion has applications in relation to the growth of partnership working in local government and, in particular, to the rise of public–private partnerships. In chapter 6 we consider the extent to which such arrangements have been developed in a UK context and suggest that, despite a number of misgivings, they have been an important source of creative autonomy. Third, regulation theory offers the important insight that fundamental changes are taking place in the organization of economic activity and the structuring of state intervention. One possible consequence of these changes is a growing role for local governance as part of a wider process of the 'hollowing-out' of the nation-state. This thesis has particular application to the increasing role being played by local authorities in implementing international environmental agreements (see chapter 9) and the growing linkages between local government and the European Union (see chapter 10).

3

British Local Government since 1979

Two Decades of Change

Introduction

In the previous chapter we noted the widely held view that the role of local government in the British state has undergone a major transformation since the late 1970s. This chapter provides a more detailed assessment of the specific nature of the changes that have taken place. Aside from cataloguing the principal reforms that were introduced in the period after 1979, it also engages with two key debates about the character of local government reform over the past two decades. The first of these is the issue of the extent to which the Conservatives' policy agenda constituted a coherent new-right project for the UK, as part of which a particular role was envisaged for a reformed local government sector. The second key debate concerns the extent to which the end product of these reforms has been a significant increase in central control, coming at the expense of local autonomy and the scope for local authorities to tailor policy to the needs of the locality.

The chapter begins by examining the notion that Thatcherism constituted a coherent political doctrine which provided the route map for a government intent on dismantling the pillars of the post-war consensus, on which local government's role was largely premised. It then turns to assess the way in which the Conservative agenda for local government unfolded, examining each of Margaret Thatcher's terms of office in turn and considering whether the policies of the Major governments of 1990–7 represented continuity or change from what went before them. The chapter also reviews the debate surrounding central control and local autonomy and examines the extent to which there is evidence of centralization. It is suggested that, while centralization has clearly been the intention, central government's success in achieving this objective has, at best, been mixed. In part, this relative failure to achieve central control is due to the government's failure to understand the constraints imposed by power-dependences in central–local relations. Just as important, however, are a number of forces operating externally to the system of central–local relations, which have opened up spaces for local authorities to pursue strategies of creative autonomy.

Thatcherism and the State

There are numerous accounts of the nature of Thatcherism and of the values and beliefs on which it drew (Hall and Jacques, 1983; Kavanagh, 1986; King 1987; Gamble, 1988). Despite considerable agreement, these assessments do evidence important differences of perspective. On the one hand, there are accounts that advance a relatively 'pure' view of Thatcherism, regarding it as a concerted attempt to recreate the UK according to the tenets of a relatively rigid set of ideological principles. Authors who have taken this view point to what they see as a distinctive new-right political philosophy, premised particularly on a powerful belief in the free market and an equally powerful critique of state intervention. Moreover, such accounts regard the Conservatives' election victory as marking a radical, overnight shift in post-war politics, designed to dismantle the post-war consensus and replace it with a new consensus built on these key new-right principles (Hall, 1979). On the other hand, there is a more 'pragmatic' view that interprets Thatcherism more in terms of its overall political strategy than in relation to the purity of its ideas. In this characterization, Thatcherism is still seen as embodying a certain set of political principles, but the extent to which these were either coherent or widely accepted enough to inform a 'masterplan' is played down. Instead, Thatcherite policies are suggested to have evolved from a general set of beliefs which, over time, gained credence among ministers and key policy influentials, resulting in a series of progressively more radical measures.

Thatcherism as a political philosophy

If Thatcherism can be characterized as a political philosophy, it is evidently one that borrowed eclectically from numerous sources of inspiration. Rather than discuss the relative importance of this diverse set of ideas, it is sufficient here to identify seven distinctive 'isms' that informed

Margaret Thatcher's politics in the 1980s. Between them, these seven principles constitute the core of Thatcherite thinking in relation to the economy, society and the state.

- *Capitalism*: a powerful belief in the virtues of market forces and a view that, rather than attempting to tame the free market, capitalism should be popularized, so that its benefits can be enjoyed by the vast majority.
- *Entrepreneurialism*: seen as the dynamic behind the operation of the market and, hence, as the motor of social progress.
- *Monetarism*: an economic policy, based on the work of Milton Friedman, which rejected the idea that the government could maintain full employment and instead recommended that the government's economic policy role should consist of providing for low inflation by controlling the supply of money.
- *Individualism*: an assertion of the primacy of individual freedom and a dismissal of the concept of equality, which lay stress not only on the individual's right to choose, but also on the individual's responsibility for personal failure. Claims based on some form of wider social responsibility were rejected, as expressed in Thatcher's view that 'there is no such thing as society'.
- *Liberalism*: the view, originating in the nineteenth century, that the interventionist state constituted an affront to personal liberty. Thatcherism reflected these Victorian ideas that state intervention should be kept to a minimum.
- *Moralism*: a traditional view of morality that praised 'Victorian values', including a belief in self-reliance, the importance of the family unit and the virtues of discipline and hard work. The state was seen as a key agent of enforcing moral standards, particularly through the system of law and order.
- *Nationalism*: the attempt to reassert the place of the British nation on an international stage, reflected most dramatically in the Falklands war, but also in the attitude taken towards European integration and in the emphasis put on providing the UK with a strong military presence.

However, the idea that Thatcherism represented the systematic translation of a coherent political philosophy into a coherent political project is problematic for three main reasons. First, the various sources of inspiration that contributed to the Thatcherite *Weltanschauung* were in many ways too contradictory to constitute a coherent political philosophy. Particular contradictions were evident between the conservative and liberal elements of Thatcherism and, as was implied above, in the attitude towards state intervention. Second, there is limited evidence that the Conservative Party as a whole or even the Cabinet shared the values espoused by Margaret Thatcher and her principal allies. A number of more moderate Conservatives continued to hold positions of influence in both the Cabinet and the party at large, and it was probably not until 1987 that Thatcher could stop asking whether some of her closest colleagues were truly 'one of us'. Third, even though a number of clearly Thatcherite policies were introduced, recognizably underpinned by new-right principles, the experience of putting theory into practice often altered Thatcherite values beyond recognition. For example, the flagship economic policy of monetarism was to prove little more than a short-lived experiment that rapidly gave way to a combination of fiscal conservatism and interest rate manipulation.

Nonetheless, the principles underpinning Thatcherism did have profound implications for the way in which the role of the state was perceived in relation to social and economic processes. Thatcherism was premised on a critique of state intervention, of which there were several strands. First, influenced by the doctrines of neo-classical economics, Thatcher and her allies espoused the belief that government intervention was a barrier to the operation of the free market and, therefore, to the achievement of the maximum social benefit. Second, the state bureaucracy was seen as inefficient and self-serving, conclusions that were made academically respectable by the work of public choice theorists such as William Niskanen (1971; 1973). Third, particular criticism was reserved for state welfare provision, which not only was regarded as being unjustifiably expensive, but more importantly was seen as self-defeating, since it was held to lead to a dependence on state provision. This was argued to have led to a dependency culture, in which those in receipt of state welfare were increasingly unable or unwilling to take responsibility for their own welfare. Finally, the state provision of welfare was seen to have led to the creation of state monopolies that restricted individual choice.

However, commentators on Thatcherism have also sought to qualify the way in which it perceived the role of the state. In particular, it has been stressed that 'less state' did not mean a 'weak state' (Gamble, 1988). As we have noted, Thatcherism saw a need for the state playing a significant role in maintaining law and order and in providing for the defence of the nation. To a large extent, this reflected the nineteenth-century idea of the 'night-watchman state': that is, one that played a minimal role but which was fundamentally concerned with protecting social order from both internal disorder and external threat. The state was seen as central to ensuring the conditions in which the free market could operate effectively. Consequently, the Thatcher governments continued to intervene in the economy, particularly in the form of supply-side measures aimed at removing obstacles to operation of the free market. As a result, Gamble (1988) has suggested that the politics of Thatcherism was typified by a belief in 'the strong state and the free market'.

Thatcherism as an attack on the post-war consensus

It has widely been argued that Thatcherism represented a definitive break with the post-war consensus that had shaped the way the UK was governed from 1945 onwards (see chapter 1). Thus, it is proposed that, following her election in 1979, Margaret Thatcher set about dismantling this consensus through a policy programme which introduced monetarism, privatized state-owned industries, restricted trade union powers and cut back on key areas of welfare expenditure. However, although this is essentially the view taken by Thatcher herself (Thatcher, 1993), there are two principal problems with it.

First, it fails to recognize that the policies which had underpinned the Keynesian welfare state had already been under pressure for a decade. The Heath government of 1970–4 had attempted to implement a number of the policies that were subsequently to be deemed Thatcherite, including the abandonment of reflationary economic measures, the reduction of state ownership and legislation to introduce trade union reform. Although the Heath administration famously 'u-turned' on its proto-Thatcherite agenda after 1972, the problems it was intended to address did not take long to resurface. As we noted in chapter 1, during the mid-1970s deep-rooted structural problems in the UK economy were exposed by the onset of the international crisis. The Keynesian policies of the Labour government rapidly succumbed to a combination of high unemployment, rising inflation and a deepening Public Sector Borrowing Requirement. Labour's decision to take out a loan from the International Monetary Fund (IMF) brought with it certain conditions, including that the government take immediate steps to reduce public expenditure and bring inflation under control. If monetarism was not yet born in 1976, Keynesianism had certainly died.

Second, the validity of the view depends on how the post-war consensus is defined (Butcher et al., 1990). There is no real evidence that the Thatcher government's agenda in 1979 went any further than a concern to accelerate the proto-monetarist policies introduced by the outgoing Labour administration and a determination to succeed where Heath had failed in relation to denationalization and trade union reform. If the definition of the post-war consensus is restricted to economic policy, then the Thatcher governments clearly did suggest a break from Keynesian demand-management, the mixed economy and corporatist bargaining. However, the main pillars of the welfare state underwent comparatively little change before 1987. Hence, there is a somewhat more measured view of the strategy employed by the Thatcher governments: namely, that they began with a concerted attempt to reverse the economic policies of previous administrations and then assumed progressively more radical ambitions in relation to the welfare state, most, but not all, of which were realized in their third term of office.

Thatcherism and Local Government

The contrasting views of Thatcherism discussed above have important implications for the way in which the experience of local government reform is interpreted. Where the 'pure' interpretation of Thatcherism holds sway, local government reforms have generally been regarded as a key element of a new-right blueprint that the Thatcher government set about implementing on the day it took office (Duncan and Goodwin, 1988a). More 'pragmatic' accounts, on the other hand, have interpreted events in less explicitly ideological terms, suggesting that the Thatcher governments' policies towards local government were developed over time. This interpretation reflects the assumption that the Thatcher governments became increasingly radical as the 1980s progressed (Stewart and Stoker, 1995b). A third, 'ultra-pragmatic' interpretation rejects ideological considerations almost entirely and argues that the Thatcher governments centralized power merely as a political strategy designed to ensure their own political survival (Bulpitt, 1989).

Thatcherism as an ideological attack on local government

The view that local government reform in the 1980s stemmed from the principles of a Thatcherite ideology is most coherently expressed by Duncan and Goodwin (1988a; 1988b). Using a theoretical framework derived from Marxist principles, Duncan and Goodwin (1988b) draw particularly on the argument advanced by Miliband (1973) that the local state could act as an obstacle to the central state and offered the possibility for some working-class gains to be made at the local level. In addition, Duncan and Goodwin argue that uneven development under capitalism has implications for the local state, in that it produces significant policy variation. The local state thus acts as a conduit for specifically local interpretations of capitalism (the interpretational role) and provides a mechanism through which local representation can seek to influence responses to that interpretation (the representational role). In certain localities, where a radical interpretative and representational role becomes dominant, the local state may develop strategies that are antagonistic to the local state, as was the case with the GLC and other new urban left councils in the 1980s. As a result, such councils are thrown into direct conflict with the central state, which may then seek to impose its own interpretation on the local state.

Duncan and Goodwin argue that because of the local state's potential to obstruct and contradict the central state, the centre will always seek to control sub-national authorities. However, they argue that until 1979 local political autonomy was tolerated 'within strict overall constraints' (Duncan and Goodwin, 1988a, p. 50). However, they suggest that even such limited local autonomy could no longer be tolerated by the Conservatives when they took power. Committed to a project of 'introducing the values of the market place into all areas of social and economic life' (p. 49), the government was determined to remove all possible obstacles to this radical policy. Consequently, the government immediately set about centralization on two fronts: control of local government finance and control of the policy areas in which local government played a significant role. This two-pronged strategy represented a direct attack on local government, which was subsequently stepped up when authorities such as the GLC mounted a direct challenge to the government's 'plan to reshape Britain from above' (p. 62).

Thatcherism as a pragmatic but progressively radical strategy

Other observers, while alert to the radical ambitions of Thatcherism, dispute the fact that this implies that the Conservatives arrived in office with a clear strategy for local government reform. For instance, Stewart and Stoker (1995b, p. 2) argue that the government had no predetermined strategy and that it 'learnt its strategy through experience'. While they accept that the government was influenced by a variety of ideological positions, they interpret the Conservatives' approach to local government reforms as an evolving one. Thus, experimental policies that proved successful were often built upon, while others floundered and had to be 'adapted and changed to overcome resistance or implementation failure' (Stewart and Stoker, 1995a, p. 192). Moreover, significant political constraints would have prevented any immediate, full-scale attack on local government, such as the views of Conservative-controlled local authorities (Butcher et al., 1990). Indeed, while Mrs Thatcher was herself deeply ambivalent, if not openly hostile, towards local government, it is equally clear that her views were not shared by the Cabinet as a whole. Thus, as Kenneth Baker makes clear in his memoirs:

> Margaret did not have much time for local councils, which she expected to be the agents of central government. She said to me once with a resigned sigh, 'I suppose we need them.' However, many activists in the constituencies were councillors, and some MPs had served as councillors, as I had done . . . So there was something schizophrenic in our attitude to local government. (1993, p. 111)

Such accounts also stress the lack of any degree of consistent application of principles to local government reform. Reviewing the Conservatives' record up to the mid-1990s, Stewart and Stoker (1995a, p. 194) suggest that 'The government's approach to changing local government has certainly been inconsistent; it is becoming increasingly incoherent.'

Local government and the politics of statecraft

An alternative interpretation of the Conservative governments' policies towards local authorities is provided by the notion of the politics of statecraft put forward by Bulpitt (1983; 1986; 1989). Bulpitt advances an account of centralization which assumes that, rather than seeking to implement a set of policies deduced from a particular ideological position, the behaviour of the political elite is primarily determined by rational considerations. Specifically, this elite will attempt 'to protect and promote what it perceives to be its own interests' (1989, p. 56). This implies that ideological considerations will only be used 'to justify, or add gloss to, behaviour and decisions already determined by statecraft considerations' (p. 56). The major factors influencing governmental strategies are therefore assumed to be 'the art of winning elections and achieving some necessary degree of governing competence in office' (1986, p. 21).

Based on these assumptions, Bulpitt presents an historical account of central–local relations which suggests that the governing elite under Thatcher regarded the traditional autonomy of local authorities as a threat to the achievement of these basic objectives of statecraft. Bulpitt's argument is essentially in two stages. First, he proposes that in the period from the 1920s to the 1960s the British state operated as a particular statecraft regime in which the roles of central and local government were clearly distinguished. This regime, the 'dual polity', established the national state's concern as the 'high politics' of economic and foreign policy, while local authorities were left to undertake tasks associated with the 'low politics' of welfare and other services. Under this model, local authorities were trusted with a relatively high degree of autonomy, which they had gained in return for not fundamentally questioning the role of the centre. However, this was a bargain that very much rested in the hands of the national elite, since for local authorities 'the survival of the autonomy they possessed rested in the hands of others, in particular the national party leaders and their continual perception that their interests did not require more central control' (1989, p. 67).

The second stage in Bulpitt's analysis is that, particularly after 1979, the governing elite was driven by self-interest to seek to restrict the autonomy of local government. Specifically, he suggests that, while the Conservatives 'did not arrive in office determined to clobber local authorities' (p. 68), local authority resistance increasingly threatened the success of the government's core statecraft objectives. In particular, the refusal of many councils to accept the logic of the government's attempt to control public expenditure, and the associated rise of a highly visible political challenge from a number of authorities controlled by the Labour left, were seen to be undermining the government's position. In this context, Bulpitt suggests that restricting local autonomy was quite simply 'the easiest option open to frustrated politicians' (p. 65). As a result, the Conservatives developed a series of policies in the 1984–7 period that would subordinate the government's policies towards local authorities to their national political objectives (Bulpitt, 1989).[1]

Local Government Reform, 1979–97

There are numerous reviews of the impact that the Conservative governments had on local government (Pickvance, 1991; Travers, 1989; Cochrane, 1993; Stewart and Stoker, 1995a; Rhodes, 1997). We do not attempt, therefore, to offer an all-encompassing account of the reforms that the Thatcher and Major governments introduced. However, we have elected to present the key changes of the period in a broadly chronological order, taking each of the Conservatives' terms of office in turn. This narrative is used to assess the competing claims made above as to whether the reforms were introduced as part of a coherent new-right or Thatcherite agenda or whether they emerged incrementally in response to changing political conditions. It also provides a means of assessing the extent to which there was continuity between the Thatcher and Major governments. However, dividing up the period of Conservative rule in this way should not obscure the fact that there were key themes running through the entire period. Reforms to the system of local government finance feature throughout, as do the introduction of market mechanisms in local government and the removal of functions from local authorities, albeit not with the same, almost obsessive, consistency.

The issue of local government finance is undoubtedly the most important in this narrative. During the Conservatives' first two terms of office, their agenda for local government was dominated by attempts to reform the way in which local authorities were resourced, and in the period from 1988 to 1992 local government finance became perhaps the key political issue of its time (see chapter 4). There are good reasons why the issue of local government finance loomed so large. To begin with, it had already been on the agenda for some time. Particularly significant was the fact that the Conservatives had a long-standing aim of abolishing the domestic rates (Butler, Adonis and Travers, 1994). At the time of the 1979 election, this policy commitment presented the Conservatives with a serious dilemma. On the one hand, there was no real policy alternative except for local income tax, which was considered politically unpalatable. Yet, on the other hand, dropping the policy entirely was equally difficult, since it was a key issue among Tory supporters. In 1979 the problem was addressed by making a vague commitment to rates reform, but during the 1980s, as rates increases brought the issue to a head, the dilemma re-emerged, resulting in a number of unanticipated policy decisions.

The wider economic policy agenda of the incoming administration also raised the position of local government finance on the government's agenda. Since local authorities account for approximately one-third of total public expenditure, any significant attempt to reduce public expenditure would have to involve local government bearing its share of the burden. Thus, even before it was forced to accept the conditions of the IMF loan, the Labour government had signalled its intent to reduce its financial support to local authorities. In a much-quoted speech in 1975, Tony Crosland, the Secretary of State for the Environment, declared: 'We have come to terms with the harsh reality of the situation which we inherited. The party's over' (Crosland, 1983, p. 295). But it was after 1979 that attempts to reduce public expenditure were to have the most profound effect on local government. The Conservatives came to office committed to cutting the overall level of public expenditure while upholding or increasing the level of spending on health, law and order, and defence. The implication, therefore, was that the savings would have to be made in areas such as social services, housing and education, all of which were key local authority functions (Travers, 1986).

The first Thatcher government, 1979–83

If the Conservatives had come to power in possession of a blueprint for the radical reform of local government, it would arguably have been evident in two of the government's earliest pieces of legislation: the 1980 Local Government, Planning and Land Act and the 1980 Housing Act. Certainly, the two Acts did portend much of the government's future agenda, but whether they were conceived as the first element of a pre-defined plan is quite another question. The Local Government, Planning and Land Act introduced new provisions relating to the three core areas of reform – finance, functions and markets – outlined above. It established central powers to control local authority spending through the introduction of financial penalties (in the form of a reduced grant) for councils that spent in excess of defined levels. It created the legal provision for urban development corporations (UDCs) and enterprise zones – urban regeneration initiatives that bypassed local authority control and stripped them of specific powers. And it introduced the first elements of competition to local government service provision by specifying that a specific proportion of work carried out by local authority direct labour organizations (DLOs) in the areas of maintenance, construction and highways had to be subject to competitive tendering. Similarly, the 1980 Housing Act also had major implications for local authority functions and finance. The Act established the right of council tenants of more than three years' standing to buy their properties from local authorities at heavily discounted rates. It also introduced far-reaching cuts in subsidies for local authority housing construction. These measures marked the onset of a decline in local authorities' role as housing providers.

At the time, all of these measures were to prove politically controversial. However, whether they represented a radical break with the past and the ushering in of a new agenda is disputable. For instance, the outgoing Labour government had adopted a policy of placing DLOs on a more commercial footing, which would require them to act as independent trading bodies, making a return on capital and subject to tendering process (Walsh, 1995). The Labour government had devised the measures in response to scandals involving inflated building costs in Labour-controlled local authorities such as Manchester and Glasgow and as a means of preventing further embarrassments. Walsh (1995, p. 30) notes that the legislation on DLOs in the 1980 Act 'followed this model closely' and that the introduction of competitive tendering 'can be seen as an expression of an existing stream of policy thinking, rather than a break with the past'. Similarly, the sections of the 1980 Local Government, Planning and Land Act that laid down the legislative framework for UDCs were taken almost directly from the provisions laid down in the

1947 Town and Country Planning Act to implement the Labour government's policy of new town development corporations. Perhaps most notably of all, with the exception of the new financial legislation, no other element of the 1980 legislation was to be significantly built on until after 1987.

Moreover, the fact that the government continued to introduce fresh changes to the way in which local authorities were financed was a product of the persistent failure of legislation to bring about the desired results rather than an attempt to make progress on a pre-defined agenda. Having formally introduced expenditure targets and grant penalties in 1981, the government rapidly became aware that such controls were not proving particularly effective. Local authorities did not reduce their expenditure, using a combination of rate increases, to make up any shortfall in income resulting from the new scheme, and creative accounting, to avoid the imposition of financial penalties (see chapter 4). In response, the Conservatives introduced a further six significant changes to the grant system in the period to 1983 in an attempt to close the loopholes that local authorities were exploiting. In addition, the government began to shift the focus of its efforts from expenditure to income controls. This shift began with the introduction of legislation under the 1982 Local Government Finance Act to prevent local authorities levying 'supplementary rates': that is, introducing rate increases more than once in a financial year. One key effect of these changes was that local authorities found themselves operating in conditions of considerable uncertainty and therefore continued to increase the rates as a means of building up reserves to guard against further, unpredictable changes in the grant regime (Rhodes, 1997).

Beyond these ongoing, and ultimately futile, attempts to reduce local government expenditure, there were few indications that the government had any obvious agenda for local authorities. The Education Acts of 1979 and 1980 removed the compulsion that Labour had placed on local authorities to establish fully comprehensive education at secondary school level and introduced a degree of parental choice. But other than these measures, and the provisions made in relation to housing, DLOs and urban regeneration referred to above, there were no significant attempts to redefine the role of local government.

The second Thatcher government, 1983–7

If Thatcher's first term of office had produced little more in relation to local government reform than a cat-and -mouse game over local authority expenditure, her second administration largely involved more of the same, but with the added drama of it taking place against the backdrop of a showdown with a small number of local authorities that had begun to advocate a politics of local socialism.

During the Conservatives' first term of office, a number of Labour-controlled local authorities in the larger English cities had begun to espouse a new set of socialist principles that distinguished them from other Labour-led councils. Typified by the rise of politicians such as Ken Livingstone, who was elected leader of the Greater London Council (GLC) in 1981, this emerging breed of local politicians was frequently termed 'the new urban left'. They were united less by a single coherent ideology than by an attempt to bring a diverse set of new left values to bear on local government. In addition to the GLC, Labour councillors influenced by the values of the new urban left were to reach positions of influence in several London boroughs as well as in Manchester and Sheffield. The new urban left not only sought to introduce a distinctive political agenda to local government, but were intent on issuing a direct challenge to the policies of the Thatcher governments (see chapter 5). Livingstone, in particular, used his position to confront the government on a number of key issues, expressed most dramatically by the GLC's decision to display a running count of the capital's jobless total from its offices at County Hall. Meanwhile, in Liverpool, a Trotskyist variant of local socialism emerged as the Militant Tendency became increasingly influential on Liverpool City Council.

It was in the context of these development that a last-minute decision was taken to include a commitment to abolish the GLC in the Conservatives' 1983 manifesto. There is little evidence that this was anything other than a combination of *ad hoc* pragmatism and a knee-jerk reaction to Livingstone and others throwing down the gauntlet to the government. Yet, the search for a replacement for the rates was, ironically, the issue that ultimately put abolition on the agenda. Flynn, Leach and Vielba (1985) report that in 1982 a Cabinet sub-committee had been established with a primary remit to find a means of abolishing the domestic rates. Chaired by William Whitelaw and code-named MISC 79, the sub-committee was also asked to look into the possibility of abolishing the GLC and the six metropolitan counties. Unable to find a suitable means of replacing the rates, MISC 79 instead made the abolition of the GLC and the metropolitan county councils its principal recommendation (Flynn, Leach and Vielba, 1985).

Meanwhile, the government's continued failure to bring local authority spending under control was compounding party demands for the replacement of the rates. The implications of this long-standing policy commitment were again to prove significant in provoking policy change: this time in the form of the 1984 Rates Act (Travers, 1986). Under the terms of this Act, more stringent controls were introduced on the capacity of local councils to raise income through rate rises. In particular, the Act gave the Secretary of State for the Environment the power to exercise 'rate limitation', a policy that became popularly known as 'rate capping'. In essence, this legislation gave the Secretary of State the discretionary power to impose an upper limit on the rates set by a local authority. Used predominantly to restrict Labour councils, rate capping raised the tensions between the Conservatives and a handful of left-wing councils to new heights (see chapter 4). But the cat-and-mouse game continued: as the tension grew, Liverpool City Council briefly managed to outmanoeuvre the government and succeeded in gaining budgetary concessions from the Secretary of State for the Environment. While Liverpool's victory was short-lived, it proved to be a major source of embarrassment for the government and raised the stakes in the growing tensions between central and local government (Parkinson, 1985).

By the end of eight years of Conservative rule, the radical new-right agenda for local government was still yet to emerge. Once again, the Rates Act and the abolition of the GLC and the six metropolitan counties were controversial political moves that were regarded by most supporters of local government as 'an attempt by central government to gain further control of local government' (Flynn, Leach and Vielba, 1985, p. iv). Yet, they still did not amount to a far-reaching agenda for the reform of local government. While they represented radical measures, they were clearly provoked more by the political context of the mid-1980s than by any clear, ideological principles. Arguably, if ideology figured significantly in government legislation towards local authorities in the period to 1987, it was in the 1986 Local Government Act, which banned the financing of 'propaganda' activities with rates revenues and which was aimed particularly at the campaigning activities of some Labour authorities.

The third Thatcher government, 1987–90

If there was ever a distinctive new-right agenda for local government reform, it emerged in the year following Margaret Thatcher's victory at the 1987 general election. In 1988 four Acts of Parliament were passed that could lay greatest claim to heralding a revolution in local government. At the heart of this legislation were a series of reforms that began to redefine fundamentally the role of local authorities by casting them in the role of enablers rather than providers (see chapter 8). However, the radical nature of these changes was overshadowed by the penultimate chapter in the story of the Conservatives' search for a replacement for the rates: the introduction of the community charge.

The 1988 legislation went far further than anything previous in extending market practices in local authorities and removing local government functions. The Local Government Act of 1988 placed a requirement on councils to submit a range of functions to competitive tender. Under the terms of this Act, local authorities were now compelled to subject park maintenance, cleaning services, refuse collection, vehicle maintenance, catering and leisure management to compulsory competitive tendering. The Act also required councils to establish separate purchaser and provider functions within their organizational structure, as a means of creating an internal market mechanism. The extension of CCT was a reflection of the notion that local authorities should act as enablers, used in this context to mean 'purchasers' of services, rather than as service providers. This idea was also central to the 1988 Housing Act, which gave tenants the right to opt out of local authority control and to choose another landlord, thereby enabling the large-scale voluntary transfer (LSVT) of housing stock to other registered social landlords, such as housing associations. The Housing Act also laid down provision for the creation of housing action trusts, single-purpose housing regeneration bodies that would take specific council estates out of local authority control.

Some of the most significant changes were introduced under the terms of the 1988 Education Reform Act. Under the terms of this Act, schools were given the right to 'opt out' of the control of their local education authority if a majority in favour could be achieved in a ballot of parents. The Act also abolished the Inner London Education Authority (ILEA), devolved significant financial and management responsibilities to schools, introduced the national curriculum, which all state schools were required to follow, and removed the polytechnics from local authority control. In addition, it provided for the establishment of city technology colleges (CTCs), schools created directly by the secretary of state and sponsored by the private sector, which would emphasize science, technology and mathematics. The implications of these changes for local education authorities were potentially enormous. As a result of the provision for local management of schools (LMS), the capacity of local authorities to influence educational practice was diminished. The scope for schools to opt out of local authority control suggested that local government might cease to become a significant provider of education. The national curriculum appeared to remove any significant scope for local government to shape the content of what was taught locally. And CTCs were expected to appeal to parents to such an extent that they would introduce a significant degree of competition with local authority-run schools.

Given the fact that housing and education are two of the largest local government functions, in terms of both employment and spending, the implications of these legislative changes appeared, at the time, to be profound. Gamble (1988, p. 240) argued that the thrust of government policy at this time was such that it 'pointed to eventual abolition of local government altogether'. However, the initial impact of the new housing and education legislation was to prove seriously muted. In the first three years of LSVT, just fifteen authorities made use of the legislation, involving the transfer of a total of 81,500 housing units, mainly in Conservative-controlled district councils in the south of England (Mullins, Niner and Riseborough, 1992). Moreover, by this stage no Labour-controlled council had transferred housing stock; nor had any metropolitan authorities or London boroughs. Given that the total local authority housing stock in 1989 consisted of 5,270,000 units, the transfer of just 1.5 per cent of the total stock in three years suggested that the demise of local government's housing function would be some time coming. Indeed, the pattern that has emerged is one of local authorities and housing associations working in partnership to provide social housing, rather than the former's role being eroded by the growth of the latter (Wilson and Game, 1998).

Similar trends were evident in education. Evidently, the introduction of LMS has reduced the capacity of local authorities to influence the direct management of individual schools, but it has not removed their importance in establishing strategic education policy. Moreover, the government's encouragement for local schools to opt out of local authority control met with limited response. Indeed, by April 1997, out of a total of some 24,550 schools only 1,118 had become grant maintained schools (GMS) as a result of parental ballots (Wilson and Game, 1998). Likewise, there was no great stampede to establish CTCs: just fifteen were in existence by the late 1990s. And while the national curriculum did take away a degree of flexibility from local authorities and schools, later reforms made it less prescriptive and restored a greater degree of local authority influence on teaching content. Thus, it appears that local education authorities continue to play a significant role despite the objectives of the 1988 Education Reform Act.

If the other elements of the 1988 legislation were to prove only partially successful in meeting their objectives, the Local Government Finance Act of that year can only be classified as a policy disaster. This Act laid down the legal provision for a radical reform of the way in which local authorities were financed, at the centre of which was the community charge, or poll tax as it popularly became known. The history of the brief existence of this tax is far too complex to deal with here in any degree of depth (for a fuller account, see chapter 4). However, its centrality to the recent history of local government demands that we at least provide the highlights of this remarkable tragi-comedy. The 1988 Act abolished the domestic rates, the local business rate and the revenue support grant, respectively replacing them with the community charge, a uniform national non-domestic rate and a system of grant allocation based on standard spending assessments (SSAs). In addition, the Act also introduced fresh restrictions on capital expenditure. The new arrangements were introduced in Scotland in April 1989 and in England and Wales a year later.

There were two significant things about the new measures. First, the poll tax was to prove almost universally unpopular and attracted unprecedented levels of popular resistance. MORI surveys showed that, between 1987 and 1990, the proportion of the population positively disapproving of the tax rose from 45 per cent to 73 per cent (Butler, Adonis and Travers, 1994, p. 259). Resistance to the tax in the form of non-payment reached such levels in some areas that it almost brought the system of local government to collapse. Non-payment was particularly acute in Scotland, where it was estimated in September 1991 that 12 per cent of the taxes for 1989/90 were still outstanding, with the figures rising to 23 per cent and 77 per cent for the financial years 1990/1 and 1991/2 respectively (p. 179). Second, taken together, this package of reforms introduced tight restrictions on local government finance. The SSAs were used by government to define appropriate levels of spending for each authority and, therefore, appropriate levels for the community charge. These definitions were then used subsequently to justify placing a cap on local authorities that set their community charge above the proposed level. And the setting of a single national business rate removed the capacity for local authorities to raise the rate to generate additional revenues or to lower it in an attempt to encourage inward investment and business start-ups.

Yet, the introduction of the new system was not only intended to restrict the financial autonomy of local authorities. Rather, the changes appeared to have two contradictory objectives, which were never reconciled, and which were central to the political fallout created by the poll tax. On the one hand, the new system was clearly the *tour de force* of the government's attempts to achieve direct control over local authority spending. Yet, on the other hand, the introduction of SSAs and the poll tax was also intended to expose the inefficiency of high-spending Labour councils and thus undermine both Labour's local political base and, ultimately, its level of support nationally. Since the latter objective could be realized only if local councils were free to set the poll tax at whichever levels they chose, it was never likely to be realized. But, more significantly, because the primary objective was to force local authorities to reduce expenditure, the attempt to shift the blame for high spending to councils themselves fundamentally backfired. The end result of SSAs and capping was that high-spending local councils were forced to set poll tax levels which, although relatively high, still necessitated significant cuts in local services. In such circumstances it was probably inevitable that voters increasingly blamed the government for this situation, rather than their local councils or the Labour Party. Opinion polls showed that in 1988, 39 per cent of voters laid the responsibility for high poll tax rates with their local councils, while 33 per cent blamed the government. Yet by 1990, the same question prompted only 18 per cent to lay the blame at the doors of their local authorities, whereas 56 per cent now regarded the government as being responsible for the situation (Butler, Adonis and Travers, 1994, p. 259).

The poll tax was flawed from the very beginning (Cochrane, 1993). But the government had invested a great deal of political capital in the policy and introduced a series of increasingly desperate measures designed to make the tax more palatable, including a number of rebates to reduce the burden on those on lower incomes. The damage had been done, however, and none of the measures was to prove enough to prevent the haemorrhaging of popular support for the Conservative Party. As we note in chapter 4, there can be little doubt that the high-profile failure of the poll tax was a central element in Margaret Thatcher's demise. Thus, if the politics of statecraft had hitherto led the Conservative elite to pursue a policy of local government reforms, it was now to result in the removal of the party's leader.

Clearly, if the Conservatives ever had a particular agenda for local government, it was largely implemented in 1988. However, whether these reforms represented the achievement of a specifically Thatcherite vision for local government is highly questionable. Certainly, by the late 1980s, the Thatcher government's policies in general were more clearly influenced by new-right ideology and particularly by ideas drawn from public choice theory (see King, 1987). As a result, there were common threads to the 1988 legislation. As Travers (1989, p. 15) notes, 'their philosophical origins were similar, deriving from the ideas of right-wing think tanks and policy units', but he adds that the measures evolved separately rather than as a collective agenda. More fundamentally, as we have seen, large elements of the 1988 legislation were to prove to be failures, at least in relation to their original objectives. We shall return to this point below.

The Major governments, 1990–7

Upon becoming Prime Minister, John Major had one urgent priority: find an acceptable alternative to the poll tax. To this end he appointed Michael Heseltine, his principal challenger in the election for the Conservative Party leadership, as Secretary of State for the Environment. Heseltine had been an outspoken critic of the poll tax throughout and approached the task of finding a replacement with some zeal. Given the origin of the Poll Tax fiasco in the search for an alternative to the domestic rates, the result was somewhat ironic. The 1992 Act introduced the council tax, ostensibly a property tax tiered according to the property's value, and therefore not significantly different to the rates. Following the intense unpopularity of the poll tax, the new arrangements were greeted, if not with enthusiasm, then at least with relief by the local government community. Yet, the sting came in the tail. The 1992 Act retained and consolidated the use of SSAs and capping and indicated that, after twelve years of persistent effort, central government control over local authority finance had finally been achieved (see chapter 4).

Heseltine was not content, however, with concerning himself solely with local government finance. One of the unintended outcomes of the poll tax fiasco was that it had served to make local government one of the major domestic political issues of the early 1990s. In the bid to replace Thatcher in November 1990, the future of local government had thus featured strongly in the debate between rival candidates, with Heseltine, in particular, using the opportunity to advocate a broader vision of local government reform. This vision encompassed not just a replacement for the poll tax but also advocacy of elected mayors as a means of strengthening local democracy and proposals to bring about more effective local government through the creation of unitary authorities. Consequently, within a week of his appointment, the new Secretary of State announced his intention to undertake a complete review of the finance, structure and internal management of local government.

Beyond the introduction of the council tax, the Heseltine agenda was to give rise to three main strands of local government reform in the period to 1997. First, the government instigated a government commission charged to look into the options for rationalizing the overall structure of local government by creating unitary authorities in those parts of England that still had a two-tier system of local government (i.e. counties and districts). The Local Government Commission was established in 1992 and was quickly to become embroiled in controversy. Although the Commission was eventually to recommend the creation of forty-six new unitary councils, this was only to occur after a series of high-profile disputes with central government and with individual local authorities (see chapter 5).

Second, there was a shift towards the use of competitive bidding among local authorities for government resources. This policy began with Heseltine's instigation of new urban policy measures, which invited local authorities to take the lead in forming public/private/community sector partnerships that would then compete for government funding. These principles were originally put forward in the City Challenge initiative, introduced in 1991 and subsequently developed by the single regeneration budget (SRB), introduced in 1994. Moreover, competitive bidding was extended to a number of other policy areas including housing investment and rural development (Oatley, 1998). Alongside these developments was a third major element of the Major governments' agenda for local government: the consolidation of a private sector role. The government announced the extension of CCT into so-called white-collar functions in local government, such as accountancy and personnel and legal services. In addition, the period saw the introduction of the Private Finance Initiative (PFI), which marked a shift towards the private sector providing the resources for large-scale capital projects in the public sector (see chapter 6).

On the whole, the Major governments continued the thrust of previous policy. Indeed, in many ways, Major succeeded where Thatcher had failed. It was in the period 1990–7 that central government control over local government expenditure was achieved. However, some of the more radical elements of the government's policies towards local government were again subject to failure. The extension of CCT, in particular, was not achieved on any significant scale and a multitude of problems were experienced in relation to the PFI (see chapter 6). Yet while the Major governments were essentially to involve more of the same for local government, there were also signs that at least a degree of policy-making responsibility was being returned to local authorities. For example, City Challenge and the SRB at least partially reversed the tendency of using mechanisms and agencies that by-passed local authorities. As we shall see, the period also saw a notable increase in local authority attempts to carve out policy spaces independently from the centre. In addition, the 1990 Community Care Act established local authority social service departments as the lead agencies in community care provision. Under the terms of this Act, local authorities are responsible for assessing needs and co-ordinating service provision. The Act has clearly led to a major increase in the involvement of other agencies in the care of the elderly and the mentally ill. However, it is local authorities that are obliged to draw up annual community care plans and assess whether the resources of the various organizations involved in service provision are being used effectively. In this sense, the SRB and community care are archetypal examples of the new local governance, in which local authorities take a lead role in co-ordinating local policy networks (see chapter 5). Such developments suggest that local government's role is changing rather than diminishing.

Assessment: Was Centralization Achieved?

There is a powerful consensus that the British polity was centralized during the 1980s. From the beginning of the decade, a series of publications pointed towards the centralizing tendencies inherent in the growing number of legislative changes affecting local authorities after 1979 (Burgess and Travers, 1980; Newton and Karran, 1985; Duncan and Goodwin, 1988b). Some accounts suggested that the programme of reforms introduced by the Conservative governments of that period were a threat to the tradition of autonomous local government in the UK (Jones and Stewart, 1985). Others regarded the centralizing tendencies as a sign that the UK was 'out of step' with its European neighbours, where moves towards decentralization were underpinning more effective attempts to reconfigure the state and to modernize public sector management (Crouch and Marquand, 1989; Flynn and Strehl, 1996). Indeed, in one account, centralization under the Thatcher governments was deemed to have gone so far that 'Britain stands in sight of a form of government which is more highly centralised than anything this side of East Germany' (Newton and Karran, 1985, p. 129).

There can be little doubt that the period of Conservative rule from 1979 to 1997 did involve concerted attempts to restrict the autonomy of local authorities. However, whether these attempts actually succeeded is quite another question. Indeed, the straightforward centralization thesis can be disputed on two principal grounds. First, there is no reason to assume that the centre always got its way in its attempt to restrict local autonomy. Rhodes (1997, p. 6) argues that 'the centre's relations with local government have been characterised more by unintended consequences than by a revolution'. In this view, the government's attempts to engineer a centralized system of control are seen to have failed to a substantial degree due to a combination of resistance and evasion on the part of local authorities and to the inherently flawed assumptions that the policies themselves made about the functioning of the British state. Second, there have been a series of opportunities for local authorities to respond to wider patterns of change external to the operation of central–local relations. As Stewart and Stoker (1995a, p. 203) note, 'there were other influences upon local government apart from central government legislation', such as wider patterns of socio-economic change, developments in management theory and the growing role of the European Union. Through such pro-active activity, local authorities have carved out new spaces for independent action. We term such activity 'creative autonomy'.

The relative failure to achieve centralization

Any discussion of the extent of government centralization is bedevilled by the fact that there are problems in the way that centralization is measured. There is no generally accepted set of criteria that may be used to measure the extent to which a political system is centralized or the extent to which it allows scope for local autonomy. Comparative studies of local government that have attempted to make such assessments have tended to concentrate on easily measurable variables such as the respective proportions of local government income that are drawn from central and local sources. Applied to the recent history of UK local government (see chapter 4), such an approach evidently suggests a decline in local autonomy, but it does not represent the whole story. The fact that local authorities receive a significant proportion of their income from central government cannot simply be read as an indicator of centralization – the key issue is the extent to which local authorities are free to use the resources that they receive. The source of local government income is therefore at best a surrogate measure of local autonomy and at worst a misleading one.

Despite this problem, the thesis that the Conservative governments after 1979 embarked on and achieved a programme of governmental centralization that contrasted to a previous period of growing local autonomy can be disputed on a number of grounds. First, the Thatcher government was not unique in attempting to curtail the scope for local autonomy. As Flynn, Leach and Vielba (1985) point out, centralizing tendencies can be traced back to the immediate post-war period. If such a long-term view is taken, it is possible to identify 'the transfer of employment exchanges, electricity production and health services from local authority control to single-purpose organisations accountable to central government as the start of the process of centralisation' (p. 12). Second, the capacity for central control has been exaggerated. The centralization thesis often suggests that, because the British constitution accords no significant degree of protection for local government, 'the power of national government to restructure local government is absolute' (King, 1993, p. 217). However, as Pickvance (1991) notes, while this assumption is certainly true of the centre's capacity to alter the overall structure of local government, the picture is quite different in relation to central government's attempts to control local authorities in their day-to-day business.

Third, the difficulties of achieving central control are illustrated by the fact that many of the government's attempts at centralization were largely a failure, even when judged on their own terms. As Cochrane (1993, p. 67) points out, 'some core elements in the market-based (new right) agenda for change in local government have proved impossible to implement'. As we saw above, a number of government reforms failed in the 1980s and 1990s. Others, such as the provision for housing action trusts in the 1988 Housing Act, were to become viable only following bargaining with individual local authorities, which insisted on specific changes to the policy (Karn, 1993). These developments suggest a lack of central capacity to achieve its objectives. Rhodes (1997, p. 133) suggests that the extent to which the centre is able to control subordinate tiers of government is increasingly being undermined by a twin process of 'internal hollowing out (for example, institutional fragmentation) and external hollowing out (for example, globalisation)'. Based on these assumptions, Rhodes argues that 'the most important consequences of central government policy towards local government since 1979 are that: it produced a policy mess . . . in which neither level of government achieves its objectives; and it compounded the problem of central steering in a differentiated polity' (p. 113).

That there has been an enormous volume of legislation since 1979 directed at controlling local authorities is clearly beyond doubt. However, as Rhodes (1997) notes, the sheer amount of legislation was at least in part due to its persistent failure to achieve the desired results. Rhodes thus characterizes much of the government's activity as 'repetitive legislation'. This was particularly the case in the field of local government finance, where 'legislation was passed, failed in the courts or in its desired impact, so prompting a new bill ostensibly to correct the defects, but in fact to create more defects and consequent legislation' (p. 120). The overall failure of the government's attempts to bring about a reduction in either local government expenditure or employment has been pointed to by a number of observers. Writing in 1993, Cochrane noted that local government expenditure as a proportion of total public expenditure had remained more or less static in the period 1980–90 at about 30 per cent. Over the same period there was a minor drop in the absolute numbers employed by local authorities, explained largely by the transfer of the polytechnics out of local authority control (Cochrane, 1993, pp. 33–4).

Fourth, while the government was intent on removing power from local authorities, not all of its reform agenda was necessarily centraliz-

77

ing (Rhodes, 1997). For instance, while the legislation to allow schools to opt out of local authority control has removed powers from local authorities, it can hardly be described as centralization, since the policy involves the delegation of responsibility to headteachers and school governors. We have also noted above how measures such as City Challenge and the single regeneration budget returned powers to local authorities. To these we might add the example of community care, a policy field in which, from the early 1990s, local authorities were given the lead role as co-ordinators of a mixed economy of welfare.

Fifth, if genuine centralization had been achieved, we would expect the outcomes to be a diminishing degree of local policy variation and the loss of any capacity for independent action among local authorities. Yet, there is clearly evidence to suggest that local government is not quite so hamstrung. Carmichael (1994, p. 242) suggests that despite the evidently centralizing efforts of central government, 'the hostile climate has provided evidence of the diversity of responses to central government policies by local government'. Moreover, where international comparisons have been made, it has been noted that British local authorities have often led the way over their continental counterparts in the pursuit of European policy initiatives and in the development of local sustainability strategies (see chapters 9 and 10). These developments may seem counter-intuitive but, on closer examination, there is no real paradox at all. Instead, it appears that the very existence of a hostile climate has led local authorities in the UK to attempt to make greater use of those resources and opportunities that they have open to them. It is to these developments that we now turn.

The rise of creative autonomy?

If the evidence of centralization is patchy, the notion that local government has been the defenceless victim of a barrage of centralizing measures and has lost any capacity for independent action is simply not sustainable. Attempts by local authorities to chart an independent course were observable in the early 1980s. The resistance of a relatively small number of councils during the 1980s may have hit the headlines, but equally significant was the fact that at that time 'many councils were setting out more modestly to explore what was possible within the limits they faced' (Cochrane, 1993, p. 42). Indeed, as Cochrane notes, these authorities increasingly sought to test where the boundaries to local initiative actually were, with the result that 'there was continued evidence of new initiatives developing at the local level' (p. 42). Chief among these was the development of local economic strategies, through which local authorities attempted to develop policies independently from national economic management (see Campbell, 1990). Moreover, these pioneering attempts to introduce local economic development policies laid the foundations for a number of important innovations later in the 1980s, such as the growth of sub-regional partnerships (see chapter 6). Other examples of local policy innovation in the 1980s include new directions in service delivery (see chapter 8) and environmental protection (see chapter 9).

Butcher et al. (1990) suggest that local authorities responded differently to Thatcherism. Thus, while some Conservative-led authorities did use the new legislative frameworks to pursue a radical new-right agenda locally, many more councils resisted government policies. Moreover, local government reform was not restricted to Conservative initiatives. Local authorities continued to innovate throughout the period, and fresh ideas came from both the left and the political centre (Butcher et al., 1990). Their ideas have spread throughout the local government community and have even, at times, been picked up by national government. Both the Citizen's Charter (pioneered by York City Council) and public/private partnerships are notable examples. The election of a Labour government has taken this process of learning from local government a stage further. The White Paper 'Local government modernisation' takes forward a series of proposals that have grown up in local government over the past decade or more. Other examples include the Local Government Association's development of the New Commitment to Regeneration. Launched in 1998, and currently at an early stage of development, this policy is attempting to recast the nature of regeneration policy by focusing on the potential of local public expenditure in its totality. The policy has been welcomed by national government and is currently being developed by twenty-two pathfinder areas.

Such examples of creative autonomy have often been overlooked in the literature on local government. They occur where local authorities are able to find avenues for independent action within increasingly tight financial constraints and the restrictions imposed by the notion of *ultra vires* (see chapter 1). Creative autonomy is a development that, if anything, has been encouraged by persistent central attempts to control the activities of local authorities. Local government has been keen to demonstrate that it has the capacity for autonomous policy making, even within a centralized unitary state. Moreover, in seeking out such spaces of creative autonomy, local authorities may have had to face the constraints of a deeply unsympathetic central government, but they have also been in a position to exploit opportunities arising from changes external to the system of central–local relations. The process of hollowing-out pointed to by a number of theorists (see chapter 2) has not only reduced the centre's steering capacity (Rhodes, 1997), but also opened up fresh opportunities for sub-national government. Three particularly significant developments may be used to illustrate this point.

First, the globalization of economic activity is seen to have undermined the capacity of the central state to manage the national economy and has instead led to a view that state intervention in the economy is best undertaken at the local and regional levels. Second, the process of European integration has offered local authorities an opportunity to obtain resources to support innovative policy programmes in relation to local economic development and regeneration (see chapter 10). Third, the rise of global decision-making arrangements to develop policies to promote sustainable development has also brought with it a recognition that the local level is the most appropriate field of action for what is essentially a global problem (see chapter 9). Admittedly, creative autonomy has not been achieved across all policy areas and all local authorities; there are huge sectoral and geographical variations in the extent to which it has emerged. And there can be little doubt that in their major service areas of social services, housing and education, local authorities have experienced a clear loss of autonomy. Yet, as we have seen, local authorities have, at the very least, successfully defended their importance as service providers while also adopting new strategic roles in a more pluralist pattern of service delivery. Just as importantly, as we show in the remainder of the book, many local authorities have begun to redefine their role by moving into new policy fields where the scope for creative autonomy has grown over the past two decades.

Conclusion

This chapter has shown that the story of local government since 1979 is not simply one of relentless centralization and diminishing local autonomy. While long-run centralizing tendencies were clearly stepped up considerably under the Conservatives, we have also seen that aspects of their agenda were also advocated by the outgoing Labour administration. It is beyond doubt that, taken as a whole, the Conservative governments after 1979 were more intent on bringing about centralization than any previous ruling party. However, it is also clear that their strategies have been only partially successful. To begin with, there is only partial evidence that the British system of government is more centralized today than it was twenty years ago. Even more fundamentally, there is clear evidence of a mismatch between these governments' objectives and the actual outcomes of the policies that they produced. The events of the late

1980s therefore appear to add a great deal of weight to the power-dependence theories advanced by Rhodes, which were discussed in chapter 2. In particular, the stream of policy failures and unintended consequences confirm Rhodes' prognosis that 'the centre's capacity to achieve its aims has deteriorated' (Rhodes, 1988, p. 8).

The developments we have charted would, however, lead us to reject the notion of local government reform constituting a specifically Thatcherite project of creating a post-Fordist local government sector (cf. Stoker, 1989). Given the evident degree of policy failure and the extent to which policy was made 'on the hoof' rather than with an eye to a new-right blueprint, such a thesis appears entirely unsustainable. However, elements of regulation theory appear to be supported by our discussion of British local government since the early 1980s. This applied, in particular, to the tendencies towards 'hollowing-out' discussed above and to the notion that the post-Fordist era has ushered in a period of policy experimentation prompted by the demise of the Keynesian welfare state. It may well be that local authorities' attempts to carve out spaces of local autonomy can be seen in this light, and this is a theme to which we shall return subsequently.

Part II

Local Government from Thatcher to Major

Three Dimensions of Change

4

The Financing of Local Government

Introduction

Local government finance has long been a complex and problematic, if not somewhat tedious, policy area. However, the election of the Conservative government in 1979 saw the whole area take on an increased saliency. In the period from 1979 to 1997, successive Conservative governments brought about a radical and qualitative change in the financing of local authorities. Local authorities became a key target of a government that aimed to roll back the overburdening public sector and liberate the forces of the market. And the attempt to undermine local government power was at its most evident in the area of local finance (Davies, 1993, p. 80). To this end, a series of increasingly restrictive measures were imposed on the amount of money local authorities were allowed to spend. The world of local government finance, previously regarded in general as a rather technical backwater, developed an increasingly controversial and political hue. A number of highly contentious policies were brought in. Most contentious of all was the community charge, or poll tax, as it became more commonly known. The community charge was intended to bring a radical and major shake-up to the way local authorities raised their own revenue to pay for local services by replacing the long-established system of local rates. Instead, it proved to be one of the greatest policy disasters in post-war British politics, leading to riots in Trafalgar Square and tremors in the Tory shires. More specifically, it was an important contributory factor in the demise in 1990 of one of its major proponents, the Prime Minister Margaret Thatcher.

This chapter considers three interrelated issues. It begins by examining how local government is funded, paying particular attention to the issue of how a balance is struck between central government support on the one hand, and the exigencies of local autonomy on the other. Second, it provides a detailed analysis of the growing financial restraints imposed on local authorities under the Thatcher and Major governments, and charts how local authorities responded to these, at times in a successful and creative way. The final section looks at the issue of domestic rates and the attempt to find a more effective and appropriate method of raising revenues at the local level.

How is Local Government Funded?

When discussing how local authorities are funded, it is important to draw a distinction between two distinct types of local authority expenditure, namely revenue and capital. Revenue expenditure is the expenditure used to keep services functioning on a daily basis. This can include staff wages and salaries, electricity bills for libraries, office stationery, school books and petrol for council vehicles. Capital expenditure relates to such things as the construction of roads and buildings, the buying of land, and large items of equipment such as refuse collection vehicles. Capital and revenue expenditure have two common areas of funding. First, local authorities can raise revenue through the levying of local taxes in the shape of the council tax. However, there have been, as we will discuss below, a number of restrictions introduced on this form of revenue. As an illustration of this, in 1980/1 local authorities raised 26 per cent of their revenue through local taxes in the form of rates. By 1995/6, council tax, which had replaced rates, amounted to only 11 per cent of total local authority income (see figure 4.1). Second, local authorities also derive income from fees and charges. These vary from local authority to local authority, but include charges for such things as home help services, meals on wheels, and the use of local authority recreational facilities.

In addition, capital expenditure is funded from three other specific sources. First, capital grants are available from central government for specific capital projects. Examples are the Single Regeneration Budget Challenge Fund and Capital Challenge. Grants are also available from the European Union, particularly via the European Regional Development Fund. Furthermore, local authorities were encouraged by successive Conservative governments from 1979 to 1997 to look at new and imaginative ways to raise funds, including forming partnerships with the

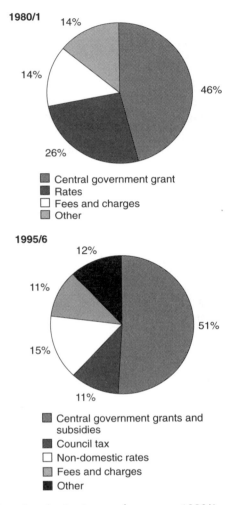

The Financing of Local Government

1980/1

14%

14%

46%

26%

■ Central government grant
■ Rates
□ Fees and charges
■ Other

1995/6

12%

11%

51%

15%

11%

■ Central government grants and
  subsidies
■ Council tax
□ Non-domestic rates
■ Fees and charges
■ Other

Figure 4.1 Local authority income by source, 1980/1 and 1995/6
Source: Local Government Financial Statistics.

private sector (see chapter 6). This policy has continued under the current Labour government. For example, in 1997 the London borough of Lambeth secured funding from London Electricity to refurbish one of its tower blocks.

Second, central government spells out to each local authority on an annual basis the maximum it can borrow to fund capital projects. It is important to note that borrowing for the purpose of funding current expenditure is not permitted. This system accounts for more than 50 per cent of the capital investment of local councils. There are a variety of borrowing sources available to local authorities. These include the Public Works Loan Board and commercial banks in the UK and Europe. Local authorities can also issue bonds and stocks. Third, local authorities can use capital receipts from the sale of capital assets such as land, buildings and housing stock. Under the previous Conservative government, however, local authorities were restricted to spending 25 per cent of receipts from housing sales and 50 per cent of receipts from the sale of other assets. The current Labour government has eased the restrictions on the use of receipts from housing sales.

In addition to fees and charges, there are two other sources that fund local authority revenue expenditure. First, income is provided by the national non-domestic rate (NNDR). The NNDR is a tax on local businesses. It is levied centrally and redistributed to local authorities on a per capita basis. It replaced the old domestic rates system in Scotland in 1989 and in England and Wales in 1990. We will return to this subsequently. Second, local authorities receive grants from central government. The largest of these grants is a general block grant in the form of the revenue support grant (RSG). Local authorities have discretion in how this money is spent, as it is not a specified grant. Traditionally, the bulk of central government grant support has taken this form. However, in recent years there has been a growing emphasis on more specific grants as central government has sought to influence the operations of local government more directly (see figure 4.2).

Local government has traditionally been dependent on central government financial support for a high percentage of its income to provide services. This financial state of affairs has implications for the autonomy of local government. The Layfield Committee (Layfield, 1976) was set up to consider the whole question of local government finance and central–local relations. It reported in 1976 and is regarded by many as the definitive analysis of local government finance (Butler, Adonis and Travers, 1994). It voiced its concern at the muddled way in which local authorities were financed. The situation needed clarification. It concluded that 'the main responsibility for local expenditure should either be placed upon the government or local authorities' (Layfield, 1976, pp. 300–1). For Layfield, local government had become too dependent on central government funding. Local autonomy was being severely undermined. The solution lay in local government being responsible for raising a higher percentage of its own revenue in the form of local taxes. A local income tax offered the best way forward. We will return to the issue of a local income tax and other forms of local revenue raising later in the chapter.

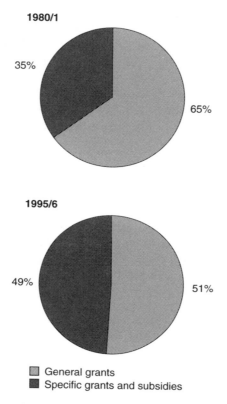

1980/1

35%

65%

1995/6

49%

51%

☐ General grants
■ Specific grants and subsidies

Figure 4.2 Percentage of general and specified central government grant, 1980/1 and 1995/6
Source: *Local Government Financial Statistics*.

However, the solution put forward by Layfield ran the risk of producing problems of resource inequality. Put simply, less affluent local authority areas are not in a position to raise the same level of resources as more affluent areas. Furthermore, poorer local authorities are likely to have greater pressures placed upon them and, as a consequence, may well require higher levels of resources. Indeed, one of the alleged benefits of central government grants is that they can be used to equalize out such resource disparities. Whether they do so in practice has been a focus for much debate. What is clear, however, is that no matter what system one adopts for raising local revenues, for the reasons outlined above some level of central government support is still required. The solution lies in devising a system that strikes an appropriate balance between local autonomy, on the one hand, and the exigencies of central support, on the other, and that it is seen to be fair and impartial. The experiences of the past twenty years have shown it to be a solution that is somewhat elusive.

The Increasing Financial Restraints on Local Government

As we noted in chapter 3, the 1980s produced a string of Conservative government initiatives aimed at reforming the financing of local government. Such initiatives did not come out of a vacuum. There had been widespread dissatisfaction for some time with the way local government was financed. There was a general recognition that the grant system was cumbersome and complex. In addition, the rates were viewed by many as unfair. However, the changes of the 1980s went beyond mere reform. Rather they produced a qualitative shift in the relationship between central government and local government. Indeed, for some commentators such reforms posed 'profound questions for the future of local democracy in Britain' (Newton and Karan, 1985, p. 114).

The reforms initiated in the 1980s and beyond have to be seen in context. Chapter 3 discussed how, prior to the election of the Thatcher government in 1979, there had existed since the Second World War a broad consensus about the value of local government and its role within the developing welfare state. In general terms, local government was seen as making a positive contribution to public policy in the UK. However, the Conservative general election victory of 1979 marked a sea change in the mentality of central government. It has been noted that 'within weeks of taking office, local government was strongly criticised by some ministers who claimed that it was wasteful, profligate, irresponsible, unaccountable, luxurious, and out of control' (Newton and Karran, 1985, p. 116). This was hardly an auspicious start. It was also the harbinger of what proved to be a stormy and tempestuous period in central–local relations.

As mentioned in chapter 3, the Conservatives returned to power in 1979 advocating a monetarist philosophy. The approach of the new government drew to a great extent on the work of two academics, Bacon and Eltis (Bacon and Eltis, 1978). This had particular significance for local government finance. The central core of their thesis was that the principal problems of the British economy lay in the fact that too few people were producing marketed goods and services. They drew a distinction between marketed outputs, which are sold, such as commercial products and services, and non-marketed products, which are not. These include social services, state education and the NHS. Bacon and Eltis went on to argue that an increasingly large proportion of the nation's resources had been directed into the non-marketed sector. As an example of this, they argued that in the period 1961 to 1975 employment in local government increased by nearly 70 per cent (p. 12). Such a growth served to crowd out the marketed sector, thereby reducing its ability to create wealth.

The Bacon and Eltis thesis has, however, been subject to criticism. Some commentators have noted that, in the reasoning of Bacon and Eltis, 'private health services are marketed and, therefore, a benefit to the economy, while the NHS is a non-marketed liability' (Newton and Karran, 1985, p. 23). Their assertion of significant employment growth in the non-marketed sector in areas such as local government is also challenged (Newton and Karran, 1985). Despite such criticisms, however, the 'crowding out' theory gained increasing respectability and acceptance amongst key Conservative policy-makers and right-wing think tanks in the late 1970s and provided academic credence for the financial restrictions imposed on local government by successive Conservative governments from 1979 to 1997.

The block grant in the 1980s

The early 1980s saw a succession of Acts of Parliament aimed at restricting the financial freedom of local government. Central government concern about local government expenditure was not, however, a new phenomenon. As part of macro-economic management, governments had traditionally sought to limit the amount local authorities spent. However, this was generally done within what have been described as 'the rules of the game'. Up to 1979, decisions about the annual level of local government expenditure were based on a multilateral approach that involved central government in consultation with the various local authority associations through the Consultative Council on Local Government Finance (CCLGF). After 1979, however, the approach became a unilateralist one with central government seeking to impose its will on local government (Dunleavy and Rhodes, 1986). Furthermore, central government had previously been concerned to control aggregate local government expenditure. The new Conservative government, while still concerned about general levels of local expenditure, increasingly sought to control the expenditure of individual local authorities; specifically, it sought to target the expenditure of a number of local authorities that it perceived as being 'over-spenders'.

While the Conservative government could seek to claim that its legislation was simply seeking to bring some financial rectitude to local government, there was nonetheless a strong ideological flavour in the cocktail of central–local relations. Writing of the proposals in June 1980, Ken Livingstone, who became leader of the Greater London Council in 1981, talked of 'Michael Heseltine's plans to crush the main Labour-controlled London Councils' (*London Labour Briefing*, June 1980). Although Livingstone's remarks no doubt contained a strong dose of political hyperbole, there was, nonetheless, some credence in what he had to say. On 28 May 1980, the *Financial Times* produced a Department of the Environment (DOE) list of twenty local authorities identified as being the highest over-spenders. The list comprised fifteen Labour-controlled London boroughs, including Lambeth. Lambeth, under the leadership of Ted Knight, had become strongly influenced by a new radical brand of 'local socialism' that sought radically to restructure local government organisation and service delivery (Atkinson, 1996). Its vision of an expanding and dynamic local government was at odds with the monetarist philosophy of central government. As the influence of this 'local socialism' expanded, especially in London, the conflict between sections of local government and central government became increasingly bitter and rancorous. It was a conflict that was to reach its apogee in the battle over the 1984 Rates Act. We shall consider this shortly.

As we noted in chapter 3, in its attempt to restrict the financial autonomy of local government, the Conservative government introduced a number of legislative changes. The first of these was the 1980 Local Government Planning and Land Act. At the heart of the Act was an attempt to reduce the amount of central government grant (so-called block grant) provided to local government. Previous government action had been concerned with total aggregate local government expenditure and block grant. However, the 1980 Act was to change this. A new concept was introduced: grant-related expenditure assessment (GREA). Under GREA, central government made detailed assessments using various local economic, demographic and social criteria in order to determine what each local authority should be expected to spend to provide a common level of service.

Under the previous system, block grant was distributed on the basis of need, and 'lacking any better measure of need, it was assumed that local authorities would spend what they needed to spend' (Newton and Karran, 1985, p. 116). There was, as some commentators have noted, 'an odd circularity to this system – grants should be distributed according to needs, needs were revealed by expenditures, and expenditures determined grants – but it had the advantage that the basis for the distribution of grants was the spending patterns set by local authorities themselves' (Newton and Karran 1985, p. 116). The new system, with central government determining the level of block grant for each local authority, was a radical departure from past practice. As such it marked a fundamental reduction in local authority power and a growing concentration of power at the centre. In addition, reference has been made to the arbitrary and indeed partial way in which the GREAs were calculated (Newton and Karran, 1985).

Under the provisions of the Act, local authorities that spent over their GREA would see their block grant reduced (grant taper). However, as we noted in chapter 3, central government attempts to reduce local expenditure were thwarted by the fact that a considerable number of local authorities simply raised their rates to make up for the shortfall in block grant. In spite of the ratcheting up of central control, local government had apparently managed to preserve its autonomy, or least some of it. The government responded to what it perceived to be an undermining of its authority with the 1982 Local Government Finance Act. The Act contained two key elements designed further to erode the financial autonomy of local government. First, a further penalty, known as grant holdback, was introduced. Through this mechanism 'overspending' local authorities would have a proportion of their grant withheld. Second, the previous right of local authorities to levy a supplementary rate in the middle of the financial year was removed, thus taking away the option to make up any loss of revenue brought about by grant taper and holdback.

Rate capping

Despite such restrictions, many local authorities continued to increase expenditure by increasing their rates (Loughlin, 1996). A number of options were considered by the Conservatives to block off this option. In 1981 the government flirted with the idea that any increase in rates would have to be agreed by local voters in the form of local referenda. This idea was soon rejected. However, as Kingdom (1991, p. 181) has noted, the 1983 general election landslide victory 'put new wind into Conservative sails'. The government sought an ever more radical and restrictive path. The eventual outcome was the 1984 Rates Act. While it may be the case, as some commentators have argued, that the introduction of the Act was dictated more by central government 'exasperation than with a sense of direction', it did have important implications for local government (Jackman, 1985, p. 170). It brought about 'a substantial weakening of the financial autonomy of local authorities' (Pratchett and Wilson, 1996, p. 6). The 1984 Act sought to control the actual rates that individual local authorities could levy. It gave to the Secretary of State for the Environment the power both to restrict the level of rates in individually specified local authorities and to impose a general limit on all local authorities in England, Wales and Scotland. Such a policy of 'rate capping' was a qualitative departure from previous practice, 'taking away for the first time since 1601 the right of local authorities to set their own rates' (Lansley, Goss and Wolmar, 1989, p. 34). As such, it marked a fundamental shift in the balance of the relationship between central and local government. With his ever-extending powers, the office of Secretary of State increasingly came to resemble that of the old French Prefect with its extensive powers of control over local government – a post abolished in the Deffere reforms of 1982.

The 1984 Rates Act provoked a bitter ideological battle between central government and a number of Labour-controlled local councils, mainly concentrated in London, where the brand of 'local socialism' identified above had gained in influence after the 1982 local council elections. As such, it makes an excellent case study of central–local power relations and demonstrates how highly political and controversial local government finance can be. During the summer and autumn of 1984, leaders of sixteen of the local authorities on the government's so-called hit list for rate capping met to discuss their response and their tactics. A number of alternative strategies were considered, including that of refusing to fix a rate. Such a tactic had been used by the Militant-dominated Liverpool City Council in 1983 when faced with the prospect of introducing cuts in public expenditure. As Lansley, Goss and Wolmar (1989, p. 36) note, 'the council refused to make a rate, hoping to press the government into financial concessions. Liverpool held out for three months forcing a nervous Patrick Jenkin (The Secretary of State for the Environment) into negotiations'. This 'success' took on a certain mythology. It was to play an important part in the ultimate choice of tactics. At the end of an often acrimonious debate, upwards of forty Labour-controlled local authorities opted for a strategy of non-compliance with 'rate capping' by refusing to fix a rate.

However, the final outcome was an apparent victory for central government as, one by one, the local authorities initially committed to the strategy of non-compliance fell by the wayside. Rhetoric gave way to reality. One of the key problems with the no rate strategy was its essential ambiguity and lack of coherence. Its rationale was outlined in 1984 by John Austin-Walker, the Labour leader of the London borough of Greenwich, who argued that it was important to develop, 'as far as possible, a common approach and seek to find tactics which can unite authorities whether at risk or not . . . The common action is the levying of a rate or precept' (Austin-Walker, 1984, p. 1).

Yet, the strategy was soon to unravel. One of the principal reasons lay in the different legal positions of the forty or so authorities committed to non-compliance. The metropolitan county councils, including the GLC and ILEA, were under a legal requirement to levy a rate precept by 10 March 1985. The other local authorities were under no legal requirement, save to set a rate within a reasonable time. Past experience in the case of Liverpool in 1983 pointed to a date somewhere towards the end of June (Atkinson, 1996, p. 222). A clear refusal by all forty local authorities would have met the exigencies of unity. Yet, as has been noted, 'this critical decision was fudged because most leaders knew they could not deliver' (Lansley, Goss and Wolmar, 1989, p. 34). Splits began to appear both within and amongst rate-capped authorities. Such splits were 'heightened by the knowledge that most councils could get by without cuts' (p. 41). Indeed, the original scale of the cuts required 'had been exaggerated to add urgency to the campaign' (p. 41).

Both the GLC and ILEA abandoned their policy of non-compliance and voted to set a rate precept, producing a bout of infighting and recriminations (Atkinson, 1996, p. 226). The whole non-compliance strategy began to crumble. By June 1985 only two of the original local authorities that had agreed on the 'no rate' strategy were still refusing to set a rate, namely Lambeth and the Militant-dominated Liverpool City Council, which, ironically, had not been rate capped. Even in Liverpool and Lambeth defiance ended in defeat, with those councillors who refused to set a rate being financially surcharged and barred from office.

This outcome marked the beginning of the end of the 'local socialism' experiment. Local government gradually became more passive, although resentment at the continually restrictive and arbitrary central control of local government expenditure did not go away. Furthermore, a number of local authorities responded in imaginative ways to the efforts of central government.

Creative autonomy

Despite the apparent 'victory' of central government over local government, we saw in chapter 3 that attempts to restrict local government expenditure did not meet with total success. It has been argued that 'like so many central offensives, rate-capping failed' (Kingdom, 1991, p. 181). While this may somewhat overstate the case, the complexity of the Rates Act coupled with the 1980 and 1982 reforms created a number of unintended loopholes in the system. During the 1980s, a number of local authorities sought creative ways to exploit such loopholes. It has been noted how 'a major "creative accountancy" industry emerged, in which local authority treasures and lawyers working hand in hand with financial institutions sought, with some success, to exploit' the complexity of the legislation (Loughlin, 1996, p. 43).

In the two years following the 1984 Rates Act, a number of 'left-wing councils were to run rings round the Department of the Environment' (Lansley, Goss and Wolmar, 1989, p. 42). A number of schemes were utilised. One of the most imaginative was the deferred purchase agreement. Under such agreements, private companies agreed to purchase assets on behalf of certain local authorities, the local authorities agreeing to pay the companies at some specified date in the future. The London borough of Camden even agreed a lease and leaseback deal involving its own town hall! By this and other mechanisms, local authorities were able to spend a great deal more than central government restrictions permitted. For example, the London borough of Islington, in the financial year 1986/7, 'spent three times more on its housing programme than the government's imposed limit' (p. 42).

However, by the summer of 1986, the rate-capped local authorities were beginning to be boxed in. The deferred purchase scheme had been outlawed by the Environment Secretary, Nicholas Ridley. In the spring of 1987, he issued warnings to the banks that central government would not back local authority loans. This caused alarm in the financial markets. As a consequence, rate-capped councils faced increasing difficulty in even securing routine loans, not to mention funding for creative accounting. Councils were therefore left with large deficits, which they could not bridge due to the rate-capping restrictions. The only option was to cut spending levels. In the two years that followed, a variety of left-wing Labour councils agreed such cuts. They included the London boroughs of Brent, Hackney, Haringey, Lambeth and Southwark, and local authorities outside London including Liverpool, Manchester and Sheffield. Despite some strong opposition to such policies from, among others, some Labour councillors and trade unionists, a new financial 'realism' was emerging. The local socialism project was on the retreat.

Reform in the 1990s

The Conservative government, following its third successive general election victory in 1987, continued its attempt to turn the screw on the finances of local government. In April 1990, a number of important changes were made to the system of local finance. These have been referred to in chapter 3. First, a uniform national non-domestic rate (NNDR) was introduced, replacing the local business rate. This was a fundamental change of process. Prior to this, each local authority had been free both to set its own level of business rate, within the overall parameters of rateable value, and to use the total sum accruing from the business rate to offset the cost of local services. Under the new scheme, the level of business rates would be set nationally. Although collected locally, the income from business rates would now be distributed nationally on a per capita basis. The consequences of this were twofold. There was a general loss of financial autonomy for all local authorities and, more specifically, the changes meant a significant loss of revenue for those local authorities with a high concentration of local businesses. Central government justified this change by arguing that it was preventing profligate and high-spending, predominantly Labour-controlled local authorities from imposing what effectively could be termed a tax on business. Expressed another way, it 'was explicitly directed towards undermining the ability of left Labour councils – particularly in London – from funding their activities from taxes paid by business, instead of taxes paid by individuals (and voters)' (Cochrane, 1992, p. 7). The new policy was met by a chorus of disapproval not just from Labour and the Liberal Democrats, but from a significant number of Conservatives in local government who argued that it undermined the concept of accountability.

Second, the GREA was replaced by a standard spending assessment (SSA). The SSA was used to calculate what each authority needed to spend to achieve a common level of service. This included an equalization element as before. It was calculated on the basis of a simpler formula and was based on needs in the following areas: education, fire, highways, social services, police, other, and capital finance (Kingdom, 1991). Third, domestic rates were to be controversially replaced by a flat-rate poll tax (see below). Under this proposal, the DOE would set a notional poll tax within which local authorities had to operate. A prediction of a local authority's tax income could be made by adding its poll tax yield to its share of NNDR. The amount that each authority would receive in RSG would then be calculated by subtracting total tax income from the SSA (Kingdom, 1991). Under this new system, RSG could not be changed once set at the beginning of the financial year. Thus as Kingdom notes, 'any marginal expenditure rises were to be passed on disproportionately to poll tax (thus a one per cent expenditure rise could mean a four per cent poll tax rise, an effect termed gearing) thereby increasing the pain on local electors' (p. 189). Finally, strict controls on capital expenditure were introduced.

Yet without doubt, by far the most radical of the proposals implemented in 1990 (1989 in Scotland) was the highly controversial decision to replace the system of domestic local rates with the community charge, or poll tax as it became known. It was a decision as reckless as it was radical. It sent shock waves through the government and was instrumental in the downfall of Margaret Thatcher, regarded by many as the most powerful Prime Minister since the Second World War.

The Question of Domestic Rates

Until the reforms of 1990, the rates system had been the basis of local taxation in the UK. It was a system that had its origins in the Poor Law of 1601. The rates were a property tax, calculated on the basis of a notional annual rent for particular properties. There were, as noted above, two kinds of rates, namely domestic and business. Despite the apparent problems associated with the rates, governments of differing political persuasions, mindful of the major practical problems and political pitfalls that might present themselves, had shied away from major reform. The election of the Conservatives under Margaret Thatcher was to change all that. However, before we consider the process that led to the ultimate abolition of domestic rates, it would be helpful to set the whole issue in context by examining the case for and the case against the system of domestic rates.

There were four main arguments in favour of retaining the rates. First, they were progressive. People who lived in larger properties, and who tended to be more affluent, paid more. Second, they were a tax on property. As a consequence, they were relatively easy to collect. Indeed, 99 per cent of rates were collected each year. Third, collection costs were low and the system was relatively easy to administer. Fourth, the rates had a long-established record as a successful way of raising local revenue. However, there were also a number of arguments against domestic rates.

First, it was claimed that the system was regressive, since the burden of payment did not fall equally on all rate payers. The oft-quoted example was that of the old lady on a small pension who paid the same level of rates as the household next door where there were four wage-earners. Second, rates being a tax on property, not everyone paid them. It has been estimated that in the region of 50 per cent of all those entitled to vote in local elections did not pay rates. Third, there was an argument that 'there was a breakdown in the chain of accountability between councillors and the local electorate. Put simply, many local people could quite happily go on voting for local services, whilst not having to pay for them' (Atkinson and Wilks-Heeg, 1997, p. 89). Finally, it was argued that there was insufficient buoyancy in the tax base as rates did not increase automatically with inflation.

Reforming domestic rates

The problems associated with the system of domestic rates had been acknowledged by both Labour and Conservative governments since the end of the Second World War. However, all had shied away from reform, given the very real practical difficulties that this would involve. The Thatcher government was to take a different tack. It was, however, to sail into stormy political waters. Domestic rates were replaced in Scotland in 1989 and in England and Wales the following year by the poll tax. Bold as the move was, it came at a high price, both politically and financially, culminating in 'popular resistance to a degree unprecedented since the General Strike of 1926' (Butler, Adonis and Travers, 1994, p. 1).

Before looking at these ill-fated reforms, it is important to set the issue in context. By the mid-1970s, central government grants accounted for 60 per cent of total local authority income. Of the remaining 40 per cent, only 20 per cent came from domestic rates. Once rebates had been taken into account, some local authorities derived no more than 10 per cent of their income from local householders (Butler, Adonis and Travers, 1994, p. 21). Such an unbalanced situation led to a 'disenchantment with local taxation' and 'gave a powerful stimulus to the development of policy in the Conservative party in the latter half of the 1970s' (p. 21). This in turn led to the Conservatives' 1974 general election manifesto commitment to abolish domestic rates. Concern over domestic rates was not, however, confined to the Conservatives. The Labour government elected in 1974 had its problems. The local government reorganisation of 1974 had been followed by rate increases as high as 30 per cent in some areas. Hostile public reaction led the government to introduce some short-term relief for domestic rate payers (Hepworth, 1976, p. 101). At the same time, the Layfield Committee, referred to above, was set up to look at the whole question of local authority finance.

By the time of the 1979 general election, however, the Conservatives' commitment to rates abolition was less clear, replaced instead by a weak commitment to reform (Butler, Adonis and Travers, 1994, p. 22). Their principal focus was on macro-economic issues such as the desire to cut income tax and public expenditure. Despite this, however, there were increasing calls on the government to do something about the rates issue. Large rate increases, particularly in 1981, 'fuelled pressure within the

Conservative Party to take action on the 1974 commitment to abolish domestic rates' (p. 29).

Local elections in the early 1980s resulted in heavy losses for the Conservatives. Labour councils came to power in a number of local authorities pledging a new style of local politics. The 'new urban left', as they were described (see chapter 3), advocated an expanding and dynamic local government. Rates were increased to fund local services. The most high profile of these attempts was provided by the GLC under the leadership of Ken Livingstone. The battle between central and local government had begun. It would prove to be a bitter affair.

There was a growing demand among significant numbers of Conservative MPs for something to be done about the rates, although there was little clear idea of what might replace them (Butler, Adonis and Travers, 1994, p. 29). Indeed, 'finding a tax which can raise enough revenue, be fair, and provide local accountability is almost impossible' (John, 1999, p. 53). In 1981, the government published a Green Paper entitled 'Alternatives to domestic rates' (DOE, 1981). It rehearsed many of the arguments of Layfield. It looked at four alternatives for local taxes:

- local income tax (LIT);
- local sales tax;
- property tax;
- poll tax.

In contrast to the 1981 Green Paper, the Layfield Committee made no reference to the poll tax. In their seminal analysis of the poll tax, Butler, Adonis and Travers (1994, p. 30) raise the question as to why the poll tax was suddenly elevated 'to a co-equal status with the three hardy annuals of LIT, sales tax, and property tax'. For them, the answer is far from clear. There was no evidence that either Margaret Thatcher or Michael Heseltine, the Secretary of State for the Environment, had promoted the idea of a poll tax. Although, as has already been noted, Margaret Thatcher hated the rates, her stated alternative while in opposition had been a sales tax. In addition, Heseltine had opposed the idea of a poll tax whenever it had been raised (p. 30). However, in the early 1980s the poll tax was being promoted in some new-right circles (Foster and Perlman, 1980, p. 220). This 'gave the right a glimmering of a policy and confirmed the DOE in its readiness to treat the idea as politically respectable, in Tory circles, at least' (Butler, Adonis and Travers, 1994, p. 32). Yet the idea of the poll tax was not pursued as a viable policy option at this stage; despite the acknowledged difficulties with the rates, the practical problems of reform were regarded as too considerable (Wilson and Game, 1998). However, the seeds of an idea had been sown

(Travers, 1986). Indeed, in an illuminating anecdote, Butler, Adonis and Travers (1994, p. 35) recount how, when a draft of the Green Paper came back from No. 10 Downing Street to Heseltine's office, there was a scribbled note by Margaret Thatcher next to a section on rising local government expenditure which read 'I will not tolerate failure in this area again.'

The Conservative manifesto for the 1983 general election again did not include a specific commitment to abolish domestic rates. Indeed, a 1983 White Paper appeared to confirm the continuation of rates (DOE, 1983). While noting that rates were far from ideal or popular, it argued that they were 'well understood, cheap to collect and very difficult to evade'. It continued by stating that 'The Government have concluded . . . that rates remain for the foreseeable future the main source of revenue for local government' (p. 14). Yet in 1986, the government issued a Green Paper entitled 'Paying for local government' (DOE, 1986). It proposed what was certainly the most radical reform of local government finance in the UK in the twentieth century. Why such an apparent volte-face? The initial impetus for change came out of the rating revaluation exercise in Scotland, which had been implemented in 1985. The outcome was domestic rate increases of up to 30 per cent. This caused an outcry among government supporters, since many of the increases impacted on the more affluent and traditionally Conservative areas.

The arrival of the poll tax

The issue of rates reform was discussed at a meeting at Chequers at the end of March 1985. Half the Cabinet were in attendance. According to Margaret Thatcher's memoirs, it was at this meeting that 'the community charge was born' (Thatcher, 1993, p. 648). Having listened to the opinions of government ministers Kenneth Baker and William Waldegrave, she was converted to the merits of the community charge 'and with the zeal of a convert, her pragmatic cynicism about the impossibility of abolishing the rates was replaced with an equally strong belief that something could be done' (Butler, Adonis and Travers, 1994, p. 76). It was one of the first signs that Margaret Thatcher was losing her political touch.

There were two principal aspects to the reform. First, as already mentioned, the system of local business rates was replaced by the national non-domestic rate (NNDR). Second, domestic rates would be replaced by a flat rate charge, known as the community charge or poll tax. Aside from a few specified exceptions (including members of religious orders and convicted criminals), it was to be paid by all local voters. As a consequence, it quickly became dubbed the poll tax (Kingdom, 1991). It has been described as 'the most radical reform in the system of local government finance ever proposed in modern times' (Loughlin, 1996, p. 44).

The philosophy underpinning the poll tax proposal stemmed from a new-right view that the rates system, whereby not all local voters paid domestic rates, lacked accountability. Of the 35 million electors in England, only 18 million were liable to pay rates. Of these only 12 million, approximately one-third of the electorate, were liable to pay full domestic rates (DOE, 1986, para 1.37). In addition, for every one pound raised from domestic rate payers, 50 pence was paid by the non-domestic sector (paras 2.14–2.18). The poll tax would, it was argued, create a chain of accountability between elected councillors and voters. Local people would now have to pay for their electoral choices. The government believed that it would reap the political benefits of such a change as what it regarded as inefficient and high-spending Labour controlled local authorities would be forced to levy a high poll tax. In the end, however, this proved to be a disastrous miscalculation. The wrath of the electorate fell not on local government but on the perpetrators of the poll tax, central government itself (see chapter 3).

The poll tax takes its toll?

Chris Patten was Secretary of State for the Environment from 1989 to 1990 and the minister in overall charge of local government. Looking back, he is scathing of the poll tax, arguing that it was 'fundamentally flawed' and 'the single most unpopular policy any government has introduced since the war' (quoted in Butler, Adonis and Travers, 1994, p. 1).

It has been argued that 'the single most crucial decision in the whole community charge saga was that it should be introduced at a single stroke, rather than phased in over a number of years' (Wilson and Game, 1998, p. 191). This represented a departure from the 1985 Green Paper (DOE, 1986), which had argued that the new tax should be introduced at a low level (a figure of £50 was suggested) and gradually increased as rates were phased out over a ten-year period in England and Wales, and a four-year period in Scotland. The 'big bang' approach adopted by the government meant that local electorates could not be cushioned against the full impact of the new community charge. Former Environment Secretary, Kenneth Baker, has described this decision, together with Chancellor Nigel Lawson's under-funding of the tax, as 'fatal mistakes' (Baker, 1993, p. 127). In addition, there was a dearth of strategic thinking around the poll tax, quite remarkable, if not without precedent, given the qualitative change to the whole system of local government that it implied. As Butler, Adonis and Travers (1994, p. 100) note, up to its introduction in 1989, 'significant aspects of the tax were being redesigned on the hoof'. Indeed, at one point it seemed that barely a week would go by before some new scheme would be devised to subsidize the poll tax and make it more palatable to the electorate.

However, as poll tax bills were delivered through the letter boxes of local voters, resentment and opposition began to mount. They were much higher than the government had wished for or anticipated, coming in at an average of £363 per person. The DOE estimate had been £278. Some households were up to £1,500 worse off. It has been estimated that there were 27 million people living in 'losing' households and only 8 million in households that gained (Butler, Adonis and Travers, 1994, p. 158). Why was there such a discrepancy? The explanation lies in the actions of both local and central government. Local authorities had increased their spending by approximately 13 per cent, roughly 4 per cent above predicted inflation. Central government, however, 'had been working to a low inflation target [and] had greatly underestimated the start up costs of the new tax' and, in addition, rate support grant had been set at too low a level. (p. 158).

It has been argued that the campaign of resistance that followed was unprecedented in Britain with so many people directly confronting the law (Burns, 1992). The most visible manifestation of this was the so-called Trafalgar Square riots of 31 March 1990: 'Filmed against the backdrop of Nelson's column and the "mother of parliaments", the riots became an international sensation' (Butler, Adonis and Travers, 1994, p. 154). Attempts by government ministers to portray the demonstrators as hooligans in the hope of a public backlash failed (Butler, Adonis and Travers, 1994). By this stage, the poll tax was deeply unpopular. An opinion poll published in *The Times* on 30 April 1990 showed only 12 per cent support for the poll tax. One in three of those interviewed wanted a return to the rates. At the end of April, the Labour opposition had an average opinion poll lead of 23 per cent. Increasingly, the problems of the poll tax were attributed personally to Margaret Thatcher. This was to some extent unfair since her Cabinet colleagues were equally to blame for the introduction of the poll tax. However, 'the government's inflexibility to calls for reform or abolition in the spring and summer of 1990 was above all her inflexibility; and with each passing week, the blame attached ever more firmly to her personally' (Butler, Adonis and Travers, 1994, p. 155). Margaret Thatcher resigned as Prime Minister the following November, having failed to secure sufficient support from her parliamentary colleagues. Her fall from grace was due in no small part to the poll tax. Her political judgement had deserted her.

The aftermath of the poll tax

The whole issue of the poll tax has been described as an 'extraordinary episode in our contemporary history' (Wilson and Game, 1998, p. 192). It not only claimed the scalp of supposedly the most powerful Prime Minister since the Second World War, but also left in its wake financial and administrative chaos. Four examples illustrate the extent of this chaos. First, the cost to central government of bringing in the poll tax totalled over £7 billion in 1991/2 alone. Second, local authorities employed an additional 15,000 staff to administer the tax. Third, there was a significant level of non-payment. In England, one year after the introduction of the poll tax, £1 billion out of a total of £12 billion had still not been collected. In Scotland, levels of non-payment reached 13 per cent in the first year, and 20 per cent in the second year. Even by the end of 1995, unpaid poll tax bills still amounted to some £1.5 billion, the single biggest debt problem facing local government (Wilson and Game, 1998, p. 192). Fourth, since the introduction of the poll tax, over one million names have disappeared from the electoral register.

The arrival of the council tax

Newly installed as Prime Minister, John Major set about the task of reforming the local tax system. Michael Heseltine, the newly appointed Secretary of State for the Environment, was charged with the responsibility of replacing the poll tax. A number of options were considered before the government settled for the council tax, which came into effect in April 1993. It is a mixed system based on both a system of property values grouped into seven bands and a headcount (single households receive a 25 per cent rebate). There are also 50 per cent discounts for those under eighteen, full-time students (those in student accommodation are excluded), the 'severely mentally impaired' and some carers for disabled people. There are also rebates of up to 100 per cent for those on low incomes.

However, the council tax has itself been subject to a number of criticisms. First, there were complaints from its inception about the flawed and rushed nature of the valuation of properties. Such a process was crucial, since a higher property valuation results in a higher council tax. Second, it was argued that the system discriminated against those living in London, where property prices tend to be higher than the rest of the country. A proposal to set up a system of regional bands, supported by opposition parties and several back-bench Conservative MPs, was rejected by the government. Third, the council tax was introduced in the context of the same grant regime. Therefore, the problem of gearing still exists, 'since high increases in local tax will still be needed to maintain any spending over the levels implicitly approved by the government's spending assessments' (Cochrane, 1992, p. 19). Fourth, the council tax was still centralising. Local government would still only collect around 15 per cent of the revenue it needed to pay for local services. The NNDR remained in place.

Despite such problems, the council tax has not drawn the same level of criticisms, or encountered the same degree of difficulties, as the poll tax. The government of John Major broadly succeeded in drawing the sting out of the issue of local government finance, while at the same time achieving its aim of keeping control of local authority expenditure. Today it is no longer the highly charged political issue it was at the beginning of the 1990s.

Conclusion

As a result of the legislative changes introduced in the 1980s and 1990s, British local government has, according to a report published by the Council of Europe, less financial freedom than almost all its European counterparts (quoted in the *Guardian*, 14 October 1998). There is certainly a great deal of validity in this argument. We have seen in this chapter how successive Conservative governments from 1979 to 1997 attempted to put in place a series of measures aimed at limiting the room for financial manoeuvre for local authorities. The capping of individual local authority budgets and the introduction of the poll tax and the NNDR marked a qualitative change in central–local relations in the UK. This is a matter of fact. Despite this, however, local government did not merely become an agent of the centre. It demonstrated its capacity, admittedly with varying degrees of success, to fight against central government diktat. Some local authorities responded to the new agenda by seeking new ways of funding public projects through the private sector (see chapter 6). Finally, central government may have demonstrated its ability to impose its will on local government, the poll tax being a good example of this. However, it came at a great cost for the Thatcher government, both politically and financially. Local government had been wounded, but lived to fight another day.

5

The Changing Structure and Shape of Local Government

Introduction

The period from 1979 to 1997 witnessed important changes in the structure and shape of local government in the UK. The aim of this chapter is to analyse these changes. First, it looks at the changing structure of local government. This includes a focus on the decision to abolish the English metropolitan counties, including the Greater London Council (GLC) in the mid-1980s, together with an analysis of the reasons behind this controversial policy. The work of the Local Government Commission, set up in 1992 with a brief to review local government structures, is also analysed. Second, attention is given to the changing shape of local government, in particular the increasing phenomenon of 'non-elected' local government. The contextual shift identified in chapter 2 from the notion of local government as a provider of local services to the more embracing concept of local governance is also considered in more detail.

The Changing Structure of Local Government

As we saw in chapter 1, changing structure has been a constant theme in the history of British local government. Indeed, it could be argued that structural change has often been viewed as a substitute for substantive policy change. Very rarely has the issue of structural change been rooted in an overall discussion about what should be the objective and purpose of local government and how structure and organization might facilitate objective and purpose. Notwithstanding this, however, the history of local government structural and organizational change teaches us one very important lesson: that there is no one best rational or scientific approach. As we noted in chapter 1, local government reorganization is an endless process. It is also highly subjective. Like service delivery, debates about local government structure are shot through with values, ideology and politics. This is nowhere better illustrated than in the debate around the abolition of the metropolitan counties and the GLC in 1986.

The abolition of the Greater London Council and the metropolitan counties

It has been argued that the abolition of the GLC and the English metropolitan counties raises important constitutional issues, in particular 'the right of central government to remove a tier of government on what almost everyone outside Government circles regards as flimsy grounds' (Newton and Karran, 1985, p. 122). While this may indeed be true, the reforms also reflected, albeit in an extreme form, the formal status of local government as a creature of central government. Such a unilateral act would be unthinkable in a federal system such as Germany, where the rights of local government are enshrined in the constitution and protected by bodies such as the federal Constitutional Court. This is not for one moment to suggest that local government remains subservient and dominated by the centre. The pattern of the relationship is more complex than that of master and servant. As has already been argued, the UK has a long tradition of vibrant and active local government which has managed, despite the formal constitutional constraints (such as *ultra vires*), to create its own space and achieve a degree of autonomy. Despite the attacks of the 1980s and 1990s, it remains an important element in the British political system.

The decision to abolish the metropolitan counties and the GLC in 1986 created a unitary system of local government in these areas (see figure 5.1). It was highly contentious, with various commentators arguing that it was a politically motivated decision (Leach and Stoker, 1997; Flynn, Leach and Vielba, 1985). The Conservatives for their part, however, argued that the decision was purely organizational (DOE, 1983). As Pycroft (1995, p. 54) has noted, the GLC, and indeed the metropolitan counties, in the view of the Conservatives, had too few functions to justify their existence, and had 'encroached upon the domain of the lower tier of urban local government (in the case of London, this was the London boroughs)'.

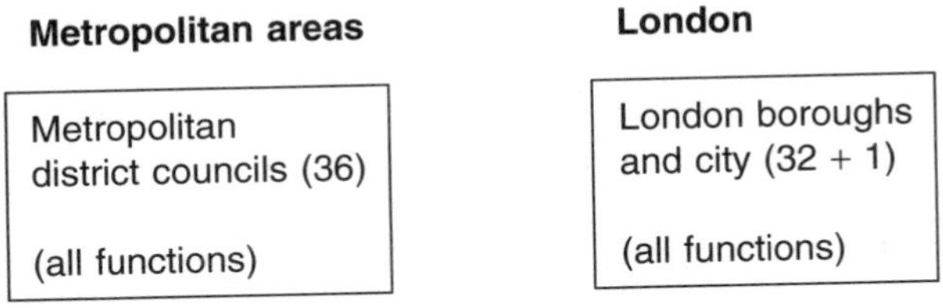

Metropolitan areas   **London**

Metropolitan district councils (36) (all functions)	London boroughs and city (32 + 1) (all functions)

Figure 5.1 The structure of local government in London and metropolitan areas after 1986

In respect of the metropolitan counties, it is worth remembering, as we pointed out in chapter 1, that they were created by the Conservative government in 1973 as a product of the Redcliffe-Maud Commission, which had been set up in 1969. The GLC was a product of the Herbert Commission on London local government, again set up by a Conservative government in 1963. Both the metropolitan counties and the GLC were set up as strategic authorities, with responsibility for strategic planning and co-ordination. Their role in direct service delivery was limited. This was the role of the metropolitan districts and the London boroughs. However, by the early 1980s, the Conservative government was arguing that both the metropolitan counties and the GLC had failed in their strategic role and had become an unnecessary and costly tier of local government. The top tier of local government in London and the metropolitan counties was no longer necessary. Removing it would 'produce efficiency savings and enhance performance' (Cole and Boyne, 1996, p. 63).

Critics of the government argued that the decision to abolish the GLC and the metropolitan counties was not based on the exigencies of rational administration but was highly political. The fact that all the metropolitan counties and the GLC were Labour controlled at the time of their abolition lends credence to this thesis. Indeed, for the Conservative government, the GLC and the metropolitan counties 'were acting outside their authority by developing highly political programmes in opposition to national government' (Pycroft, 1985, p. 54). The GLC enjoyed the highest profile. As Elcock (1991, p. 39) notes, 'the GLC leader, Ken Livingstone had emerged as a colourful and effective antagonist with his headquarters just across the Thames from Mrs Thatcher's'. The abolition of the GLC was presented in some quarters as the product of a personal conflict between Livingstone and Thatcher. Ken Livingstone, in his account of the events of the time, disputes this (Livingstone, 1988). For him, it was a political clash with a new brand of local socialism (see chapter 3). 'There was a huge gulf', argued Livingstone, 'between the cultural values of the GLC Labour Group [in areas such as anti-racism, promoting gender politics and gay rights, and the creation of nuclear-free zones] and everything Mrs Thatcher considered right and proper' (p. 251). Thus the decision was taken to abolish the GLC and indeed the metropolitan counties.

Livingstone himself had cast doubt on the value of the GLC, arguing that its record up to 1981 had been one of failure and that it had not secured a proper role (Livingstone, 1987). Thus, he appears, to some extent, to share some of the analysis of the Conservatives. Yet Livingstone saw in local government, and in the GLC in particular, the opportunity to act in imaginative and creative ways to promote social change. The GLC, with its large resource base, strategic position and limited responsibility for direct service provision, provided a unique opportunity for policy innovation and development. This took many forms. Funding was provided to community, gay and women's groups. Decentralization of services was promoted. There was an attempt to increase the participation of Londoners in the services that affected them. The GLC became active in economic development in an attempt to safeguard and promote job opportunities. While the success or otherwise of these initiatives is a matter of debate (Mackintosh and Wainwright, 1987; Atkinson, 1996), there is no doubting the radically different and positive style that the GLC, and indeed a number of other Labour-controlled local councils, brought to the world of local government. The fact that abolition, coupled with internal divisions in the 'local socialism' project, largely brought the experiment to an end does not negate this conclusion.

There was also a positive response to the Conservative government's abolition policy. The GLC, in particular, through the 'Save the GLC' campaign, fought a vigorous and imaginative battle. Clearly, it would be a nonsense to suggest that this represented a victory for the GLC; it was, after all, abolished. Yet public opinion was on the side of the GLC. An opinion poll in the *London Evening Standard* newspaper in October 1983 showed that 54 per cent of Londoners opposed abolition, while only 22 per cent were in favour. A MORI opinion poll in September 1984 found 55 per cent of respondents saying they would vote Labour at a full GLC election. This compared to the 42 per cent that the Labour Party achieved at the 1981 GLC election. The GLC may have lost the abolition battle, but it won the public relations battle.

What of the administrative aftermath of the abolition of the GLC and the metropolitan counties? Their functions and responsibilities were taken over to some extent by the London boroughs and the metropolitan district councils. However, a considerable amount of their work was divided between a variety of joint committees, joint boards, central government departments and *ad hoc* agencies. A study by Hebbert and

Travers in 1988 found that in the region of 100 bodies had responsibility for delivering services in Greater London, with twenty-one different ways of raising money (p. 198). There were over twenty centrally appointed bodies, such as Greater London Arts and London Regional Transport. In addition, there were sixteen London-wide nominated bodies. These included the London Fire and Civil Defence Authority and the London Waste Regulatory Authority. Important changes also took place in education. The education service in the twelve inner London boroughs (the boundaries of the old LCC) was the responsibility of the Inner London Education Authority (ILEA). ILEA was in effect a sub-committee of the GLC. With the abolition of the GLC, ILEA became a directly elected single-purpose authority, something quite unusual in the history of twentieth-century British local government (Wilson and Game, 1998). However, ILEA itself was subsequently abolished, with responsibility for education being transferred to the inner London boroughs as from 1 April 1990.

The picture in the metropolitan areas was less complex. However, although fewer functions were transferred to quasi-government agencies, those that were tended to be the high-spending and high-profile services. For example, joint boards were established for the three areas of passenger transport, police, and fire and civil defence. Joint committees were also established for areas such as recreation, arts and economic development.

It has been argued that the abolition of the GLC and the metropolitan counties resulted in a 'degree of complexity that can be seen not so much as a streamlining of our cities as a return to the administrative tangle of the 19th century' (Wilson and Game, 1998, p. 54). As we have seen, this applied particularly to London. The new arrangements in London came in for criticism in relation to both the lack of democratic accountability and the fragmentation of services. London, it was argued, lacked a strategic voice. As such, it was suffering as a city. Areas such as public transport, the environment and planning required a pan-London approach. This criticism was not just confined to Labour politicians, but also came from business leaders and other political parties. Michael Heseltine, the former Conservative Secretary of State for the Environment, proposed the idea of a mayor for London. However, changes to the structure of London local government were unlikely as long as the Conservatives remained in power nationally. They had invested much political capital in the abolition of the GLC. Labour's 1997 general election victory was to change the picture (see chapter 12).

The abolition of the GLC and the metropolitan counties resulted in a broadly similar organizational pattern. A range of services had been removed from directly elected local government and transferred to a variety of either appointed or indirectly elected bodies. Indeed, the removal of a variety of functions from directly elected local authorities became a key feature of the Conservatives' local government policy in the 1980s. We shall return to this issue shortly.

The Local Government Commission

In November 1990, as the shock waves of the poll tax continued to cause political tremors, John Major replaced Margaret Thatcher as Prime Minister. Major sought to distance himself from the local government policy of his predecessor (Pycroft, 1995). He turned to Michael Heseltine, his defeated opponent in the Conservative Party leadership battle, to handle the high-profile local government portfolio. Hesletine had a well-known interest in local government finance and organization. A key part of the new Secretary of State for the Environment's brief was to find a replacement for the discredited poll tax. However, he also announced a review of the structure and internal management of local government. This represented a significant shift in government policy. Indeed, Heseltine's predecessor had argued in the summer of 1990 that local government 'needs a reorganisation like it needs a hole in the head' (Leach and Stoker, 1997, p. 1).

As part of the review process, the Local Government Commission (LGC) was established in July 1992 under the chairmanship of Sir John Banham (see chapter 3). It was expected to complete its task within five years, producing final recommendations in 1997. The work of the Commission tells us as much about the nature of public policy making in the UK as it does about the problems associated with local government reform.

In England, the process of local government restructuring was to be guided by consultation with local authorities, business organizations, voluntary groups and other interested parties. In Scotland and Wales, the task of local government reorganization was the responsibility of the Scottish and Welsh Offices under the guidance of the Secretaries of State for Scotland and Wales respectively. Three principal factors underpinned the desire for change. First, there were concerns on the part of central government about the existing functional, administrative and geographical disparities of the local authority map. The government's preferred solution to this problem was the creation of a system of unitary local government. Second, the government pointed to what it perceived to be the lack of community identity and democratic accountability of existing structures. Third, the government spoke of the costly duplication and waste resulting from the two-tier system (Pycroft, 1995). As we noted earlier, such demands for local government reform were by no means new. Indeed, debates on the structure and shape of modern local government have been a constant theme since its inception. Doubtless, they will continue to be so.

Sir John Banham set out what he saw as the three key objectives of the Commission in a letter to the *Financial Times* on 7 July 1993. First, the LGC was to deal with any problems that had resulted from the reorganization of 1974. Indeed, it has been argued that some of the main problems of local government, namely its unaccountability, inefficiency and remoteness, were not dealt with then (Byrne, 1994). Second, the Commission was to seek to 'streamline the confusing and wasteful two-tier system of district and county councils'. Third, it would 'equip local government to meet the challenges of the early decades of the next century'. These were ambitious and far-reaching objectives.

The Commission, however, was entitled to begin its work in an optimistic mood. After all, both the Labour and Liberal Democratic parties had supported the reform process in 1991 and were broadly in favour of unitary authorities, a key tenet of Conservative local government policy. The setting up of the Commission was seen as an attempt by the Conservatives to deflect attention from the poll tax fiasco. However, from quite early on, the work of the Commission and the strategy of the government met strong resistance from 'a disparate but remarkably effective agglomeration of interests' (Pycroft, 1995, p. 49).

The principal task of the Local Government Commission was to test the case for the introduction of unitary authorities. It 'explicitly eschewed blueprints for the whole country' (Leach, 1999, p. 59). Each of the thirty-nine English counties was to be looked at on an individual basis. The review process was to be divided into five tranches and was to be completed in no more than four years. Such an approach, producing recommendations for particular geographical areas, was to create a number of problems and tensions. We shall return to these shortly. As part of the consultation process, the Commission used a number of mechanisms. These included consultation with local business groups and various other organizations as well as large-scale opinion surveys of local people.

The work of the Commission attracted a great deal of controversy. Indeed, it has been variously described as 'inept' (Sinnott, 1997) and a 'fiasco' (Leach and Stoker, 1997). There are several explanations for these judgements. First, its final recommendations fell well short of what many, including the government, had anticipated. It proposed the abolition of only seven of the existing thirty-nine English county councils, 'despite the government's stated preference for unitary authorities' (Pycroft, 1995, p. 49). It is true that the Commission did recommend the creation of fifty new unitary authorities, principally in urban areas.

However, they were to exist within the dominant established framework of two-tier local government. Second, while the Commission's early recommendation for the abolition of Cleveland and Durham county councils and the creation of a single unitary authority for the Isle of Wight appeared uncontroversial, it was apparent as it carried out its consultation process that there was increasing opposition to the creation of unitary authorities. In Durham, for example, a MORI poll found a clear majority in favour of retaining the county council. Such a finding was important for, as Pycroft (1995, p. 58) has argued, Sir John Banham 'was prepared to accept that the electorate was "the jury" ' for all proposals'. However, there was a problem here. While other commentators concede that 'the Banham Commission made strenuous efforts to canvass local opinion', voter apathy and relative ignorance meant that the 'process was dominated by established interests, particularly existing local authorities and their respective associations' (Leach, 1997, p. 65).

Third, the retention of a largely two-tier system itself met with opposition from a number of large towns and cities, many of which had been unitary county boroughs before the reorganization of 1974. Places such as Bristol, Leicester and Nottingham actively lobbied the Environment Secretary, John Gummer, to reject the recommendations of the Commission and award them unitary status. The Association of County Councils was, not surprisingly, broadly in favour of the Commission's proposals, while the Association of District Councils pressed for the unitary solution. Fourth, the fact that the review was carried out in stages 'inevitably drew attention to inconsistencies in approach' (Leach, 1997, p. 65). For example, Hull was to be awarded unitary status, while larger cities such as Bristol and Nottingham were initially denied.

Fifth, the opposition of a number of shire Conservative MPs to proposals to abolish their county councils added to the complexity and confusion. The most vocal opposition came from Somerset, where all four of the county's Conservative MPs raised strong objections to the abolition of their county. They included junior government minister David Heathcoat-Amory, who threatened to quit the government over the matter. The Environment Secretary, John Gummer, rejected the Commission's recommendation for a unitary system in Somerset in October 1994. Finally, a number of other bodies stated their opposition to unitary authorities which, they argued, would be under-bounded, under-resourced and, as a consequence, unable to deliver effective local services. These included teacher unions, the local government officers' union, NALGO, and the Association of Directors of Social Services.

Leach and Stoker (1997, p. 2) have argued that, unlike the abolition of the GLC and the metropolitan counties in 1986, the Local Government Review from 1992 onwards was 'more open ended and less driven by central government'. They also argue that it was driven less by ideological concerns than by the introduction of the poll tax. There is clearly validity in this argument. Yet, as has been pointed out, there was 'continuing Government involvement at every stage in the review process' (Leach, 1997, p. 65). Indeed, Leach and Stoker (1997, p. 2) concede that the government 'was never too far from the steering wheel'.

Such close government involvement led to confusion and policy shifts. The timetable was altered and various recommendations were either rejected or referred back to the Commission for further consideration. For example, second reviews were carried out in 1994 in Derbyshire, Durham and Gloucestershire. The Commission produced its final recommendations for the Secretary of State in January 1995. They can be summarised in the following general terms:

- twenty counties where no change was proposed;
- eleven counties in which one or two unitary authorities were proposed, but the overall pattern of change was limited;
- eight counties where a unitary solution was recommended.

Most of these recommendations were accepted by John Gummer, although there were a few exceptions: unitary solutions for Bedfordshire, Buckingshire and Dorset were rejected. However, Gummer also identified twenty-one local authorities where the case for unitary status should be re-examined by a new commission. Growing tensions between Sir John Banham and the Secretary of State soon became apparent, culminating in the former's forced resignation in March 1995. Following this, a second Local Government Commission was created. It soon set about its work, which was in essence a tidying-up exercise on the work of the previous Commission. In January 1996, it made recommendations for eight new unitary authorities, all of which were accepted by John Gummer. The final outcome can be summarised as follows:

- Forty-six new unitary authorities were created.
- From an original total of 296, 238 districts remained as part of a two-tier system.
- Fourteen counties remained unchanged.
- Twenty other counties remained largely intact, but lost one or more unitary districts.
- Four counties were abolished.

The Local Government Commission in perspective

The way the review of local government structures was conducted has been described as shambolic by some commentators (Leach and Stoker,

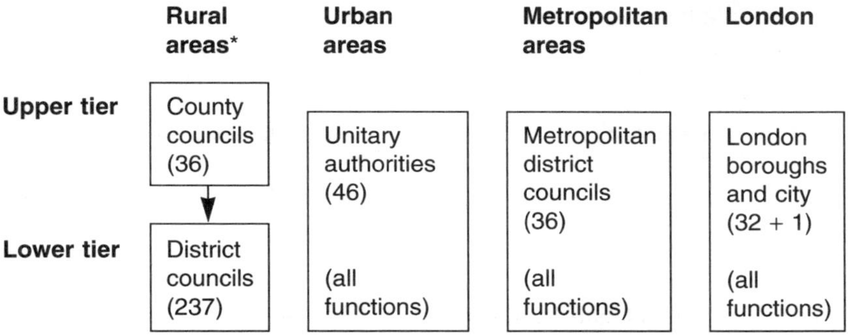

	Rural areas*	Urban areas	Metropolitan areas	London
Upper tier	County councils (36)	Unitary authorities (46)	Metropolitan district councils (36)	London boroughs and city (32 + 1)
Lower tier	District councils (237)	(all functions)	(all functions)	(all functions)

*Note that not all rural areas are two-tier, e.g. Herefordshire is a unitary authority.

Figure 5.2 The structure of local government in England after 1998

1997). Clearly, it was a very complex process, fraught with a number of organizational, personal and political difficulties. There can be little doubt that it was badly handled. However, difficulties are almost inevitable when trying to reform British local government structures. History and experience have taught us this. There are always going to be disagreements over objectives, since there are a myriad of differing interests competing with each other in what is essentially a zero-sum game. The work of the Local Government Commission simply underlines this point. However, the Commission also demonstrated the determination and capacity of local authorities to defend their corner when their interests were threatened.

Reorganization in Scotland and Wales

Although no formal commission was set up to look at the structure of Scottish and Welsh local government, central government did carry out a type of consultation exercise, having stated its own preference for a unitary system. The principal bodies consulted included individual local authorities, local government associations and professional bodies. The government then proceeded to ignore the results of the consultation 'by implementing its original plan, albeit with a few marginal changes' (Boyne, 1997, p. 65). As a result, the process of local government restructuring went much more smoothly, resulting in the creation of a totally unitary system. In Scotland, the nine regions and fifty-three districts set up after the 1974 reorganization were replaced by twenty-nine unitary authorities. The three island councils created in 1974 retained their unitary status. In the case of Wales, the eight county councils and thirty-

115

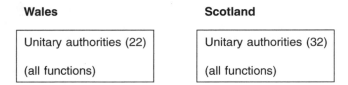

Wales

Unitary authorities (22)
(all functions)

Scotland

Unitary authorities (32)
(all functions)

Figure 5.3 The structure of local government in Wales and Scotland after 1998

seven districts that had been created in 1974 were replaced by twenty-two unitary authorities (see figure 5.3).

The changes in Scotland and Wales thus proceeded with little difficulty. It has, for example, been argued that in the case of Scotland 'the process of implementation was successful', with services continuing 'to be delivered with little adverse comment in the media' (Midwinter and McGarvey, 1997, p. 87). However, it is unlikely that the situation will remain static. During the 1997 general election campaign, the Labour Party announced its intention, if elected, to set up an inquiry into the relationship between local and central government. With the Labour Party now in office, and a new devolved Scottish Parliament now in place (see chapter 11 for further discussion), there is certain to be ongoing debate about the role and nature of Scottish local government. It might well 'change the political landscape in which Scottish local councils operate' (Boyne, 1997, p. 87). For example, in the aftermath of the May 1999 elections to the Scottish Parliament, the joint Labour/Liberal Democrat administration agreed to consider the introduction of proportional representation for local elections. If this were to be implemented, it would have important implications for local politics in Scotland. In Wales, the new Assembly has taken on responsibilities for local government. New patterns and relationships are likely to develop. We will consider these in chapter 11.

The Changing Shape of Local Government

Local governance

Increasingly, the term 'local government' has become inadequate as a concept for describing the complex pattern of interactions at the level of sub-national government. Developments in the 1980s and 1990s have created new patterns of local policy making and service delivery (Clarke and Stewart, 1994; Painter, Isaac-Henry and Rouse, 1997). Likewise, it is 'no longer possible to equate local politics with the politics of local government', since many key decisions are now taken in fora other than local government (Cochrane, 1993, p. 124). The term 'local governance' better reflects this new reality (see chapter 2). It is 'a term which seeks to capture the shift away from a system in which local authorities were the key actors in their localities to one where decision making authority and service provision is shared amongst a range of agencies' (Pratchett and Wilson, 1996, p. 3). It involves a network of actors operating in a complex environment, with a blurring of the boundaries of responsibility (see chapter 2). Allied to this, the late 1980s and 1990s saw a reduction in the role of local government as a direct service provider and a move to what has been termed the 'enabling authority' (see chapter 8 for further discussion). The government set out its rationale in 1991:

> The Government's model for local government in the 1990s and into the 21st century is that of the enabling authority. Here the task of local authorities lies in identifying requirements, setting priorities, determining standards of service and finding the best way to met these standards and ensuring they are met. This implies a move away from the traditional model of local authorities providing virtually all services directly and a greater separation of the functions of service delivery from strategic responsibility. (HM Treasury, 1991, p. 22)

Such an approach had an important impact on local government in the 1980s and 1990s. Elected local government is but one part of 'a complex mosaic' encompassing a wide variety of actors involved in the delivery of local services (Pratchett and Wilson, 1996, p. 6). The move towards local governance would seem to imply a reduced role for local government. Indeed, voluntary and private sector agencies have been afforded a greater role in the delivery of local services. The introduction of compulsory competitive tendering (CCT) means that the private sector has been brought more into the delivery of local services. However, the trend towards local governance also presents elected local government with opportunities. As we have noted, local governance involves a complex network of actors and organizations. Those involved in the network are mutually dependent on each other to achieve desired outcomes. Local government will continue to have an important role to play as such networks are characterized by power-dependence relationships. More fundamentally, it has been argued that local authorities, because of their strategic position, have the scope to become network managers. This opens up interesting possibilities for local authorities to develop and extend initiatives (Painter, Isaac-Henry and Rouse, 1997). Local public/private sector partnerships are an example of this scenario (see chapter 6). Viewed from this perspective, it is perhaps better to see the role of elected local government as a changing, rather than a reduced, one.

The world of non-elected local government

One of the consequences of the development of local governance has been the growth of agencies over the past fifteen to twenty years, which can be collectively described as 'non-elected local government'. This term refers to a variety of organizations that stand outside the formal system of elected local authorities, but which provide public services at a local level that are financed by the state. Such agencies are frequently described as 'quangos' (quasi-autonomous non-governmental organizations). While the development of the so-called quango state has been associated with successive Conservative governments since 1979, it is by no means a new phenomenon. For example, the Labour government of 1945–51 set up the new town development corporations. These were imposed directly on top of existing local government structures. Likewise, the 1974–9 Labour government created a number of similar agencies, including the Scottish and Welsh Development Agencies. While in opposition, the Conservatives were often critical of such developments, pledging to roll back the quango state. However, the Conservative election victory of 1979, far from stemming the tide, actually produced a strengthening of this trend.

The 1980s and early 1990s saw numerous examples of responsibility for service delivery shifting from directly elected local authorities to single-purpose agencies. One of the most prominent examples was the creation of urban development corporations (UDCs). The UDCs were founded on the back of the 'impatience' of the Thatcher government with elected councils. As such, they were typical of the Thatcher governments' attempts to overcome the problems of power dependencies in central–local relations by bypassing local authorities altogether. There were twelve UDCs in total, the largest being the London Docklands Development Corporation (LDDC). Their role was to speed up the business of acquiring land, preparing it for development and selling it. Paradoxically, this entrepreneurial role was to recreate the problem of central–local power dependency in another form. Due to the 1980s property boom, the LDDC was able to acquire considerable profits from land sales. As a result, the LDDC consequently became involved in development projects, most notably Canary Wharf, which prompted unplanned national shifts in regeneration and transport policy and the failure of which became a major embarrassment for the government (Wilks-Heeg, 1996). The UDCs always being intended as short-life organizations, their functions passed back to the local authorities and successor bodies such as English Partnership from 1998.

Other agencies included London Regional Transport (LRT), training and enterprise councils (TECs), housing action trusts (HATs), grant maintained schools (outside the control of local education authorities) and the Funding Agency for Schools. In the field of education, the role of local authorities was gradually reduced. A number of schools opted out of local authority control (see chapter 3). These grant maintained schools receive their funding directly from the Department of Education. City technology colleges (CTCs) were also introduced. In the field of higher education, polytechnics were taken out of local authority control to become free-standing bodies. We can also include the so-called joint boards under the general heading of non-elected local government (Leach, 1996, p. 64). Examples include the London Fire and Civil Defence Authority (LFCDA). Joint boards are indirectly elected bodies, consisting of elected local councillors nominated by local authorities.

In total, it has been estimated that the world of non-elected local government comprises some 4,800 bodies with an estimated budget of £37 billion. This amounts to almost two-thirds of the equivalent allocation of central government money to local government. In England and Wales, there are in excess of 50,000 people working in such bodies compared to 23,000 elected local councillors (Greer and Hoggett, 1996, p. 150). Unsurprisingly, a number of criticisms have been levelled at this state of affairs in relation to democratic accountability. Some commentators have argued that it has 'meant replacing democratic decision-making and control with the free market' (Kingdom, 1991, p. 45). It has been argued that the 'growth of the local unelected state' has been 'at the expense of local representative democracy' (Painter, Isaac-Henry and Rouse, 1997, p. 230). Stewart (1996) has maintained that the existence of non-elected local government, which he terms the 'New Magistracy', creates problems of public accountability. Even in relation to joint boards that are entirely composed of elected local councillors there have been criticisms. For Leach, such councillors are nothing more than appointees, since they are not directly elected to the joint board. Rather they are elected to district councils or London boroughs, which, in turn, nominate them for joint board membership. For Leach, 'it is fallacious to argue that a joint body is accountable in the same way that a local authority is just because it is composed of councillors' (1996, p. 64). While this may be true, the presence of such local councillors still gives elected local authorities a voice and potential for influence.

In relation to the quango state, Gray (1994, pp. 65–6) notes the shift in the public debate from notions of democratic accountability to ideas of economic accountability and the commodification of local services through market forces and the right to choose. For instance, Waldegrave (1993) has argued that accountability to the individual customer can meet the requirements of public accountability. However, Stewart (1996, p. 171) takes issue with such a perspective: 'In public services there can and should be responsiveness to the customer, but within the limits set by public policy and the allocation of public resources. Accountability to the individual customer cannot replace the need for collective account-ability for that policy and that use of resources.' Other commentators strike a somewhat less critical tone. For example, Stoker concedes that, seen from a traditional perspective, reducing the role of local authorities may reduce local democracy. 'On the other hand,' he argues, 'the form of direct participation offered through some of the new agencies of local governance might be seen as a gain for local democracy' (Stoker, 1995c, pp. 4–5).

Conclusion

Local government underwent significant change in both its structure and its shape from 1979 to 1997, causing much controversy. The abolition of the GLC and the metropolitan counties in 1986 attracted perhaps the greatest controversy. It was argued by some that it was a highly politi-cal decision on the part of the Conservative government. The fact that all the abolished local authorities were Labour controlled may be said to back up this argument. The decision may have been driven in part by politics, but it was also a reflection of the problematic nature of local government structure. The GLC, in particular, had come in for criticism almost from its inception. However, despite the apparent ease of struc-tural reform (cf. Pickvance, 1995), the centre did not always get its own way. The workings of the Local Government Commission in the 1990s demonstrated once again that local government structure and its reform is a very thorny issue that has the potential to mobilize powerful coali-tions opposing change. It demonstrated the key role of politics and, in particular, the determination and ability of local authorities to defend their corner when their interests were threatened.

The nature of the local policy process has also changed. As we noted in our discussion of theoretical perspectives (chapter 2), there has been a transition from local government to local governance. Elected local government is now just one of a number of actors involved in the shaping and delivery of local services. The role of the private sector and the voluntary sector has expanded significantly. The involvement of new agencies in service delivery and the development of 'non-elected' local government have given rise to concerns about both democratic account-ability and the future of elected local government. Such developments can be viewed as a challenge to local government, but also as an oppor-tunity. Local governance does not necessarily imply a reduced role for local government. Indeed, as we noted in chapter 2, local governance involves a complex network of actors and organizations involved in a power-dependence relationship. Local government has the potential to play a key role in this relationship.

6

Local Government and the Private Sector

Introduction

The involvement of the private sector in local authorities' activities has been one of the central aspects of the shift towards local governance over the past decade. Commercial interests have become involved in the work of local authorities in a number of ways, ranging from the contracting-out of service delivery to private companies through to the participation of business leaders in strategic regeneration partnerships. These developments have widely been interpreted as the imposition of a private sector ethos on local authorities by a government committed to the introduction of market-based approaches throughout the public sector (Farnham and Horton, 1996; Wood, Valler and North, 1997). Moreover, it is generally suggested that, following initial local authority opposition to such policies, councils have pragmatically and somewhat begrudgingly accepted that they will need to work with the private sector in the way envisaged by government.

There is a certain amount of truth in such interpretations. The initial attempts to enhance the role of private sector interests in local governance did originate from central government reforms in the 1980s. These included the introduction and extension of CCT, which enhanced the role of the private sector in service delivery and the creation of business-led, special-purpose agencies, such as urban development corporations and training and enterprise councils, which handed important policy functions to private sector representatives at the expense of local authorities. Moreover, although initially the source of considerable conflict in central–local relations, such attempts to boost private sector involvement appeared to have been widely accepted by local authorities by the late 1980s. Consequently, the requirement placed on local authorities to form partnerships with the private sector in order to access government regeneration funding has become an accepted part of local governance in the 1990s (Parkinson, 1996).

However, there are also reasons to dispute the idea that the enhanced private sector role in local government affairs represents the realization of concerted government attempts to recast the role of local authorities in a distinctive new-right mould. First, the degree to which the Conservatives succeeded in transforming the nature of local government through private sector involvement is likely to have been exaggerated. The private sector's direct role in local governance has certainly been enhanced, but only as a result of persistent central government effort, and it remains a patchy rather than a universal phenomenon. Second, local authorities have themselves taken the initiative in building better working relationships with the private sector, particularly through partnership mechanisms. In many cases, these partnerships have been initiated by Labour councils (Dobson, 1995) and have harnessed private sector support in order to address specific local policy priorities, through activities that the scarcity of resources would otherwise not permit. As such, rather than representing a further decline in local autonomy, local government's growing engagement with the private sector is a further example of the limits of central diktat and of the scope for the local pursuit of creative autonomy. It also reflects the central propositions of regime theorists (see chapter 2) which suggest that local public and private actors have a mutual interest in seeking to co-operate more formally.

To support these propositions, this chapter analyses the recent experience of three distinctive forms of relationship between local authorities and private companies: compulsory competitive tendering, the Private Finance Initiative and public/private partnerships. In addition, to illustrate the significance of these developments to the work of a local authority, we briefly consider the extent to which Liverpool City Council has entered into new types of relationship with the private sector over the past decade. In conclusion, we suggest that, to date, central government attempts to bring about a decisive shift of responsibility for service provision and for undertaking large capital projects from local authorities to the private sector have proved more difficult than originally envisaged. By comparison, local authority efforts to initiate partnership arrangements, although rarely problem-free, have met with rather more success. Moreover, the value of this experience is shown by the fact that the Labour government has subsequently drawn on the experience of local authorities, resulting in a commitment to extend the capacity of local councils to enter into partnership arrangements and in the relaunch of the Private Finance Initiative.

Compulsory Competitive Tendering

In chapter 3 we noted how compulsory competitive tendering (CCT) became an increasingly important feature of the Conservative government's efforts to remodel local government in the late 1980s and early 1990s. Introduced by the Local Government, Planning and Land Act of 1980, CCT was subsequently extended during the Conservatives' third and fourth terms of office. It has widely been argued that CCT was at the very heart of the government's attempts to engender change in local authorities. Indeed, to many observers CCT was an attempt progressively to transfer responsibility for service delivery to the private sector. Following this view, Walsh (1989, p. 30) suggests that 'it is quite possible to envisage the local authority of the future as a set of contracts, and a network of internal and external trading'. Ten years on, the provision that has been made for the abolition of CCT and for its replacement through the Best Value initiative, indicate that such a scenario is unlikely (see chapter 12). CCT is nevertheless indicative of the blurring of boundaries between the public and the private sector that has taken place in recent years and it is of key importance to any account of how relationships have developed between local authorities and the private sector over the past two decades.

We saw in chapter 3 that, following the initial introduction of competitive tendering for construction, building maintenance and highways in 1980, subsequent legislation progressively expanded the number of local government services subject to competition from the private sector. Thus, the 1988 Local Government Act introduced CCT for a range of maintenance, cleaning and catering services. The tendering process for these functions, and for the management of sports and leisure facilities which was added by the government in December 1989, was phased in over a two-and-a-half-year period, beginning in April 1989. Despite this staggered approach, through which different authorities were required to put different services out to tender at different times, the extension of CCT came to represent a period of turmoil in many local authorities. Almost immediately after the end of this thirty-month period, the 1992 Local Government Act made provision for the further extension of CCT to a number of professional, financial and technical services.

Not only did the number of functions subjected to CCT grow significantly from the late 1980s, but progressively stricter measures were also introduced to try to increase the extent of contracting-out of service provision. The 1980 Act had established that where functions were not contracted out to the private sector, local authorities would be required to award contracts to direct labour organizations (DLOs), which would operate on a commercial basis, independent from the local authority's financial and organizational structures. To ensure a level playing field with the private sector, DLOs were also required to make a surplus equivalent to a 5 per cent return on capital. Furthermore, if they failed to do so for three years in a row, they could be closed down. Yet, despite these provisions, most local authorities that actively sought to keep contracts in-house were generally successful in doing so. Between 1980 and 1985 the total value of contracts awarded to DLOs fell, but only modestly, from £1.8 million to £1.5 million (Stoker, 1991). Inevitably there was a price to be paid for this success and the consequences were largely experienced by local government employees. Thus, 1980–5 saw a decline in the numbers employed by DLOs from 156,606 to 121,381 as well as a downward pressure on wages and a deterioration of working conditions (Stoker, 1991).

Although a small number of Conservative local councils, most notably Wandsworth, market-tested a wide range of services through voluntary competitive tendering in the early to mid-1980s, the government was evidently disappointed at the scale of contracting out and sought to introduce new mechanisms to promote its take-up. Thus, the 1988 Local Government Act introduced a significant tightening of the regulations concerning so-called anti-competitive tendering among local authorities. Contracts were to now to be awarded on a strictly commercial basis, with little or no room for councils to cite social considerations as a reason for awarding contracts to direct service organizations (DSOs). There were also to be strict rules preventing councils from restricting, distorting or preventing competition. To ensure these rules were adhered to, each local authority was to submit an annual report to the Secretary of State for the Environment, detailing what decisions they had taken in the areas subject to CCT. If not satisfied by the content of an annual report, the Secretary of State now had powers at his or her disposal to act against a local authority. Specifically, he or she could serve a written notice on local authorities requesting further information or requiring an explanation. If the Secretary of State also found this response to be unsatisfactory, he or she could issue a direction against the DSO concerned, requiring work to be retendered or imposing specific performance conditions.

Yet, despite these relatively draconian measures, in-house bids continued to win the majority of contracts. At the end of the first year of CCT, a survey by the *Municipal Journal* found that 76 per cent of contracts had gone to DSOs, while a similar survey carried out by CoSLA found that the figure in Scotland was 85 per cent (Wilson and Game, 1994). Similarly, a survey carried out by Shaw, Fenwick and Foreman (1994) found that, in the period up to 1992, the private sector won only 13 per cent of contracts tendered by authorities in the north of England. According to the LGMB's fifth survey on CCT, the private sector had won just 17 per cent of all tenders, with these frequently being restricted to smaller contracts. Indeed, even though the LGMB's seventh report on CCT found that the private sector was winning 40 per cent of tenders by 1993, this represented only 17 per cent of the total value of all contracts. Thus, in terms of value, DSOs had collectively been awarded £1.5 billion of the £1.8 billion worth of contracts put out to tender (Wilson and Game, 1994, p. 330). Moreover, there was little or no evidence that the success of in-house bids had been achieved through anti-competitive practices among local authorities. By the end of 1991, a total of twenty-three councils had been served notices under the 1988 Local Government Act, resulting in just twelve decisions to impose a fresh tendering process, constituting less than 1 per cent of all contracts awarded (Wilson and Game, 1994, p. 329).

In part, the success of DSOs in winning tenders can be attributed to the considerable expertise that they bring to the market-place as well as to the professionalism with which they have approached the task of providing effective services at competitive market prices. Yet, the single most important explanation for the low proportion of contracts awarded to the private sector is the low level of bids submitted by private companies. Indeed, many contracts have been awarded to DSOs by default as no private sector bids have been submitted. In December 1996, the DETR published research that showed low levels of awareness of CCT in four of the sectors covered by the 1988 legislation: sports and leisure management, building cleaning, catering and vehicle maintenance. The research also showed an even lower level of understanding of the CCT regime in these sectors, with just 25 per cent of catering and 9 per cent of vehicle maintenance firms surveyed claiming to know 'a lot' or 'a fair amount' about CCT. Most fundamentally of all, the researchers found that a relatively small number of firms were involved in some of the CCT markets, particularly sport and leisure management, citing the complexity of the process and low profit margins as key barriers to companies tendering (BMRB International, 1996). The growing evidence that there were relatively few companies willing or able to absorb the costs associated with competitive bidding led the Business Services Association in 1996 to argue for the replacement of CCT with voluntary procedures (Atkinson and Wilks-Heeg, 1997). In their view, voluntary tendering would serve to restrict the tenders on offer to authorities that were genuinely convinced of the potential benefits of contracting out to private companies.

The extension of CCT to the 'white-collar' areas of legal, financial, IT, personnel, housing management and construction-related services has proved to be most fraught of all. For every authority, a minimum level of work carried out by each service area was to be subject to CCT: 70 per cent for IT services, 65 per cent for construction-related services, 45 per cent for legal services, 35 per cent for finance and 30 per cent for personnel services. However, because of the complex issues involved in contracting out such services, and in view of the added complication of the outcome of the Local Government Review, the government under-took lengthy consultations with the local government sector, beginning with the 1991 consultation paper 'Competing for quality' and involving some sixty meetings between civil servants and the local authority (Cirell and Bennett, 1996). On the basis of this consultation, it had been agreed to phase in white-collar CCT, beginning with the non-reorganized authorities and those which had been established in April 1995, and sub-sequently extending it to the remaining unitary authorities, established in April 1996 and April 1997. The first deadlines were imposed on the English metropolitan councils and the London boroughs, which were required to have met the agreed targets for legal and construction-related services by April 1996. The final stage in the timetable was scheduled to be the October 2000 deadline for subjecting IT services to CCT, imposed on the unitary authorities created in April 1997.

However, it again became evident at an early stage that things were not going according to plan. Following complaints from the private sector that councils were avoiding competition, the Environment Minis-ter, Paul Beresford, wrote to eighty local authorities in December 1995 asking them to explain why they had awarded contracts to in-house teams. This was then followed in February 1996 by a request to twenty-four of these councils asking for further information and the issuing of fresh guidance on anti-competitive behaviour in March of that year. Despite these steps, however, it had become clear by March 1996 not only that were far fewer contracts being put out to tender than the gov-ernment had anticipated, but also that the proportion being won by private companies was as low as 9 per cent in some service areas. The government responded with a series of measures intended to ensure higher levels of private sector penetration. Finalized in November of that year, the fourteen new regulations included significant increases in the proportion of work in most of the service areas to be submitted for tender, a decrease in the minimum value of contracts in personnel and construction-related services, and a reduction in the minimum number of properties that can be included in a housing management contract.

The level of private sector success in winning contracts under the white-collar CCT regime has been even lower. Figures from the LGMB database in November 1996 showed that, in the area in which most contracts had been awarded, housing management, the private sector had won just 9 per cent of tenders, representing a total of just nineteen contracts. While the private sector had gained a higher proportion of the contracts put out to tender in legal services (23.7 per cent) and construction-related services (43.9 per cent), the small number of contracts going to tender in these areas meant that the total number of contracts awarded to the private sector were fourteen and fifty respectively. As a result, by the end of 1996, a total of just 200 contracts had been awarded in the six white-collar service areas (*Local Government Chronicle*, 22 November 1996). Given that this represented an average of 0.5 contracts for each local authority in England and Wales, the low level of market penetration was evident.

Consequently, other than in a small number of local authorities, such as the London boroughs of Wandsworth, Westminster, Brent and Bromley, there is little evidence of private companies becoming significant providers of local government services. Indeed, there is general agreement that the most significant implications of CCT for local authorities are not that it has led to the demise of their role as service providers, but that it has impacted on their internal organization and culture. First, CCT has required local authorities to distinguish between client and contractor roles. This means that there must be an identifiable part of the organisation that specifies and monitors service provision (the client) and another that is directly responsible for the direct delivery or provision of the service. Since such a distinction has not been easy to incorporate into the traditional structures of departments and committees, CCT has been associated with a degree of internal reorganization among local authorities. A survey of chief executives carried out by the LGMB in 1992 found that 91 per cent felt that the introduction of CCT had led to 'changed management processes across the authority' (Young, 1996, p. 355). However, the extent to which CCT has directly led to fundamental changes in local authority internal organization is disputable, since there have been other important drivers of organizational change (see chapter 8).

Second, there is widespread evidence that a more commercial culture has taken hold in many local authorities. Again, in the LGMB's 1992 survey, 80 per cent of chief executives either strongly agreed or agreed with the statement that 'responding to competition is changing the culture of this authority' (Young, 1996, p. 355). There is also wider evidence that CCT has prompted the adoption of new values within local government. In particular, several authors have pointed towards the development of a commercial culture. Based on their interviews with officers and members in local authorities in northern England, Shaw, Fenwick and Foreman (1994) found that many interviewees spoke of a commercial ethos replacing a more traditional service or social welfare focus. Allied to this, they found that 'in the majority of cases there was a momentum building up behind efforts to promote customer values' (p. 213).

It is within the context of this growth in a customer-service culture in local government that Labour's decision to abolish CCT and replace it with Best Value should be seen (see chapter 12). Best Value recognizes that local authorities are committed to delivering quality services and seeks to enable them to move away from a contracting model that places cost concerns above issues of service quality. The extent to which the transition to Best Value is likely to alter the level of private sector involvement in service delivery remains unclear. On the one hand, Best Value creates a policy framework within which individual local authorities can determine the balance of public, private and voluntary sector provision that they see as most appropriate. As such, Best Value is certainly likely to result in more long-term, stable partnership arrangements between local authorities and private sector providers. Equally, however, assuming that fiscal pressures on local authorities will remain, most local authorities are likely to increase the level of contracting out to private companies in a bid to reduce the costs of service delivery.

The Private Finance Initiative

The Private Finance Initiative (PFI) was launched in 1992 by the Chancellor of the Exchequer, Norman Lamont, to encourage private sector investment in large-scale capital projects. Under the terms of the PFI, companies are contracted by the public sector to finance and provide infrastructure, such as roads and rail links, or buildings. In most cases, these companies will also take on the responsibility for any necessary running and maintenance of the facilities concerned. Such projects are generally termed DBFO schemes (Design, Build, Finance, Operate) and involve the transfer of risk for the procurement and operation of capital assets to the private sector. The company or consortium bearing this risk then makes a return on its investment by leasing the facility to the contracting public sector agency.

Despite the fact that its provisions were used to finance the construction of the channel tunnel rail link, the PFI had a very low profile until 1995. Take-up proved very slow, with just £500 million raised in 1992/3 and 1993/4. Most projects originated from organizations already operating in the twilight world between the public and private sectors, and included the extension of the Docklands Light Railway by the London Docklands Development Corporation and the construction of new hospital buildings for a number of hospital trusts. However, in November 1995 Lamont's successor as Chancellor of the Exchequer, Kenneth Clarke, announced his intention to extend the PFI throughout the public sector, including local government. Clarke set a target of £5 billion to be raised through the PFI in 1996/7 – almost a quarter of the government's total planned capital investment – and indicated that he aimed to secure £14 billion through the PFI by 1999. Increasingly upbeat about the PFI's potential, Clarke told the CBI Conference in July 1996 that 'the PFI is about delivering better services by combining the strengths of the public and private sectors working in partnership'. Six months later, in a speech to the Private Finance Annual Conference, Clarke declared that the PFI would herald a sea change in the provision of public services, arguing that 'the essence of the PFI is about transforming the public sector role from being an owner of assets to being a purchaser of services'. In short, the implications of the PFI for local government were that it would reinforce the trend towards public–private partnership and underpin the more general shift towards the enabling authority.

However, once again, things were not to prove quite so simple. Although the PFI was formally opened to local authorities in October 1996, it took some time before the first local authority PFI agreements were signed. To a large extent, this time-lag was caused by legal uncertainties about the scheme. The City of London's Financial Law Review Panel suggested that banks might face risks resulting from legal uncertainties associated with the PFI. The panel expressed the view that there were no clear guarantees that PFI projects could not be declared illegal under the principle of *ultra vires*, thus causing agreed contracts to be declared void. As a consequence, the PFI continued to flounder and, by the time of the 1997 general election, just one local authority PFI agreement had been signed. In May 1997 the PFI thus became the subject of one of the numerous reviews launched by the incoming Labour government. The Bates Review, which reported just one month later, put forward twenty-nine recommendations designed to streamline the operation of the PFI and remove the barriers that had delayed progress in its first five years of operation. The government accepted the recommendations in full and, of particular importance to local authorities, made an immediate decision to pass the Local Government (Contracts) Act. This Act, which came into force in December 1997, provides a degree of assurance to investors regarding the legal capacity of local authorities to enter into PFI arrangements. Under the terms of the Act, clarification is given that local authorities have the powers to enter into long-term service contracts with the private sector and that, in the event of a contract being set aside by judicial or audit review, the contractor would be entitled to compensation.

The promotion of the PFI to local authorities has also been helped significantly through a number of other changes. The first of these was the establishment, in April 1996, of the Public Private Partnership Programme Limited (4Ps), a company set up by the local authority associations and dedicated to helping local authorities develop PFI projects and other partnership initiatives. It works closely with the DETR, the Treasury and other central government departments, and disseminates best practice within local government to encourage further take-up of the PFI. Second, the Paymaster-General announced in November 1997 that £750 million of capital resources would be made available to PFI projects put forward by local authorities in England and Wales in the 1997/8 and 1998/9 financial years. Third, an interdepartmental Project Review Group was established, bringing more certainty to the process by guaranteeing revenue funding from the relevant central government department. Through these changes, the PFI process has been streamlined, although it remains complex. For local authorities wishing to submit a PFI bid, 4Ps is its first port of call. The local authority and 4Ps then work together to submit the bid to the relevant government department. If provisionally endorsed by the department, the bid is then forwarded to the Project Review Group (PRG), an interdepartmental committee chaired by the Treasury Taskforce, which 4Ps attends. Once endorsed by the PRG, the bid becomes eligible for revenue support and, assuming the partners remain committed, the agreement can then be signed.

Despite a significant number of teething problems experienced in its development, the PFI looks destined to become a significant element of local government finance. One of 4Ps' first acts was to publish a list of thirty pathfinder projects for the PFI in February 1997. These projects covered a number of local government service areas, including schools, social services, waste management and libraries (see table 6.1). By May 1998, eighteen of these had either been signed or secured endorsement from the Project Review Group. However, PFI activity in local government has gone far beyond these pathfinder projects. In its first two years of office, the Labour government has agreed local authority PFI schemes at a rate of about fifty per annum. Thus, by August 1999, some four years after the PFI had been extended to local government, a total of 103 local authority PFI schemes had been approved by ministers and twenty-eight contracts had been signed (*Local Government Chronicle*, 6 August 1999, p. 7).

Table 6.1 Local authority PFI pathfinder projects

Service area	Council	Project	Status as at May 1998
Education (schools)	Dorset County Council	Replacement of Colfox Secondary School	Signed
	Westminster	Replacement of Pimlico School	PRG list
	Manchester City Council	Replacement of Temple School	PRG list
	Dudley	New IT system for the entire schools estate	PRG list
Energy/housing	Manchester	Community heating scheme	PRG list
Waste	Hereford and Worcester	New waste management and recycling system	PRG list
Public transport	Nottingham	Light rail transit scheme	Awaiting transport White Paper
	South Yorkshire Passenger Transport Executive	Transport interchange in Doncaster city centre	Awaiting transport White Paper

Other transport and highways	Maidstone	Car park	Financed from own resources
	Brent	Replacement of all on-street lighting	PRG list
	Doncaster	Northern Bridge relief road	Awaiting roads review
	Essex	Upgrading on the A130	Awaiting roads review
	North Yorkshire	Three road schemes	Awaiting roads review
	Devon	Upgrading of Kingskerswell bypass	Awaiting roads review
Social services	Westminster	Replacement of a 60-bed residential home with a 90-bed dual registered home	Signed
	Surrey	Refurbishment and replacement of 17 residential care homes for the elderly	Signed
	Dudley MBC/ Priory NHS Trust	Development of a polyclinic to provide community health centre services	PRG list
	Harrow	Replacement of a resource centre for the elderly	PRG list
Economic development	Norwich	Link road	Pursuing other public/ private partnerships
IT	Harrow	Document image processing system	Signed
	Kent	IT systems for library services, public access systems and corporate services	PRG list

Continued

Table 6.1 *continued*

Service area	Council	Project	Status as at May 1998
Housing – non-HRA	Berwick	Development of new non-HRA social housing	Seeking PRG listing
	Redbridge	Replacement and refurbishment of sheltered accommodation	Funded via other means
	Derby	Improvement of privately owned rented accommodation	Seeking PRG listing
Libraries	Bournemouth	New central library and IT system	PRG list
Council accommodation	Sheffield	New office accommodation as part of a regeneration project	Seeking PRG listing
Home Office	Derbyshire Police Authority	Procurement of Ilkeston police station	Signed
	Wiltshire Police Authority	Procurement of a police helicopter	Signed
Greater Manchester Fire Authority		Procurement of a new fire station at Stretford	PRG listed
Local chancellor's department		Procurement of a new magistrates' court	PRG listed

Source: Local Government Chronicle, 29 May 1998, p. 14.

Public–Private Partnerships

If the private sector has been relatively cautious about becoming involved in the delivery of local services or the financing of local public sector capital, the converse appears to be the case when it comes to engagement in strategic partnerships. There has been a proliferation of public–private partnerships over the past ten to fifteen years, most of them concerned particularly with regeneration and economic development issues. Indeed, the term 'partnership' has become so prevalent in the local government lexicon that, to some observers, it has become almost completely meaningless (Edwards, 1997). However, it has also been suggested that one of the key reasons for the appeal of the concept of partnership is its very ambiguity (Roberts et al., 1994). Partnerships do not need to conform to any particular regulations or statues, and they can take any of a number of organizational forms, ranging from relatively informal talking shops through to incorporation as jointly funded companies with paid staff and offices. Public–private partnerships are therefore characterized by enormous diversity, as noted in a detailed review of partnership working in local government carried out for the LGMB: 'They [partnerships] are not characterised by distinct fiscal regimes, organisational structures or modes of operation. There is no single easily transferable model of partnership. They vary in scope, purpose, membership, the degree of formality of their organisational structures, the level of resources they command and their actual and potential impact' (Roberts et al., 1994, p. 5).

The logic behind partnership working is that independent organizations coming together around shared objectives means that, while they will need to give up a degree of control over their own resources and compromise their organizational objectives to a degree, they can expect to gain as a result of the synergy made possible by acting in concert with others (Mackintosh, 1992). While the lead roles in partnership formation have generally been played by local authorities and private companies, voluntary and community sector interests also play a part, as do a range of other state and para-state organizations (such as the NHS Trusts, TECs and housing associations). Consequently, partnerships can be based on a number of alternative structures, depending on the nature of the partners and, the extent to which the individual partners are prepared to commit resources and/or undertake responsibility for the delivery of specific projects or programmes. From the wide range of partnership forms that exist, five main types of organisational form can be identified:

- *Companies limited by guarantee* Where partnerships involve the placing of legal commitments on individual partners, establishing a limited company is usually the preferred option. Most public–private partnerships that involve any significant pooling of resources to provide specific services take this form. Examples are a large number of economic development companies such as Nottingham Development Enterprise and Knowsley Development Partnership.
- *Joint ventures* This is a form favoured in partnerships between local authorities and developers, and similar partnerships concerned with development of land or buildings. An example is the Victoria Dock Company in Hull.
- *Regeneration-led partnerships* These include partnerships funded by the single regeneration budget.
- *Trusts* These are set up between statutory bodies and private sector partners to provide infrastructure or arts facilities.
- *Forums* Where partnerships are intended to bring public and private interests together to provide strategic input or advice, legal incorporation is not necessary. Such partnerships may involve individual partners paying a membership fee, but there is unlikely to be any significant pooling of resources or any attempt to undertake projects or to provide significant services. However, relatively loose forum arrangements may be used as a basis for submitting bids for funding from central government and/or the European Union, and may consequently develop a more formal structure if such bids are successful.

There is a conventional wisdom that these partnerships have arisen because local authorities have been coerced into such arrangements by central government and European funding requirements. A number of partnerships have indeed grown up in this way, often with the consequence that they have essentially been temporary marriages of convenience, intended to secure funding and little else (DETR, 1998g). However, such an interpretation belies both the previous development of partnership initiatives by local authorities and the cases of local councils that have recently formed partnerships with private companies without any particular motives to secure government funding. Indeed, to the extent that central government policy has acted as a catalyst for partnership development, it has often been in a negative sense: local authorities have often sought to develop partnership arrangements to overcome resource constraints or to avoid the imposition of central government special initiatives.

The concept of local government working in partnership with other organizations initially arose in the 1970s, although this was almost entirely a vision of partnership based on closer co-operation between local authorities and other public sector agencies in the context of inner-city regeneration (Parkinson and Wilks, 1986). The emergence of public–private partnerships is very much a product of the 1980s and 1990s, and has been brought about by a changing political and economic context. Roberts et al. (1994) suggest that local authorities have been prompted to enter into partnership arrangements in response to a number of changes in the external operating environment of local authorities. These changes primarily include the reduced control that local actors have over economic processes as a result of the internation-alization of the economy, the problems of policy co-ordination brought about by the fragmentation of local governance and a growing recogni-tion that some of the most pressing policy challenges can be addressed only through a multi-sectoral, and thus by implication a multi-agency, approach (Roberts et al., 1994).

These macro-changes were in turn amplified by significant develop-ments in regeneration policy during the 1980s. First, the progressive erosion of local government financial autonomy and the growing use of central government arm's-length agencies such as UDCs, increasingly reduced local authorities' capacity to undertake independent policy ini-tiatives. Second, the Conservative government's commitment to promot-ing private sector leadership in urban regeneration and the growing interest among the business community in regeneration issues, as reflected by the foundation of Business in the Community, had raised the profile of local economic and social development on corporate agendas. Third, the property boom of the late 1980s provided mutual opportu-nities for local authorities and business interests alike. For local author-ities, the property boom offered them a means of raising revenue from the sale of land and buildings, while, for the private sector, it obviously presented the opportunity to undertake potentially profitable investment (Harding, 1991).

The outcome of these developments was that partnerships were initi-ated without any formal requirements or incentives being offered by central government. Several partnerships were founded by the private sector in the late 1980s and early 1990s. For example, the East London Partnership was initially established in 1990 by Business in the Com-munity, with five major companies constituting the founding members and contributing £30,000 each. Others, such as Business Opportunities on Merseyside, were private sector initiatives that were able to draw on significant public sector financial and organizational support, in this instance from the Merseyside Task Force. However, the majority of part-nerships have been initiated by local authorities. During the late 1980s, the opportunities provided by the property boom meant that these often had a physical development focus. Consequently, prominent examples included Birmingham Heartlands Ltd (a body created by Birmingham City Council, five private developers and the Birmingham Chamber of Commerce) and the Victoria Dock Company (a partnership between Hull City Council and a private developer formed to regenerate a disused dockland area in the centre of the city). However, numerous partnerships have increasingly been formed with a view to contributing to the 'soft' elements of regeneration through initiatives aimed at improving training provision or enhancing the quality of business support services. One pioneering example is Mansfield 2010, a partnership funded jointly by Mansfield District Council, Nottinghamshire County Council and the local private sector in 1991 to provide business support functions and promote inward investment (Roberts et al., 1994).

Significantly, although the growth of public–private partnerships occurred under two periods of Conservative government, 1987–92 and 1992–97, many of the earliest partnerships were initiated by Labour-run local authorities. Both Birmingham Heartlands Ltd and the Victoria Dock Company were established by Labour councils in 1987, as were similar initiatives such as Nottingham Development Enterprise (Roberts et al., 1994). While these authorities were clearly responding pragmatically to the Conservatives' victory at the 1987 general election and its implications for local government, such partnerships were also a proactive attempt by the councils concerned to initiate, and to retain a degree of control and influence over, local policy developments. In particular, the government's proposals to establish a number of urban development corporations were seen by many Labour-run cities as a threat to local autonomy, since experience in London and Merseyside indicated that local authorities had little or no capacity to influence the policy process. By seeking to develop their own partnership arrangements, local authorities were able to establish specific policy objectives that a UDC might have regarded as secondary. Thus, in establishing the Victoria Dock Company, Hull City Council was able to ensure that development in classic UDC territory allowed for the provision of affordable housing in the city centre, including a number of housing association properties.

Partnerships have been established in a wide range of policy areas, although most have tended to be concerned with aspects of regeneration and economic development that the public and private sectors have mutual interest in pursuing. Thus, the activities undertaken by public–private partnerships are typically intended to address policy issues such as housing, place marketing, tourism, inward investment promotion, community care, education and training, infrastructure development and improvement, cultural strategies, environmental improvement, business support and city centre management. In addition, local authorities participate in partnerships operating at multiple spatial scales, since different initiatives are best addressed at different geographical levels. Thus, while housing partnerships are likely to have an estate or neighbourhood focus, partnerships focusing on infrastructure or place marketing are likely to focus on the area covered by the local authority as a whole or, as is increasingly the case, on the wider sub-region.

The tendency towards a 'scaling-up' of partnership working was one of the most significant developments of the 1990s and is serving to bring about significant institutional change at a sub-national level. It is reflected in the growth of sub-regional partnerships, through which coalitions of local authorities have combined with private sector interests to advance an agreed set of economic development initiatives (Fordham et al., 1998). Again, much of the initiative has come from local government, and several partnerships have been important catalysts for sub-national institutional change. For example, the Northern Development Company (NDC) was established as a partnership between the north-east's local authorities, trade unions and business leaders to promote inward investment to the region. Funded through a combination of membership subscription and central government support, the NDC's success provided an important impetus for the formation of inward investment agencies elsewhere in England. In 1999 it was absorbed into the North of England Regional Development Agency.

Again, it is important not to exaggerate the importance of these developments. In 1998 there was still considerable geographical variation in the coverage of sub-regional partnerships. Thus, while areas such as the north-east of England and Greater London could point to a comprehensive set of sub-regional partnerships, in other areas their coverage was found to be patchy. In addition, the extent to which such partnerships could point to any significant degree of success varied enormously. Thus, while the NDC claimed to have secured, over a ten-year period, 12.5 per cent of all new jobs created by inward investment in the UK, other partnerships could point only to less tangible (if not vague) outcomes, such as increased synergy and organizational leaning (Fordham et al., 1998). However, despite these shortcomings, the establishment of regional development agencies (RDAs) in the English regions in April 1999 has led to an explicit recognition of the significance of sub-regional partnerships. Most significantly, RDAs have indicated that they will generally seek to work through sub-regional partnerships rather than delivering policies and programmes directly.

Partnership is no panacea for local government. Success is far from universal and there have been many potent critiques of partnership working. Critics have pointed particularly to two main issues. First, concerns have been raised about the accountability of partnership. It is argued that the influence which the private sector has gained over local decision making is a fundamental challenge to the democratic legitimacy on which local government is based. With decisions made in partnership fora, away from the public eye, partnerships are seen by some to represent a new corporatist localism that reinforces the shift of power away from elected representatives. However, a second set of criticisms appears to mitigate many of the issues raised in relation to democratic accountability. Rather than pointing to local authorities and the private sector locked into tight corporatist relationships, some critics highlight the ineffectiveness of public–private partnerships. Here critics have focused on the failure of such mechanisms to deliver any significant degree of mutual action, with partnerships being dismissed as talking-shops and seen to be lacking commitment from key players. Consequently, as partnership working continues to grow at a variety of spatial scales, the challenge for local authorities is to lead the process of promoting open and transparent partnerships whose activities are consistent with the council's local political mandate and which are strong and effective enough to reap the benefits of joint working.

The Case of Liverpool

Choosing Liverpool to illustrate the way in which local authorities have successfully sought to work with the private sector might be considered a case of exaggeration to prove a point. In many ways it would have been difficult to find a locality in the UK where relationships between the business community and the local authority were as acrimonious as they were in Liverpool in the mid-1980s. During the 1980s, Liverpool City Council became one of the most prominent proponents of a revived municipal socialism, directed against the policies and politics of the Conservative government. The Militant Tendency, which gained the upper hand on the city council in 1983, took a particularly hostile stance towards the private sector, advocating a large-scale programme of public sector expenditure to compensate for the massive job losses caused by private sector withdrawal from the city. During this period, the Labour-controlled council explicitly rejected central government policies premised on private sector involvement in city politics and pursued a strategy of resisting expenditure cuts through a combination of creative accounting and setting illegal budgets (Parkinson, 1985). The result was a showdown between Liverpool City Council and central government in 1985, culminating in the city making its entire workforce redundant as it teetered on the brink of bankruptcy. Against this background, if

Liverpool can be shown to have embraced the private sector as a valued partner, it would serve to underline the significance of the trends referred to in this chapter.

Unsurprisingly, Liverpool has not bucked the national trend in relation to CCT: the private sector has not, to date, become a major provider of local services in the city. In common with many other large, Labour-run local authorities, Liverpool sought to respond to the CCT legislation by legitimately retaining service provision in-house. Thus, by the mid-1990s the extent of private sector penetration was limited to refuse collection. Under the Liberal Democrat administration that took control of the council in 1998, contracting out has since been extended to other service areas, such as grounds maintenance and housing maintenance. But the majority of contracts awarded by the council have been won by DSOs and, in view of the limited degree of contracting out, the CCT unit that the council established in the early 1990s has since been abolished. Furthermore, Liverpool is hoping that under the Best Value regime it will be able to contract out services to the community and voluntary sectors, rather than to private companies.

As has been the case elsewhere, it is in other areas that the private sector has become engaged in the work of local government, particularly through a variety of partnership arrangements. The first significant step towards partnership working was Business Opportunities on Merseyside (BOOM), founded as a joint initiative between the Royal Institute for Chartered Accountants and the Merseyside Task Force in 1986. With its roots firmly in the private sector, BOOM focused its efforts on countering the negative image that Merseyside had acquired during the 1970s and 1980s. In the view of its founder, one of the most significant achievements of BOOM was to bring the council leader, Keva Coombes, on to a platform with Merseyside business leaders and to secure the public commitment of the council leadership to work with the private sector (interview with Geoffrey Piper, 15 January 1999). Following the impetus provided by BOOM, Liverpool City Council was to join with the four other Merseyside local authorities in a subsequent initiative, the Mersey Partnership. Growing directly out of BOOM and the wider promotional efforts of the Merseyside Development Corporation, the Mersey Partnership defines its role as one of 'investment marketing', which embraces a range of related functions including the promotion and co-ordination of inward investment, place marketing, media management and tourism. Although it undertakes a number of functions on behalf of the local authority, it is predominately private sector funded.

Liverpool City Council now operates in a wide variety of partnership arrangements with the private sector. While the extent of partnership working has been increased under the Liberal Democrats, it began with the previous Labour administration. Three examples demonstrate the range of partnerships involved. First, beginning with City Challenge, the council has increasingly sought to use partnership arrangements to lead the regeneration of Liverpool city centre. In 1999, these efforts led to the establishment of Liverpool Vision, the first of two national pilot schemes in the use of urban regeneration companies. Liverpool Vision constitutes a single-purpose body intended to provide a strategic approach to city-centre redevelopment, which will harness public and private sector resources to bring about the comprehensive regeneration of the area in relation to an agreed masterplan. Second, Liverpool has also sought to make use of the PFI, and in June 1999 the government gave its backing to a scheme intended to fund the renovation of thirty-two schools in the city. Through this arrangement it is anticipated that £46 million will be invested by the private sector over a three-year period beginning in 2001. The commercial interests concerned will then manage the properties for a period of twenty-five years in return for an annual fee. Finally, the private sector has also been involved in the debate about the modernization of local government in Liverpool through the work of the Liverpool Democracy Commission. Chaired by James Ross, the director of Littlewoods, the Commission includes representation from other private sector concerns as well as other public bodies, the universities, the community and voluntary sectors.

Conclusion

This chapter has suggested that, despite the fact that some forms of private sector involvement in local governance were imposed on local authorities by a series of central government initiatives, some of the most important forms of local public–private co-operation have taken place where local authorities have actively pursued their own policies of involving private sector interests. While a handful of radical Conservative councils seized on the CCT legislation to contract out significant service-delivery functions to the private sector, it has often been Labour councils that have led in the development of strategic partnerships with the private sector aimed at promoting local economic development and regeneration.

There can be little doubt that such councils were invariably responding pragmatically to the constraints imposed on them by a Conservative government and that, for some Labour councillors, entering into partnerships with the private sector involved an almost total ideological volte-face. However, this does not negate the point that partnerships have been pursued as an opportunity to develop autonomous local strategies, albeit with significant dependence on private sector interests. The significance of the initiatives pioneered by a number of Labour-run local authorities was recognized by the Labour Party in opposition (Dobson, 1995), and there can be little doubt that it has subsequently informed the government's modernization agenda for local government. Further evidence that the local government community is taking the lead in partnership working is provided by the Local Government Association's recent initiative, the New Commitment to Regeneration. As was noted in chapter 3, the New Commitment to Regeneration has seen the establishment of twenty-two pathfinder areas that will seek to approach regeneration from a joined-up government perspective. Although there are no resources attached to the initiative, each of these pathfinders has created partnership structures that allow for significant private sector participation.

Evidently, local authorities have used partnership working to influence the national policy agenda, which, under the new Labour government, has resulted in notable national policy change. For instance, the government's commitment to extend the scope for local councils to enter into a variety of contractual relationships with the private sector, particularly in the form of joint venture companies, is a clear recognition of councils' complaints about the 'unreasonable obstacles which the law places in the way of councils trying to promote partnership' (Dobson, 1995, p. 9). Similarly, revisions to the PFI have reflected local authority concerns about the policy and enabled councils to make far greater use of private investment potential. Given the government's unambiguous commitment to partnership working, the private sector's role in local governance is only likely to increase. Assuming that constraints on local authority finance remain broadly the same, the extension of partnership working is likely to increase rather than constrain local authorities' ability to pursue autonomous local policies. In many ways, therefore, local partnerships reflect the attempt to assemble a 'capacity to govern' pointed to by regime theorists (see chapter 2). The concern, however, is that this capacity to govern will come at the expense of local accountability.

Part III

Local Government Reinvents Itself?

7

Local Elections, Political Realignment and Change in Local Authorities

Introduction

This part of the book is concerned with ways in which local government has reinvented itself. The focus in this chapter is on local electoral trends in the 1990s and the major impact these had on the pattern of party politics. First, the rapid decline of the Conservatives and the increasing dominance of Labour in local government will be analysed. Among the issues to be considered will be the factors behind this decline and whether the marginalization of local Conservatism in the mid-1990s is a permanent or transitory phenomenon. Second, the rising profile of the Liberal Democrats is considered. Third, the chapter focuses on another interesting phenomenon of the 1990s, namely the large increase in the number of so-called hung councils: that is, councils in which no party has a majority. Fourth, and this links to the third point, attention is given to another development in local politics in the 1990s: the rise of Labour–Liberal co-operation in the shape of various power-sharing agreements at the local level. Consideration is given to whether this marks a permanent shift in the local political landscape towards a new kind of politics, and its potential implications for national politics are also discussed. Finally, the chapter considers the decline in voting at the local level, the factors behind this trend and the implications of low electoral turnout for local politics.

Table 7.1   The state of the parties in local government, May 1996

Party	Number of councillors	Councils controlled
Labour	11,326	218
Liberal Democrat	5,182	56
Conservative	4,415	12
Other	2,558	31
No overall control	–	140

Conservative Local Politics in Decline and the Growing Dominance of Labour

The period of Conservative government from 1979 to 1997 witnessed many changes in the world of local government. This was no more evident than in the declining influence of the Conservative Party in local politics. Its decline has been referred to by some commentators as cataclysmic in nature (Game and Leach, 1996, p. 131). In 1985, the Conservatives, despite six years in office at the national level, had majority control of more councils in Britain than the Labour Party. It was only in 1986 that the Labour Party overtook the Conservatives as the largest party in local government, for the first time since the 1974 local government reorganization. The Conservatives did relatively well in the 1992 local elections, partly as a result of Labour's demoralization after its fourth consecutive general election defeat. However, from 1993 onwards, the Conservatives experienced a rapid decline in their local base. In 1995, the Conservatives suffered their worst ever local election results, winning outright control in only twenty-one local authorities. By contrast, the Labour Party now controlled 210 local councils. In 1996, the nadir of Conservative politics at the local level, the Conservative Party controlled only twelve local councils in England and none at all in Scotland and Wales (see table 7.1).

Local politics in England had moved from an effectively two-and-a-half party system to what can be characterized as a three-party system with the Liberal Democrats as the second party of local government. By the mid-1990s, the Labour Party was by far and away the biggest force in local government. In Scotland and Wales, the pattern of local politics is obviously different due to the presence of the two nationalist parties, the Scottish National Party (SNP) and Plaid Cymru.

By the end of the 1990s, the credibility of the Conservative Party as a political force at the local level was clearly at stake. For Game and Leach, writing in 1996, it had become 'apparent that Conservative influence in local government had been well and truly marginalised' (Game and Leach, 1996, p. 132). The question that needs to be asked is whether this marginalization of the Conservatives at the local level is a permanent phenomenon or merely transitory, being a product of the deep unpopularity of the Conservatives at the national level from the early 1990s. If it is permanent, it will have major implications not only for the local political landscape, but for national politics. The lack of a significant local base for the Conservatives poses real questions about their ability to fight national elections effectively. Local councillors are an important political resource, providing a bedrock for parties in terms of both organization and credibility. Without sufficient numbers of councillors, the Conservatives face potentially very serious problems.

The May 1999 local elections did produce something of a recovery in Conservative fortunes. They gained 1,400 council seats and took control of a further forty-eight councils. They now controlled seventy-four councils and had overtaken the Liberal Democrats as the second party of local government (see table 7.2). However, such an apparent upturn in Conservative fortunes needs to be treated with some caution. These elections took place at the mid-term point of the Labour government, generally regarded as the most vulnerable time in electoral terms for an incumbent. The Conservative position at the local level still remains fragile. After all, in 1983, the year of its worst ever general election performance, the Labour Party still controlled 142 local councils. These included fourteen county councils, twelve London boroughs and most cities outside London. After the May 1999 English local elections, the Conservatives controlled only eight county councils, four London boroughs and no large cities. Their overall national percentage of the vote stood at only 33 per cent. They failed to recapture former heartlands such as Ashford and Thanet in Kent, and Castle Point in Essex. In Scotland and Wales, the Conservatives controlled no local councils.

The 1999 local elections produced a mixed picture for the Labour Party. Its claim that it achieved the best set of local election results at the mid-term of any parliament this century may be open to the challenge (Rallings and Thrasher, 1999). It did, however, beat the Conservatives into second place nationally, securing 35 per cent of the popular vote. Not all the gains from 1995, an extremely good year for Labour, were reversed. It remained the largest party of local government, in terms of both council seats and councils controlled. It did, however, lose control of thirty-two local authorities and it also lost more than a thousand council seats. It was also 'hit by a tornado in some places' (Rallings and

Table 7.2 Party control in local government, 1999

	Conservative	Labour	Liberal Democrat	Independent/ Other	Nationalist	No overall control	Total
Scotland	0	15	0	5	1	11	32
Wales	0	8	0	3	3	8	22
London	4	18	2	0	0	8	32
Mets	0	29	3	0	0	4	36
Counties	8	8	2	0	0	16	34
Districts	59	60	16	10	0	93	238
Unitaries	3	29	4	0	0	10	46
Total	74	167	27	18	4	150	440

Source: Local Government Information Unit.

Thrasher, 1999). It lost control of Sheffield City Council for the first time since 1968 and suffered a large loss of seats in a number of councils in the north of England, including Carlisle, Hyndburn, Lancaster, and Cleveland and Redcar. In Wales, it lost control of its former strongholds Caerphilly, Cynon Taff and Rhondda, to a resurgent Plaid Cymru.

The Labour Party's loss of Sheffield illustrates well that local politics are not merely a function of national politics. The Labour Party, with a high national opinion poll rating and control of all but one of the parliamentary seats in Sheffield, still could not retain control of the city council. National factors do have an impact on local elections, but other factors such as history and local circumstances are also important. A good example of this is the 1998 London borough elections. Labour made large gains in the borough of Harrow and now controls what was once considered a Conservative stronghold. However, on the same night it suffered heavy losses in one of its own traditional strongholds, Islington, and only controls the council on the casting vote of the mayor.

The decline in local Conservatism in the 1990s examined

A number of explanations can be put forward to explain the decline in Conservative support at local government level. First, it is due in no small part to the eighteen-year dominance of the Conservatives in central government. In recent times, voters have viewed local elections as an opportunity to pass judgement on the record of government at the national level. In 1968, for example, the Labour government of Harold Wilson was severely buffeted at the local polls. The Conservative Party's long period in office 'has served to magnify this tendency' (Atkinson and Wilks-Heeg, 1997, p. 30).

However, this offers only a partial explanation. Various commentators have noted how the powers of local government were reduced to such a degree in the period from 1979 to 1997 that its role and capacity for action were considerably diminished (Wilson and Game, 1998; Chandler, 1996). As a result, local voters were less inclined to express their views on their local council's record, but viewed local elections as an opportunity to express their dissatisfaction, or otherwise, with the policies and actions of central government. There is a great deal of validity in such a viewpoint. While we seek to argue in this book that local government was not as emaciated after eighteen years of Conservative government as some might suggest, responding in a positive and imaginative way to create some autonomy and a defensible space, there was nonetheless a public perception that its role had been significantly reduced. In such a context, local elections acted more and more like referenda on central government performance, since local voters perceived local politics to be increasingly irrelevant. In this sense, the Conservatives may have reaped what they sowed, and, with consistently low opinion poll ratings from 1992 onwards, suffered accordingly. The current Labour government, by contrast, still enjoys relative popularity, if measured by opinion polls. As a consequence, its local government base, though it has shrunk to some degree of late, still remains extensive.

The Liberal Democrats on the Rise?

The mid-1990s witnessed an increasingly strengthened position for the Liberal Democrats at the local level. In 1994, the number of councils that they controlled had increased from twenty-eight to forty. By May 1996, they controlled some fifty-six local councils compared to the Conservatives' twelve. They had become the second party of local government. While it is true that the number of Liberal Democrat-controlled councils had been reduced slightly after the May 1997 local elections, it could still be argued that they 'were in an unambiguous second place' ahead of the Conservatives, who still controlled only thirteen local councils (Wilson and Game, 1998, p. 264). The Liberal Democrats held sway in a number of previous Conservative strongholds. These included Horsham, the New Forest, Woking and Worthing. However, their success was not confined to former Conservative areas. In 1998 they finally took control of Liverpool City Council, which had previously been a hung council. In the same year, the Labour Party fought off a strong challenge from the Liberal Democrats in the London borough of Islington. Labour, as we noted above, still runs the borough, but only on the casting vote of the mayor. The strength of the Liberal Democrats at the local level has provided a spring board for advances at the parliamentary level. In the south-west of England the Liberal Democrats built on their local success at the 1997 general election with parliamentary gains in such seats as Devon West and Torridge, Somerton and Frome, and Taunton. However, their success was not just confined to the south-west. In London, for example, Liberal Democrat control of the London borough of Sutton was followed by the capture of the borough's two parliamentary seats, Sutton and Cheam, and Carshalton and Wallington.

However, the May 1999 local elections produced a mixed picture for the Liberal Democrats. It has been argued that their vote held up reasonably well and that 'two party politics is now a distant memory in many local authorities' (Rallings and Thrasher, 1999). While this may be true, the Conservatives managed to establish themselves as the second party of local government, ahead of the Liberal Democrats. The Liberal Democrats still remain a force at the local level, controlling some twenty-seven local authorities and having just under 4,500 local councillors. However, it is a much weakened position compared to that of 1997. In the south of England, the Liberal Democrats lost control of seven local councils to the Conservatives. In parts of the north of England, they performed well, making gains in some fifty-five local councils, largely from the Labour Party. Most spectacularly, they seized control of the former Labour stronghold of Sheffield. However, they also made important inroads in Labour-held areas such as Bradford, Chesterfield, Doncaster, Kirklees and Leeds.

What explains this differential performance by the Liberal Democrats? First, it is due to some traditional Conservative voters returning to the fold at the expense of the Liberal Democrats. It is hardly surprising that this should be the case. The Conservatives reached their lowest ebb in 1995 and 1996 at the local level. Some kind of electoral recovery was always likely. Second, the gains from Labour are in part the product of a protest vote among some traditional Labour supporters, who would not be prepared to vote Conservative, against the Labour government. This, together with the Liberal Democrats' brand of community politics, has provided a rich seam of support.

The Politics of Hung Councils

One significant development in local government politics has been the phenomenon of hung councils: that is, councils where no party has a majority. As has been noted, such councils 'have become a prominent feature of local government during the last twenty years as the politicisation of local government and the reduction in the two party dominance of English local government in particular has developed' (Arnold, 1999, p. 3). In 1996, the year of the last council elections before the 1997 general election, the total number of hung councils stood at 140. After the May 1999 local elections the figure stood at 150.

Various studies have looked at how such councils are administered politically (Leach and Stewart, 1992; Leach and Stewart, 1994; Rallings and Thrasher, 1995). Four broad categories of political administration have been identified:

- no administration;
- minority administration;
- formal coalition;
- informal coalition or power sharing.

153

In a system of no administration, committee chairs may be rotated between the various political parties, or they may be elected on a much more *ad hoc* basis. In a minority administration, a single party forms an administration, with the explicit or tacit support of another party or parties, this without the guarantee of long-term support. In the case of a formal coalition, two or more parties agree to form an administration based on a joint policy programme with an agreement on the sharing-out of committee chairs. In an informal coalition or power-sharing arrangement, there is no commitment to a joint policy programme, but committee chairs are shared out (Arnold, 1999, p. 4).

There is, however, some overlap between these categories. As Game and Leach (1996, p. 135) have noted, 'there is a grey area between power-sharing and formal coalitions where the two become difficult to distinguish'. For them, the main difference 'may lie in the use of labels rather than the extent of co-operation, or commitment to shared programmes' (p. 13). Arnold further notes that both formal and informal coalitions, together with most minority administrations, may be characterized as politically integrated hung councils. Hung councils with no administration may be characterized as politically fragmented (Arnold, 1999, p. 4). Research in 1995 found that in nearly 51 per cent of hung councils there was a formal coalition or power-sharing arrangement (Rallings and Thrasher, 1995). Leach and Stewart (1994) found that in 54 per cent of hung councils there was some agreement to share committee chairs.

There are conflicting views on the efficacy of hung councils. Temple (1993, p. 25) strikes a positive note, arguing that 'hung councils work, and provide some measure of proof that British politicians with contrasting philosophies can work together to resolve difficult political issues'. Adonis and Twigg (1997) agree, arguing that many hung councils produce stable and effective government (p. 12). Other commentators argue that while hung councils 'may well have the capacity to make the policy process more democratic in some respects (for example, by preventing one group from dominating the policy agenda), the experience of balanced local government in the UK has been mixed' (Pratchett and Wilson, 1997, p. 21).

Labour/Liberal Democrat Co-operation: The Emergence of a New Local Politics?

By the mid-1990s, Liberal Democrat influence was not just confined to the local councils that it controlled with a majority. The increasing number of hung councils gave it an important grip on power, with power-sharing or other arrangements being made with other political parties. It has been noted that 'the overwhelming number of instances of co-operation between political parties in hung councils, especially in the 1990s, has been between Labour and Liberal Democrats'. Co-operation between the Labour Party and the Conservatives, or the Liberal Democrats and the Conservatives has been very limited (Arnold, 1999, p. 5). One reason for the limited role of the Conservatives in local co-operation is political history. In the majority of cases where councils have been hung, it is the Conservatives who have lost power. This tends to produce 'a reaction that they have been defeated and (even if the largest party) should not be permitted or in some cases seek to run the council, even on a minority basis' (Leach and Stewart, 1994, p. 543).

The growing policy convergence of Labour and the Liberal Democrats at the national level, brought about in no small measure by the modernization programme of New Labour led by Tony Blair, played an important part in this process. The inclusion of Liberal Democrat MPs on a key Cabinet sub-committee on constitutional matters after the 1997 general election, though it did meet criticism from some quarters in both parties, was a clear reflection of this development. Another important factor was the decision by the Liberal Democrats at a national level to abandon their policy of 'equidistance' between the two main parties. This facilitated the growing *rapprochement* with the Labour Party. The Labour Party's decision to change its position on co-operation with other parties at the local level in the mid-1990s was also not without significance. The sharing of committee chairs is now allowed so long as they do not constitute a formal coalition arrangement. However, it is not always easy to make such a clear distinction. Indeed, it has been pointed out that some local Labour/Liberal Democrat co-operation has come close to such a formal arrangement (Leach and Stewart, 1994, p. 544). There are a number of examples of local Labour/Liberal Democrat co-operation. In the London borough of Bromley, for example, although the Conservatives are the largest party, the council leader is a Liberal Democrat due to co-operation with the Labour Party. Suffolk County Council had a Labour leader in 1998 but a Liberal Democrat vice-chair of the council.

Do these developments point to the emergence of a new kind of politics at the local level? Certainly, the emergence of Labour/Liberal Democrat co-operation in a significant number of local councils, does seem to suggest a shift away from what has been generally regarded as the traditional British model of adversary politics. However, Labour/Liberal Democrat tensions at the national level are replicated at the local level. In a number of local councils, the pattern is not one of Labour/

Liberal Democratic co-operation but of competition, sometimes border-
ing on overt hostility. Reference has already been made to Liverpool City
Council, where the key battle is between Labour and Liberal Democrats,
with the Conservatives long since a spent force on the local council.
Liberal Democrats are the key challengers in a number of traditional
urban Labour 'strongholds'. One such 'stronghold', Sheffield City
Council, was wrested from the Labour Party for the first time in 1999
after a bitter and acrimonious battle. We have already noted above the
electoral battle between Labour and the Liberal Democrats in parts of
the north of England. Rochdale Council in the urban north-west, for
many years a Labour stronghold, has seen clashes between the two
parties. Indeed, the town's former Liberal Democrat MP, Liz Lynn,
has been an outspoken critic of national Labour/Liberal Democrat
co-operation.

Indeed, when considering the issue of party co-operation it is important to stress the 'importance of differences in local circumstances, which
can still be crucial in the development of specific outcomes. Locally, the
political culture of party groups may vary' (Leach and Stewart, 1994, p.
544). Norfolk County Council is a good example of this. While we noted
above Labour/Liberal Democrat co-operation in neighbouring Suffolk in
1998, in Norfolk the Conservative and Labour parties shared the positions of chair and vice-chair of the council respectively. In Oxfordshire,
Labour held the chair and the Conservatives the vice-chair.

The national organization of local government: the local authority associations

The changing nature of party politics at the local level has had an important impact on the national organization of local government. In order
to provide themselves with a collective voice to negotiate with central
government, and increasingly with the European Union (see chapter 10),
local authorities have combined to form associations. Before the recent
review of local government structures (see chapter 5), there were five
principal local authority associations in England and Wales:

- the Association of County Councils (ACC);
- the Association of District Councils (ADC);
- the Association of Metropolitan Authorities (AMA);
- the London Boroughs Association (LBA);
- the Association of London Authorities (ALA).

Scotland, by contrast, had one association representing all local councils: the Convention of Scottish Local Authorities (CoSLA).

The division of local authority associations in England and Wales, while serving a functional purpose, was also a product of politics. Until the early 1990s, the county and district councils tended to be dominated by the Conservatives and the metropolitan councils by the Labour Party. However, as we have discussed above, local election results in the early to mid-1990s dramatically reduced the number of district and especially county councils that the Conservatives controlled. Such a dramatic shift of political control, combined with the impact of the review of local government structures during the same period, led to merger discussions among the three associations: the ACC, the ADC and the AMA. As a result of this process, the Local Government Association (LGA) was launched in 1997.

Similarly, in London following the abolition of the GLC, the boroughs divided along party political lines to form two separate associations. The London Boroughs Association (LBA) consisted predominantly of Conservative councils and the Association of London Authorities (ALA) consisted of Labour-controlled boroughs. As in other parts of Britain, local elections in London in 1994 saw a big drop in the number of London boroughs controlled by the Conservatives. There was resultant pressure for a merger of the two bodies. This happened in 1995 when the Association of London Government (ALG) was created. As a result of these changes, there are now three principal local authority associations; the LGA, the ALG and CoSLA. Over the longer term, this rationalization offers the prospect of greater unity among local authorities.

The Decline In Electoral Turnout

It was noted in chapter 1 that one of the key arguments put forward in favour of local government is that it helps foster democracy by giving opportunities for people to participate in the political process. However, such an argument would appear to be undermined by the fact that 'local election turnout in Great Britain is almost at the bottom of the international league table' (Goldsmith and Newton, 1986, p. 146). Wilson and Game have noted that turnout has rarely exceeded 45 per cent and only on two occasions (both in Wales) has it gone above 50 per cent. Yet, as they also note, it was also equally rare for turnout to drop below 40 per cent (Wilson and Game, 1998, p. 204). However, in 1992, local election turnout stood at approximately 37 per cent, the lowest in ten years. From 1992 to 1995 there was an upturn in voter turnout to an overall level of 43.5 per cent. The picture changed in 1996 with turnout dipping sharply to 34 per cent. By 1997, it had fallen as low as 30 per cent. In

Local Government Reinvents Itself?

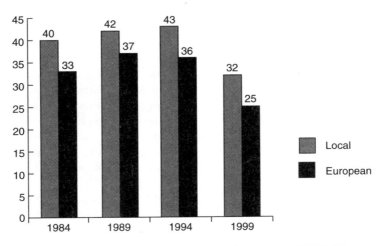

Figure 7.1 Local and European election turnout, 1984–99
Source: Adapted from *Local Government Chronicle*, 11 June 1999.

the May 1999 English local elections, turnout was on average just over 32 per cent.

The causes of declining local turnout

It is possible to identify a number of possible explanations for the general decline in voting at the local level from the mid-1990s. From 1992 to 1996, there was a heightened political atmosphere in the UK. The popularity of the Major government never recovered from the fiasco of 'Black Wednesday' in September 1992 when the country fell ignominiously out of the European Exchange Rate Mechanism. The Conservatives' reputation for economic efficiency had been severely damaged. Voters, it was argued, were willing to use local elections as a protest against the Conservative government. This increased interest in local elections and helped increase voter turnout. There may be some validity in this argument. However, it does not explain the low turnout in 1996 when the Conservative government was still extremely unpopular.

By contrast, since Labour's landslide victory in 1997, the political atmosphere has been far less heightened. This can be attributed in part to the nature of New Labour under the leadership of Tony Blair, which has generally sought to build a consensus politics in the UK. This has taken some of the edge out of politics. Peter Kellner, speaking on BBC Radio's *PM* programme on 8 June 1999, argued that Tony Blair has managed to send the British electorate to sleep. Linked to this is an argument put forward by, among others, Labour politicians, that voters have not been inclined since 1997 to vote against Labour as they were against the Major government. There is, it is argued, a 'politics of contentment' among the electorate, or more specifically Labour voters, who do not see the need to vote. Hence the fall in electoral turnout. However, there is no clear evidence to back up such an assertion. Indeed, the Labour government in official documents expresses concern at the low turnout, arguing that local democracy is not working well. Turnout is 'far too low and falling' (DETR, 1999b, para. 1–18).

It should be noted that such a fall is not confined to local elections. Turnout for the June 10 1999 European elections stood at 25 per cent, the lowest figure for any national British election. Indeed, turnout for local elections stands up reasonably well by comparison with the last four European elections (see figure 7.1). On the same day as the European elections, a parliamentary by-election in Leeds Central produced a turnout of 19.6 per cent, the lowest since 1945. What we appear to be witnessing is a general decline in voting. Whatever the reasons for this, and they are indeed varied, it is not just an issue for local politics. The vote in the 1997 general election was the lowest in the UK since the mid-1930s.

What can be done?

Can anything be done to halt the slide in voting at the local level? Or approaching it from another angle, does it really matter? Wilson and Game (1998) note that the UK has never been a high-voting country even at a national level. They go on to argue that, although it may be regrettable, 'it may be seen as a measure of at least tolerable satisfaction with the performance of our governmental institutions' (p. 208). However, when turnout reaches levels of 30 per cent (of those actually registered to vote), it is almost inevitable that questions will be raised about the legitimacy and validity of democratic local government. Are there any remedies at hand?

Three possible solutions have been put forward. First, it has been argued that a change to the electoral system is one important element in increasing voter turnout at the local level (Adonis and Twigg, 1997, p. 12). At present, the electoral system for local elections in England, Scotland and Wales is that used for parliamentary elections: namely, first past the post (FPTP). In Northern Ireland, the single transferable vote system (STV) is used. It has been argued that there is widespread resentment of the clear deficiencies of FPTP (Wilson and Game, 1998, p. 199). Rallings and Thrasher (1991, p. 5) have argued that 'local voters are poorly served by existing methods of electing local councils'. Yet despite its stated aims to modernize local government (see chapter 12 for further details), the new Labour government has so far shied away from general reform of the voting system at the local level. With the exception of elections for the new Greater London Authority in the year 2000, which will use a variant of proportional representation, the system of FPTP still remains in place in England and Wales at present. In Scotland a different picture is emerging, with the joint Labour/Liberal Democrat administration, in office since the May 1997 Scottish Parliament elections, considering the introduction of some form of proportional representation for Scottish local elections.

However, it is worth making the point that the recent introduction of variants of proportional representation to certain British elections has not backed proponents' claims of increasing voter turnout. For example, as mentioned above, the June 1999 European elections, fought on a regional proportional system, recorded a turnout of just 25 per cent.

Second, it has been argued that the weakened power of local government has turned off voters. For example, Hale (1999, p. 11) questions 'whether it is realistic to expect a significant proportion of the electorate to vote in local elections . . . when the centre has so much power over local government'. The solution is 'a wider local government tax base and more control over funding' (p. 11). So far the current Labour government has only made tentative moves in this respect. Universal capping has been removed, but considerable controls still exist. There are no plans for any significant widening of the local tax base, although a number of pilot studies on local congestion charges are to be undertaken. Calls for reform to the NNDR have met with only a limited response.

Third, there have been calls for reforms to the way we vote at the local level. Possibilities include more postal voting and elections at the weekend or spread over several days. The Labour government has put forward a number of suggestions in this regard (see chapter 12). There have already been a number of innovations. For example, at the 1998 London borough elections, some Croydon voters were able to vote at their local Tesco supermarket.

Conclusion

The mid-1990s saw a dramatic decline in support for the Conservatives and a concomitant rise in support for the Labour Party and the Liberal

Democrats. By 1996, the Liberal Democrats had overtaken the Conservatives as the second party of local government. Commentators argued that Conservative influence at the local level had been marginalized. How correct is this? While it is true to say that the Conservatives did make something of a recovery after the 1999 local elections – they had overtaken the Liberal Democrats as the second party of local government – they remain in a relatively weak position. This has implications for the Conservatives nationally as well as locally. Both the Labour Party and the Liberal Democrats still enjoy positions of relative strength.

One significant phenomenon in the 1990s was the developing pattern of co-operation between the Liberal Democrats and Labour in a number of councils where no party enjoyed a majority. Two principal factors have facilitated this: the growing policy convergence between the two parties at the national level and the change to the rules of the Labour Party which allows greater co-operation with other parties. However, while the pattern of local co-operation at the local level is predominantly Labour/Liberal Democrat, there have been examples of Labour/Conservative and Liberal Democrat/Conservative co-operation. Moreover, as we have already noted, within the overall pattern of Labour/Liberal Democrat co-operation, there are areas of strong and sometimes bitter rivalry, Liverpool and Sheffield being two of the best examples.

Reference has also been made to the low turnout at recent local elections and some of the potential factors involved in this process. While concern has been expressed at the implications for local democracy, low turnout has affected national as well as local elections. That said, however, turnout as low as 32 per cent at the local level is worrying. A number of proposals have been put forward to remedy the situation. These include giving local government greater autonomy and reforming voting procedures. How effective such proposals will be is a matter for debate. We will return to this issue in chapter 12.

8

Getting Their Own Houses in Order

New Directions in Local Government Internal Organization

Introduction

This chapter considers recent changes to the way in which local authorities are organized internally. Although this may initially appear to constitute a technical, management issue, it is also a fundamentally political one. Local authorities are a unique type of organization in that they are responsible for the delivery of multiple services to a local population to whom they are democratically accountable. One of the most significant implications of this role is that all local authorities face the challenge of balancing the need to provide for professional, business-like management of services with mechanisms that will enable local political choice to be exercised. As Leach, Stewart and Walsh (1994, p. 5) put it, 'The challenge for organisation and management in local government is to achieve both organisational effectiveness in service delivery and an effective political process.' Local authority management is, therefore, inseparable from the politics of local government.

This chapter begins by outlining the traditional, functional model of a local authority and the assumptions that lay behind it. This model is characterized by a strict vertical separation of authority (hierarchy) and a strict horizontal separation of functions (departmentalism). It has proved remarkably resilient in the face of concerted and mounting criticism. However, beginning with the Maud and Bains committees of 1969 and 1972 respectively, the character of this model has been gradually recast. Modified partially by the corporate management recommendations of the Bains Report, the traditional model was challenged more fundamentally in the 1980s. These challenges came initially in the form of decentralization and then subsequently in the radical new-right conception of the enabling authority put forward by Nicholas Ridley. However, it is the concept of community governance, a particular variant of the enabling authority, which has become increasingly ascendant in local government. In many ways, community governance, which has effectively been endorsed by the Labour government, has returned local authorities to the unfinished revolution begun by the Bains Committee. The chapter concludes that the local government community has successfully responded to the Conservative governments' attempts to define the purpose and role of local government by advancing its own, alternative view of internal organization.

The Politics of Local Authority Organization

There has never been a single, accepted way of approaching the challenge presented by the 'dual' role of local authorities as service providers and democratically elected bodies. Indeed, a number of alternative approaches have been advocated since the late 1960s. Yet, although these approaches have been diverse in nature, they have tended to address the same basic set of questions. These questions are:

- What role should councillors play and how should the councillor–officer relationship be defined?
- To what extent should the local authority be governed through strong, central direction?
- What principles should guide the way in which services are delivered to and received by their recipients?
- Should the basic building blocks of a local authority be based on individual services or on general, authority-wide objectives?
- How is accountability best achieved?

Aside from demonstrating that there is a strong degree of continuity in the issues which have been raised in discussions about local authority internal organization, these questions also make it clear that the way in which local authorities are structured is an important reflection of the way in which the role of local government is defined more broadly. As a consequence, local authority internal organization has been at the centre of political debates about local government over the past three decades. These debates have been political in both the institutional and ideological senses of the word. First, local authority internal organization has been a key issue in central–local relations. Every national government since 1964 has expressed its intent to modernize local government. While many of these attempts have focused on the overall national structure of local government, central government has attempted to influence local authority internal organization in a number of ways. The past twenty-five years have thus borne witness to a number of alternative models of local authority organization advocated by special commissions and government ministers. At the same time, principles of internal organization have also become a key issue for the local government community, which has increasingly sought to intervene pro-actively in a debate that has gone to the very heart of what local government should be about. Second, the issue of local authority organization has been of special political importance because, at particular points in time, it has taken on an explicitly ideological edge. The ideological dimension has been expressed most evidently in competing models of local authority organization, such as the new urban left's policy of decentralization and the new-right conception of the enabling authority. Since the latter part of the 1980s, the debate may have become less polemical, but important philosophical differences have nonetheless been observable, particularly in the ensuing debate about the notion of the enabling authority.

The debate about how local authorities are organized internally has not only been a source of ongoing tension between central and local government – it has also constituted a key testbed for the capacity of local authorities to bring about change autonomously from the centre. Given that local authorities have not been left to determine their internal structures, free from central government influence, they have also had to respond to the challenge of reforming traditional structures within the context of a shifting, and frequently hostile, national political climate. Even if central government has not specified that local authorities should implement particular organizational forms, various bodies of legislation have had a profound impact on how councils organize their own affairs, whether these be reforms of the structure of local government, the introduction of CCT or numerous changes to the functions for which local authorities are responsible. Since much of this legislation in the 1980s was underpinned by a desire to limit the autonomy of local government, the extent to which local authorities have been able to respond with an alternative view of their own role is a critical test of the creative autonomy thesis.

It is, however, necessary to insert an important caveat at this stage, namely that an organization which undertakes a programme of internal reform is not necessarily one which is charting out avenues of autonomous activity. Indeed, there is a danger that an organization constrained by its external operating environment will focus almost solely on organizational reform as the one sphere in which it can exercise control and engender change. Organizational restructuring is a means to an end rather than an end in itself and should reflect a prior process of agreeing organizational priorities and commitment to a particular set of values and culture. The acid test, therefore, is the extent to which local authorities have been able to achieve genuine self-transformation.

The Traditional Model and its Discontents

Had this book been written in the mid-1960s, our task of explaining the internal organization of local authorities would have been a relatively straightforward one. At that time, local authorities conformed, virtually without exception, to a common model that could be captured easily on a two-dimensional organisational chart. From top to bottom this chart would show that local authorities were based on a strict, vertical organization of authority and accountability. The full council – that is, the elected members – would occupy the uppermost position in the organizational chart, to signify its position of supreme authority. A series of lines would then show how authority was delegated from the full council to a range of sub-committees of councillors, each charged with overseeing the activities of a particular department of council employees. Conversely, lines of accountability would then run up from the individual departments, through the sub-committees, to the full council, which was ultimately responsible for the council's affairs. The diagram might also make reference to the town clerk, usually a lawyer, whose task was to advise the full council on legal issues. The second dimension of the chart, from left to right, would demonstrate how local authorities were based on a clear, horizontal separation of functions. Thus, for each major function that the local authority was charged with, such as education, housing or social services, there would be a separate council committee and a separate council department. Finally, each department would be headed by a specialist who would work closely with the chair of the relevant committee.

The UK was by no means unique in developing a system of local government based on hierarchy and departmentalism; much the same can be said of most, if not all, European countries (Batley and Stoker, 1991). However, there were particular historical and political factors that led to an entrenched culture of departmentalism in the British context. Thus, the origins of British local government in the single-purpose agencies of the early nineteenth century established a culture of functional separation which, following the Municipal Corporations Act of 1835, led to strict functional separation being observed in local authorities established to provide multiple services. This trend continued after the Second World War as local councils grew into their new role as part of the welfare state. The growing importance of welfare functions meant that most local authority departments came to be dominated by professionals. The character and ethos of individual departments increasingly became characterized by these distinctive professional groupings, thereby reinforcing departmental boundaries (Leach, Stewart and Walsh, 1994). At the same time, hierarchical modes of operation were further underpinned by a view of accountability that stressed the need to ensure observance of proper procedures and by the principle that there should be uniformity in the provision of welfare.

The deeply rooted attachment to the traditional model is remarkable when we consider that local authorities have always possessed a high degree of freedom about how to organize their own affairs. There are few organizational requirements that local authorities have to observe, other than the fact that education authorities must have a chief education officer and councils charged with social services must have a director of social services (Wilson and Game, 1994). Moreover, the resilience of the model, which is still recognizably intact in a number of local authorities, is all the more surprising given that it has long been attacked for being 'over-bureaucratic, inward-looking, insensitive to the real needs of clients, self perpetuating' (p. 344). However, there has been a progressive, if not entirely pervasive, shift away from the traditional model since the late 1960s. Initially, this shift took the form of modest, incremental changes that resulted from national commissions and were implemented by most local authorities during the 1970s. More far-reaching changes occurred during the 1980s and 1990s, as the result of which numerous local authorities are now attempting to dispense almost entirely with the traditional model.

All Power to the Centre? The Rise of Corporate Management

The initial attempts to bring about change in the internal organization of local authorities were bound up with wider concerns in the late 1960s and early 1970s to modernize the operation of local government. In the period from 1967 to 1973, seven separate commissions were established to consider reform options for particular aspects of British local government (Maud, 1967; Mallaby, 1967; Redcliffe-Maud, 1969; Wheatley, 1969; Macrory, 1970; Bains, 1972; Paterson, 1973). The ground covered by these commissions included not just matters of internal organization but also the overall structure of local government in the UK as well as staffing and personnel issues. The sheer scale of activity indicates the extent to which the operation of local government was subject to critical scrutiny in a period of just over half a decade. There was a conscious attempt to ensure that the various commissions produced an integrated set of proposals for local government reform. Thus, the Maud and Mallaby commissions worked alongside one another, sharing a common secretariat, to consider internal management and staffing as related issues. Similarly, the Bains and Paterson commissions were established to consider the internal management arrangements of the local authorities set up by the 1972 Local Government Act, itself a product of the Redcliffe-Maud, Wheatley and Macrory commissions.

These attempts to map out a comprehensive programme of local government reform did not fundamentally question the assumptions of departmentalism and hierarchy on which the traditional model was based (Leach, Stewart and Walsh, 1994). However, they did identify many of the problems that lay at the heart of the existing system. Thus, the Maud Committee criticized the fragmentation of local authorities into too many individual departments, pointed to the absence of effective central administrative direction and the lack of strategic policy making from councillors swamped with paperwork detailing the operation of the authority in minutiae. At the centre of its criticisms was what it saw as 'a nineteenth century tradition that council members must be concerned with actual details of day-to-day administration' (Maud, 1967, p. ix). The Maud Report made six main recommendations. First, it proposed that councillors should be more engaged in strategic policy making and put forward a series of recommendations to achieve this. Second, it suggested that there should be a greater separation of the roles of councillors and officials. Third, it was proposed that committees should focus more on policy determination and should delegate more powers to their chair and chief officer. Fourth, Maud recommended that the total number of committees in most authorities should be reduced to around six. Fifth, with the exception of small local authorities, it was argued that all councils should appoint a management board made up of between five and nine members and which would be delegated significant powers. Finally, the report recommended the appointment of chief executive officers.

Local authorities largely resisted the recommendations of the Maud Report. In particular, there was universal hostility to the proposal for management boards, which councillors saw as creating an implied elite within their own ranks (Hampton, 1991). There was also widespread scepticism about the scope for reducing the number of committees (Wilson and Game, 1994). Yet, despite their resistance, local authorities were already beginning to introduce organizational changes at the time of the Maud Report, many of which went some way towards furthering Maud's agenda. Consequently, the Bains Committee and its counterpart in Scotland, the Paterson Committee, reiterated much of the Maud Commission's conclusions, but also went some way to challenging departmentalism. Bains argued that 'the traditional departmental attitude within much of local government must give way to a wider-ranging corporate outlook' (Bains, 1972, p. 6). Unlike the Maud Report, Bains proposed that both councillors and senior officers should share policy-making responsibilities. Specifically, Bains made three key recommendations. First, it reiterated the recommendation that local authorities should appoint chief executives. Second, it advocated a break with the tradition of linking committees to departments, proposing that the committee structure should be determined in light of the authority's objectives rather than in accordance with the services it provided. Finally, to drive forward this more corporate approach, it proposed the creation of a cross-sectoral policy and resources committee and the establishment of a senior corporate management team.

The bulk of the Bains Report's recommendations were implemented by the new local authorities established by the 1972 Act, with most others quickly following suit. Thus, by the late 1970s, virtually all local authorities had appointed a chief executive and most had established policy committees and management committees. However, there was one main exception – programme committees did not replace the traditional departmental structure. More importantly, those changes that did occur appeared to mask a continuation of the traditional culture and values. As Wilson and Game (1994, p. 75) note, 'organisational charts changed but often political realities hardly moved'. In his analysis of the outcome of the Bains Report, Alexander (1982) suggested that corporate management teams had generally been constrained by the continued dominance of professionalism and departmental boundaries, and that policy committees did not always receive the support of other sub-committees. Alexander concluded that the significance of the report might have been 'more apparent than real, more form than substance' (p. 76). In an even more devastating critique, Dearlove (1979, pp. 181–2) argued that corporate management was doomed to failure: 'There are good grounds for suggesting that it will not be possible to implement the corporate approach . . . Fragmentation is inescapable. It certainly cannot be solved or willed away to be replaced by co-ordination simply by reducing the numbers of committees and departments and beefing up the power of central services'. It was against this background that the principles of corporate management were to come under increasing attack. Yet, as we shall see, the concerns that Bains had raised were soon to return to the local government agenda.

Decentralization: from New-Left Alternative to the Local Government Mainstream

The principal outcomes of the local government reviews of the late 1960s and early 1970s were twofold. First, local authorities were now much larger than they had been previously. Second, attention within local authorities was focused particularly on enhancing the role of the centre to enable a more corporate approach. These arrangements were based on the assumption that they would have notable advantages, stemming particularly from the capacity of such authorities to mobilize greater resources to support a more strategic approach to service delivery. However, certain drawbacks also became rapidly evident. In particular, concerns were expressed that local government was becoming too big, overly bureaucratic and distanced from the people it was designed to serve (Benington, 1976). As a result, it was proposed by a number of observers that corporate management should be supplemented by innovation at the neighbourhood level; that the 'big is beautiful' philosophy of Redcliffe-Maud should be tempered by a dose of E. F. Schumacher's 'small is beautiful' (Burns, Hambleton and Hogget, 1994).

Although a number of experiments with neighbourhood management were undertaken during the 1970s, including a series of initiatives funded by the Department of the Environment, their influence on local authority organization was minimal (Burns, Hambleton and Hogget, 1994). However, with criticism of corporate management growing in certain quarters (Alexander, 1982), arguments in favour of decentralization were increasingly heard in local government debates. Initially, decentralization was advocated particularly, although not exclusively, by a new breed of Labour-controlled local authorities that subsequently became known as 'the new urban left'. As decentralization emerged, it therefore became more than just a response to the perceived problems of corporate management: it was also one of the leitmotifs of a group of local authorities expressly opposed to the Thatcher government's policy agenda. As a result, the decentralization movement was to become embroiled in the intense political conflict over local government during the 1980s.

That decentralization initiatives became wrapped up with ideological conflicts about the role of local government should not, however, obscure the fact that the motivations for decentralization have stemmed from a variety of political and non-political convictions. The justifications for decentralization have been as diverse as anarchist-inspired arguments in favour of participatory democracy through to management philosophies that advocate decentralized operations as part of a customer-centred approach. Moreover, over time these different perspectives have tended to converge around a general consensus about the benefits of decentralization. This trend is shown particularly in relation to neighbourhood housing offices, which were first introduced in 1981 by Walsall District Council. Seen as a means of achieving better integration of services at the neighbourhood level (social services and environmental health also had a presence in the offices), Walsall's experiment was to last a mere two years as a result of Labour losing control of the authority in 1983. Yet, although Walsall's pioneering efforts were to prove short-lived, the principles of decentralized housing management were subsequently taken forward by authorities such as Islington and are today applied by most local authorities with a significant housing function. Indeed, it is no exaggeration to say that, ten years after the rise of the new urban left, decentralization had become part of the local authority mainstream. Thus, most councils applying to the Local Government Commission (LGC) for unitary status indicated that they would introduce decentralized structures (Burns, Hambleton and Hogget, 1994).

Although advocates of decentralization have had a common target in the increasingly bureaucratic and unresponsive local authorities that emerged in the era of corporate management, the diversity of motivations for decentralization have naturally translated into highly diverse forms of decentralization. These various approaches are characterized by a number of important distinctions. First, the most basic distinction that can be drawn is between those approaches which seek to decentralize responsibility to particular geographical units, such as neighbourhoods, and those which are concerned with providing for flatter organizational hierarchies and with empowering lower-level officers to take decisions and manage budgets. Second, there is an overlapping distinction between approaches which define local residents as citizens and those which define them as consumers or customers. In the case of the former, decentralization is likely to seek to engage residents in a more active role by creating opportunities for them to voice their general opinions about local services. By way of contrast, in the latter scenario decentralization is generally allied with mechanisms through which individual residents can make specific complaints if services are sub-standard or which offer them some form of customer choice. In both cases, decentralization is seen as a way of enhancing the accountability of local authorities to those they serve.

On the basis of these distinctions, it is possible to identify a vast array of approaches to decentralization. Within the category of neighbourhood decentralization alone, three main types of approach may be identified (Elcock, 1996). First, there is departmental decentralization, which involves a single department, such as social services or housing, devolving provision to neighbourhood offices. Second, many authorities have followed a policy of corporate decentralization, which brings together staff from several departments to provide a 'one-stop shop' or similar office at neighbourhood level, designed to meet the broad range of service needs that local residents may have. Finally, there are examples of political decentralization, which involve some form of neighbourhood political input into the content of service delivery. Within these three types, further distinctions can be made. Thus, political decentralization can be provided for either by linking neighbourhood offices to mechanisms aimed at encouraging participatory democracy or by placing neighbourhood offices under the control of local ward councillors. Moreover, given that it is possible to 'mix and match' different forms of decentralization, the list of alternative approaches is almost endless. Consequently, we concentrate here on assessing the significance of some of the most radical decentralization experiments and on analysing the longer-term significance of decentralization for local authorities (for more detailed accounts, see Burns, Hambleton and Hogget, 1994 and Leach, Stewart and Walsh, 1994, chapter 6).

The most ambitious decentralization schemes attempted to date have combined the decentralization of service provision to multi-functional neighbourhood offices with some form of neighbourhood democratization initiative. The London boroughs of Islington and Tower Hamlets undertook such initiatives during the 1980. In Islington twenty-four neighbourhood offices were established in 1984, each providing housing, social services and environmental health functions. In addition, neighbourhood fora were established to work alongside the neighbourhood offices. Although these are effectively limited to advisory and consultative functions and exercise no real power over policy, they constitute a significant attempt to enhance public participation in the neighbourhood decision-making process. In Tower Hamlets, seven neighbourhoods were established in 1986, when the Liberal Democrats took control of the borough. Significant powers were devolved to each neighbourhood, which took responsibility for housing, social services, environmental health, planning and development control, arts, libraries and leisure facilities. As a result, the neighbourhoods became responsible for all direct services other than highly specialist functions and only two borough-wide committees remained: policy and resources, and social services. Each neighbourhood office had its own chief executive and a full complement of senior officers. In addition, every neighbourhood office was home to a First Stop Shop, which acted as a first point of contact for local residents, while neighbourhood committees, made up of local councillors, were delegated full powers to determine policy at a neighbourhood level. Various forms of neighbourhood consultative committee were also established. It was a bold and radical move, particularly as three of the neighbourhoods had Labour majorities.

Decentralization in Islington and Tower Hamlets thus constituted far-reaching organizational experiments that combined many of the distinctive approaches to decentralization outlined above. However, decentralization in both Islington and Tower Hamlets has been subject to extensive criticism, and, in some cases, serious policy failures have been exposed. The high costs associated with such policies have meant that the number of neighbourhood offices in Islington has progressively been cut: in April 1998 the total number of neighbourhood offices was reduced to eleven. Most fundamentally, decentralization was held to be at fault when Islington's child care was found to be seriously wanting by an independent report in 1995, while in Tower Hamlets, neighbourhood autonomy led to criticism of the borough's housing policies, with the council standing accused of allowing racist principles to determine housing allocation in certain neighbourhoods (Dowding et al., 1995). As a result, social service functions have been taken out of neighbourhood control in Islington and have instead been integrated into the remit of five community care centres. Similarly, on regaining control of Tower Hamlets, Labour have recentralized many of the functions previously carried out at a neighbourhood level.

Despite the problems experienced by these more far-reaching attempts at decentralization, there can be little doubt that decentralized organizational arrangements are now widely accepted and used in local government. However, the promise of decentralization to provide a means of enhancing local authority accountability through increased citizen participation has not been realized. As Jeffrey (1997) notes, there are a number of reasons for the failure of democratization relative to the success of decentralization. First, where democratization objectives have been part of the decentralization agenda, they have generally been 'bolted on' to existing structures and, as a result, have not fundamentally altered the nature of the overall decision-making process. Second, many local authorities have been cautious about devolving any significant decision-making power to local or community fora because of a concern about the representativeness of such groupings, which often become dominated by a small community elite. Third, there have been associated problems in developing mechanisms that do enable councils to seek the views of a more representative body of citizens, and which are integral to the decision-making process. However, while the hope that decentralization might provide for a more participatory local democracy may have failed, a number of more innovative mechanisms intended to enhance local democracy have emerged in recent years (Jeffrey, 1997; Stewart, 1997). We examine these below in relation to the notion of community governance.

Towards the Enabling Authority?

The concept of the enabling authority emerged in the late 1980s and is most usually associated with a pamphlet written in 1988 by the Secretary of State for the Environment, Nicholas Ridley. Entitled *The Local Right: enabling not providing*, Ridley's pamphlet envisaged a minimalist, residual role for local government. It advocated that local authorities should, by and large, cease to provide services directly. Instead, he advocated that they should specify the services which were required and the standards to which they should be provided, and then contract out responsibility for delivering them to private sector companies, voluntary organizations and para-state organizations such as housing associations. Most famously, Ridley envisaged a scenario whereby a local council would meet only once a year, to hand out the contracts for its various services.

Despite the widespread association of the enabling authority with Ridley's specifically new-right interpretation, he did not invent the concept. As Leach, Stewart and Walsh (1994) note, the idea had already appeared in the Duke of Edinburgh's Inquiry into Housing in 1985 as well as in the government's 1987 White Paper on Housing. What was significant about Ridley's notion of the enabling authority, however, was that it represented a vision of the logical outcome (from a new-right perspective) of the government's legislative programme for local government in the period after 1987 (see chapter 3). During 1988 the Conservatives passed three major pieces of legislation that cast local authorities in an enabling role: the Local Government Act, the Housing Act and the Education Reform Act. Respectively, these extended the range of local authority services subject to competitive tendering, made provisions for the voluntary transfer of local authority housing stock to housing associations, enabled schools to opt out of local authority control and introduced local management of schools. All of these changes were inspired by a vision of local government in which local authorities would specify service content and plan for future needs, but in which they would not be directly responsible for the delivery of services. In the words of

Table 8.1 The changing role of LEAs, 1988–94 (proportion strongly agreeing or agreeing with the statement)

	1988 (%)	1992 (%)	1994 (%)
The LEA sees its principal role as that of:			
Traditional provider	76	20	31
Leader/strategic manager	80	88	77
Partner	54	95	82
Enabler	46	93	72
Adviser	76	95	80

Source: Young (1996), p. 354.

Osborne and Gabler (1992), local authorities would be 'steering not rowing'.

To what extent did the 1988 legislation lead to local authorities redefining themselves as enablers rather than providers? Young (1996) uses the LGMB surveys to assess the extent to which the 1988 legislation has moved local authorities towards an enabling role. Despite the rapid erosion of their capacity to implement autonomous housing policies, it appears that local authorities have been reluctant to let go of the housing function altogether. In 1994, 69 per cent of respondents said that they were 'neither considering nor implementing voluntary transfer' of their housing stock to housing associations. As we noted in chapter 3, even with the recent surge of voluntary transfers, local authorities remain significant housing providers. In education, there was initially strong evidence of a switch from local education authorities (LEAs) seeing their role in terms of provision to their acting as a strategic manager and enabler. Table 8.1 shows that whereas 76 per cent of LEAs saw themselves as providers of education in 1988, by 1992 this has fallen to just 20 per cent. Over the same period, the proportion of LEAs that saw themselves as operating in an enabling function grew from 46 per cent to 93 per cent. Interestingly, however, the data for 1994 suggest that this trend towards LEAs seeing themselves as enablers rather than providers may have been over-stated. Thirty-one per cent now saw themselves as acting in the role of a traditional provider, while the proportions defining themselves as strategic managers and enablers had fallen to 77 per cent and 72 per cent respectively.

The evidence that CCT has pushed authorities towards an enabling role is also patchy. We noted in chapter 6 that, despite concerted attempts to prevent them doing so, local authorities have retained a significant number of services in-house. Whether CCT has resulted in significant organizational change is also open to question. In a study of the way in which local authorities in the north of England responded to the CCT requirements introduced by the 1988 Local Government Act, Shaw, Fenwick and Foreman (1994) suggest that a third of councils had begun to introduce change in management structure and in the delivery of services *before* the extension of CCT was announced. To illustrate that the organizational impact of CCT may have been over-stated, the authors cite the chief executive of a large district council:

> CCT didn't require us to dramatically re-think the way we were organised. Before CCT arrived we had already begun to recognise the value of the client–contractor split and had established a DSO operating within a more commercial culture. Some of the things people have done because of CCT we have done for other reasons. (p. 203)

Neither is there a great deal of evidence that Ridley's particular interpretation of the concept had been developed to any significant degree, other than by a handful of flagship Conservative local authorities, such as the London boroughs of Brent and Wandsworth. Instead, the new-right view of the enabling authority has become one of several possible interpretations and, in the context of the late 1990s, one that lies at the fringe of the debate. Indeed, ten years after the publication of Ridley's pamphlet, a quite different idea of the enabling authority had gained widespread acceptance, albeit in a different guise. That a concept which was initially anathema to the local government community could subsequently become its guiding light requires some explanation. To understand these developments it is necessary for us to strip away some of the new-right rhetoric from Ridley's proposals. Evidently, despite his obvious antipathy towards local government, Ridley pointed to a trend with which many in the sector could express sympathy. Specifically, he proposed that local authorities 'will need to operate in a more pluralistic way than in the past, alongside a wide variety of public, private and voluntary agencies. It will be their task to stimulate and assist those other agencies to play their part instead of, or as well as, making provision themselves' (Ridley, 1988, p. 8). This was a starting point that supporters of local government felt comfortable with and from which alternative views of the enabling authority could emerge (see Brooke, 1989; DoE, 1991). It was in this context that the enabling concept could be recaptured by the local government community.

Strategic Management and Community Governance: the Belated Impact of Bains?

As the debate about the enabling authority has progressed, it has become increasingly enmeshed with wider strategic management concerns and, in particular, with the rise of the notion of community governance. Until recently, this debate had largely been conducted within the local government community. Influenced particularly by the work of Professor John Stewart, the LGMB and a number of pioneering authorities have progressively steered the enabling concept away from the new-right conception. These developments may, somewhat ironically, be read as the belated triumph of Bains.

Strategic management

The notion of strategic management derives from a military context, where a strategy represents a plan of action that is flexible enough to adapt in light of changing circumstances. Central to the strategic management approach is the adoption of a mission statement, which is backed up by a regularly revised strategic plan for the organization. Strategic management is essentially a latter-day equivalent of corporate management, which recognizes that organizational planning will need to be able to adjust to an uncertain and changing operational context. In practice, the similarities between corporate and strategic management are such that the two terms are often used almost interchangeably. For instance, both approaches advocate the adoption of a cross-sectoral approach to local government policy making, recommend the streamlining of committee structures and propose that councillors spend more time on policy rather than on detailed management issues. The essential difference then, as Young (1996) notes, is that strategic management posits a less mechanistic approach.

Over the course of the 1990s there has been a progressive growth in the number of authorities seeking to apply the strategic management approach. Table 8.2 shows that while 61 per cent of local authorities had adopted mission or 'core values' statements in 1992, this had risen to 74 per cent by 1994. Over the same period, the proportion of local authorities that had agreed corporate or strategic plans rose from 52 to 59 per cent. LGMB surveys also reveal that between 1992 and 1994 the average number of committees and sub-committees fell from 7.4 and 16.6 to 5.6 and 14.2 respectively (Young, 1996). While there is no straightforward means of assessing whether local councillors are oper-

Table 8.2 Local government adoption of strategic management principles

	Mission or 'core values' statement		Corporate or strategic plans	
	1992	*1994*	*1992*	*1994*
Adopted	61	74	52	59
Considering/in preparation	21	7	25	17
Neither	18	19	23	24

Source: Young (1996), p. 359.

ating in a more strategic role, a useful surrogate is provided by data on the frequency of committee meetings. It is reasonable to assume that, if councillors are relinquishing their role as monitors of the day-to-day activities of council officials, the frequency of committee meetings will be reduced. Again, the LGMB survey provides evidence that such a trend is occurring. Between 1992 and 1994 the proportion of committees meeting every six weeks or more frequently declined from 55 to 47 per cent (Young, 1996, p. 363). Over the same period there was a marked increase in the average number of deliberative fora used by local authorities, which again adds weight to the argument that the balance has shifted towards strategic concerns (Young, 1996).

Moreover, there is further evidence of strategic management belatedly ushering in key elements of the Bains agenda. In the last few years, the trend towards a reduction in the number of committees has been greatly accelerated in several local authorities. For example, Wycombe has replaced twenty-seven committees and panels with a structure made up of four committees that focus on the key issues identified in the council's strategic plan. There is also evidence that, in the forty-six new unitary authorities created following the Local Government Review, the basic principles of corporate management have enjoyed a remarkable rebirth. Fenwick and Bailey (1998a, p. 92) note that in a number of the new unitaries 'there has been a growth of the chief officers' corporate board or similar body. There is also a tendency to group together service areas into wider directorates, with a central policy/strategy function provided.' Indeed, there is widespread evidence that large numbers of local authorities are now attempting to move away from traditional structures. A number of councils are in the process of radically restructuring their internal organizational structures, with a particular focus on moving away from the traditional departmental structure (Local Government Association, 1998).

Community governance

The community governance model is associated particularly with the work of Michael Clarke and John Stewart and has been propagated widely by the LGMB (Clarke and Stewart, 1988; Stewart, 1989; Stewart, 1995; Local Government Management Board, 1993c). A distinctive form of strategic management, community governance draws on many of the same principles as the corporate management approach advocated by Bains. In particular, it retains the corporate management principle that the role of local government goes beyond its provision of separate services. Bains' advocacy of corporate management was importantly based on the view that local government should move from a focus on individual services to a focus on the well-being of the area as a whole (Hampton, 1991). Consequently, the Bains Report argued that local government is 'not limited to the provision of services. It is concerned with the overall economic, cultural and physical well-being of the community' (Bains, 1972, p. 122). In a similar vein, community governance also advocates that the primary role of local authorities is 'a concern for the problems and issues faced by local communities' (Stewart, 1995, p. 254).

However, community governance is not just about reinventing the wheel; it is very much a product of the contemporary context in which local government operates. In particular, it is framed as a response to the fragmentation of the local provision of public services and the perceived attempt of central government to undermine local authorities to the point that their role would consist of little more than local administration of services. Community governance recognizes that the local authority is just one of several service providers present in a locality, but argues that their democratic remit distinguishes their role from that of other organizations. Hence, it is proposed that local authorities should seek to ensure that the diverse needs of the populations they serve are met using whatever combination of service providers, whether local authorities, private companies or voluntary sector bodies, is regarded as being best suited to achieving this basic objective. As such, community governance offers an alternative view of the enabling council, advocating a pluralist approach to service delivery that is sustained by the overall strategic role of the local authority. The influence of decentralization initiatives is also evident, since community governance implies that a local authority 'works not merely through traditional departments, but in decentralised offices and with user organisations, community groups and tenant co-operatives' (Stewart, 1995, p. 254).

Finally, the model is also premised on the view that local authorities should be accountable to the communities that they serve, and that this will require important innovations in the way in which democratic accountability is achieved. As a result, a series of proposals for democratic innovation have been spawned by the notion of community governance (Stewart, 1997; Cairns, 1996). Among the principal mechanisms put forward are citizens' juries and citizens' panels. Developed in Germany and the USA, citizens' juries involve a small number of local residents examining a series of expert witnesses in relation to a particular policy issue, at the end of which the panel makes a recommendation to the local authority or the relevant body that has established the jury. In recent years, citizens' juries have received growing attention and have successfully been used to discuss issues such as waste management in Hertfordshire (Kuper, 1997) and the pros and cons of Liverpool having an elected mayor. Citizens' panels, by way of contrast, involve local authorities regularly consulting with a representative sample of several hundred local residents on a range of policy issues in order to gain a picture of the views of the community at large (Stewart, 1997).

Over the past ten years, the community governance model has achieved widespread currency in the local government community. Endorsed and actively promoted by the LGMB, community governance has received the support of the local government associations and has been adopted by a growing number of local authorities. In particular, a number of the new unitary authorities have used the opportunity of starting with a *tabula rasa* to adopt the model (Fenwick and Bailey, 1998a). Indeed, some observers have suggested that the basic principles of community governance have been endorsed by most individual local authorities (Wilson and Game, 1994). The appeal of community governance is, at least in part, to be explained by the fact that local authorities were already attempting to find ways of responding to external changes. The introduction of CCT, in particular, acted as a catalyst for organizational change in local authorities (p. 311). In the context of the large-scale restructuring of their role, simple preservation of the status quo was not an option for local authorities. Similarly, the Local Government Review also acted as a significant catalyst for change. Local authorities wanted to present themselves in a good light to the Commission, whether they were district councils making their case for unitary status, or county councils or metropolitan districts arguing for their continued existence, and many used the opportunity to undertake far-reaching internal reorganization (Wilson and Game, 1994). Given its contemporary appeal, community governance was adopted by a number of councils.

Milton Keynes is one of several authorities to have committed itself explicitly to the community governance model. The Local Government Review was a significant factor in the decision to adopt this approach. In 1995 the former Milton Keynes Borough Council convened a conference for key partners which established community governance as 'the guiding principles around which the new unitary council was subsequently designed and built' (Local Government Association, 1998, p. 19). On taking up its work in April 1997, the new unitary council thus defined its own role as one of community leadership and immediately set about producing a community plan for 1997/8 (Fenwick and Bailey, 1998a). In line with the community governance approach, the authority sees one of its main tasks as 'bringing together all the key local players to tackle complex issues facing the area which can only be tackled by organisations working together, by pooling resources and by sharing common objectives' (Local Government Association, 1998, p. 19).

To operationalize these principles, Milton Keynes has undertaken two major organizational tasks. First, it has sought to link the community planning process to strategic management structures that establish strategic aims and objectives for the authority as a whole as well as service plans and targets for individual council services. Second, it has played a pro-active role in bringing together its main partner agencies. This has been achieved on two levels. Formally, a common partnership agenda was established by the first community conferences in February 1995 and was taken forward by a second conference in March 1998. At the latter, a planning group made up of fourteen partner organizations was constituted, including the council, the health authority, the police authority and the council for voluntary organizations. Second, Milton Keynes has actively pursued partnership working in a number of specific policy areas, such as lifelong learning where services are delivered through a partnership of the local authority, local universities, the Chamber of Commerce, further education colleges and local business training centres (Local Government Association, 1998). Third, the council has sought to adopt a management structure in which traditional service areas are cross-cut by a number of strategic directorates. For instance, a 'learning and development' directorate seeks to make links between the education and social services directorate (Fenwick and Bailey, 1998a).

Although Milton Keynes represents one of the more developed and comprehensive applications of community governance, numerous other authorities have embraced the concept, including Middlesbrough, Southampton, Portsmouth and Stevenage. In the main, community governance has found particular favour with newly created, Labour-controlled unitary authorities, especially in the period since the 1997 general election (Fenwick and Bailey, 1998a). However, the significance of the model has recently been enhanced by the government's White Paper, 'Modern local government' (DETR, 1998d). Chapter 8 of the White Paper argues that local government's role is fundamentally one of 'community leadership'. It points to the government's intention to 'introduce legislation to place on councils a duty to promote the economic, social and environmental well-being of their areas and to strengthen councils' powers to enter into partnership' (p. 80). This duty will be operationalized through the requirement that local authorities produce a community plan, to be developed in partnership with all relevant local stakeholders. The white paper thus indicates that the community governance model has effectively become government policy.

Conclusion

It has often been assumed that, such was the extent of the centre's intent to control local government in the 1980s, local authorities were increasingly forced to implement internal organizational change in line with central government requirements. For instance, Young (1996, p. 364) suggests that the changes in internal management and organization pointed to by the LGMB surveys were overwhelmingly 'driven by national, legislative requirements' and that 'the overwhelming impression . . . was of local government engulfed in a tidal wave of centrally inspired change'. There are good reasons to dispute this conclusion. This chapter suggests that the causal relationship between central government reform and changes in local government organization are not as straightforward as Young seems to suggest. While the introduction of CCT, for instance, has certainly had a significant effect on local authority organization, its impact has been as a catalyst rather than as a template. Local authorities have been required to introduce a distinction between client and contractor roles, but the legislation leaves the issue of how this is to be achieved to the individual authority. Similarly, no legal requirements have been placed on local authorities to reduce the number of committees or to move away from a traditional departmental structure, although many have chosen to do so.

Looking back over the past two decades, it is evident that significant organizational changes have occurred at the initiative of individual local authorities. Decentralization policies and the adoption of the community governance model stand out in particular, since these have emerged from within the local government community itself and have gained increasing acceptance in the 1990s. The rise of the community governance model is especially significant, as it can be seen as a direct attempt by local authorities to respond to the negative consequences of two decades of central government reform. These new organizational principles are an attempt to provide a more holistic approach to local service delivery in the face of a process of centrally driven organizational fragmentation. Moreover, they represent a direct response to the conception of the enabling authority put forward by the Thatcher government in its last term of office, which was widely interpreted as a direct attack on the very notion of autonomous local government. As such, local authorities' efforts to 'put their own houses in order' represent a vital prerequisite for wider attempts to reinvent the role of local government in a new political and institutional content. The success of community governance, which has been recognized through the endorsement of the Labour government, indicates that local authorities have actively sought to exercise autonomous control over their own affairs. In the context of concerted centralization efforts, this is a significant achievement

9

Global Problems, Local Solutions

Local Government and Sustainable Development

Introduction

Over the past decade, the rise of the notion of sustainable development has increasingly brought environmental issues closer to the centre of the local government policy agenda. Significantly, the dynamic behind the sustainable development agenda has largely come from international institutions rather than national political systems. Since the late 1980s, the United Nations and the European Union have been particularly active in promoting sustainable development and it has widely been suggested that such efforts represent a shift towards an internationalization of policy making (Wilks and Hall, 1995). Equally notable, however, is the fact that, in more recent years, this same process of global governance has laid increasing stress on the role of local government in implementing policies concerned with the achievement of sustainable development (Taylor, 1998). Thus, while national governments are still seen to have a key role to play in environmental policy, the rise of sustainable development is often cited as an example of the rise of 'the new political economy of global–local relations' (Munton, 1997) or of the hollowing-out of the nation-state. In this context, it is suggested that sustainable development presents local authorities with a major opportunity to re-define their role (Stewart and Hams, 1992; Ward, 1993).

In this chapter we consider how UK local authorities have responded to the challenge of sustainable development and assess the extent to which this agenda shows evidence of a pursuit of creative autonomy at the local level. We begin by charting the way in which environmental policy has progressively moved from a concern with the regulation of pollution to an approach centred on the promotion of sustainable development. We also suggest that sustainable development has provided local authorities with the opportunity to move away from their previous role as (generally reluctant) environmental regulators to one of directing the process of drawing up local policy responses within the context of wider sustainable development agendas. We consider the principal ways in which local authorities have attempted to address sustainability issues, with particular attention to the role that they have been given in implementing the United Nation's Agenda 21 initiative. This analysis suggests that, while many UK local authorities have been among the most enthusiastic proponents of Agenda 21, there is also considerable variation in the extent to which sustainable development principles have penetrated the local policy process. Even where local authorities have responded positively to the requirement to produce a Local Agenda 21 strategy, there have often been significant barriers to further progress. We nonetheless conclude that, in light of the complexity of the issues it seeks to address, the pursuit of sustainable development adds to the weight of the creative autonomy thesis.

From Environmental Policy to Sustainable Development

Prior to the early 1970s, there was only very limited discussion of environmental issues. While problems such as air and water pollution were recognized to a degree, it was typically assumed that these could be tackled through government regulation. During the 1970s, the nature of the debate was fundamentally altered by the rise of a radical environmental movement that stressed what it saw as the inherent tension between the short-term pursuit of economic growth and the long-term survival of the planet. In 1972, the *Ecologist* published a *Blueprint for Survival* which argued that, if the prevailing patterns of economic growth continued, it would lead to 'the breakdown of society and the irreversible disruption of the life-support systems on this planet, possibly by the end of the century' (cited in Reid, 1995, p. 29). Later that year a team led by Dennis and Donella Meadows at the Massachusetts Institute of Technology published *Limits to Growth*, a report to the Club of Rome. In line with the *Ecologist's* conclusions, the authors argued that economic trends, if unchecked, would mean that 'the limits to growth on this planet will be reached sometime within the next one hundred years' (Meadows et al., 1972, p. 23).

The analysis provided by Meadows et al. prompted considerable debate, which generally polarized between outright rejections of the assumptions on which it was based and calls by many environmentalists for 'zero growth'. Inevitably, these debates had limited impact on environmental policy: if a choice was to be made between economic growth and environmental protection, the former was always likely to emerge victorious. The nature of this tension was also reflected internationally in a north–south divide, as evidenced at the United Nations Conference on the Human Environment held in Stockholm, again in 1972. Initiated as a result of concern in the industrialized nations of the north about rising pollution levels, the conference was interpreted by many developing countries as an attempt to restrict their capacity to develop economically. While the conference did agree to the Stockholm Declaration on the Human Environment, which suggested that development and environmental protection could be mutually beneficial, there was little to suggest that this was anything other than a pragmatic compromise. Consequently, the second document to come out of the conference, an Action Plan for the Human Environment, gave little indication of how this might be achieved and 'had little to say either about development issues or about an approach to environmental issues that placed them in a context of development activity' (Reid, 1995, p. 37).

As a result, the direct policy implications of the emergence of environmental concerns in the 1970s were not to prove profound. There was a growth in the degree of environmental regulation, allied to an increased use of 'end of the pipe' solutions intended to minimize the extent to which industrial by-products were released into air and water. Beyond these relatively modest attempts to reduce specific types of pollution, governmental actors paid little attention to environmental issues. However, the debate of the early 1970s did trigger two important subsequent developments, albeit indirectly and with a significant time-lag. First, the 1972 United Nations conference had put environmental issues on the international agenda and had established the United Nations Conference on Environment and Development (UNCED). Although frustrated by an initial lack of progress, these international efforts to promote environmentalism came to fruition during the 1980s. It was at this time that countries which had led the field in developing environmental regulation at the national level increasingly realized that many of their efforts were proving futile because pollution is no respecter of national boundaries. During the 1970s, researchers in Sweden found that as much as 50 per cent of the UK's sulphur dioxide emissions were being received in other European countries, while 82 per cent of Sweden's acid rain came from elsewhere in Europe (Booth, 1998, p. 116). Moreover, it became clear that many problems could be solved only through binding global agreements which would remove the danger of countries seeking to secure a degree of competitive advantage by free-riding on the back of others' efforts to reduce pollution. As a result, key international agreements on air pollution were reached during the 1980s, such as the 1987 Montreal Protocol, which established an international framework for the reduction of CFC emissions in response to ozone depletion.

Second, increasing attention was paid to the relationship between economic and environmental issues, particularly in the context of the agreement reached at the 1972 conference that development and environmental protection could go hand in hand. In 1980, the term 'sustainable development' first appeared in the *World Conservation Strategy*, published by the World Conservation Union (Reid, 1995). However, it was to rise to prominence through the work of the World Commission on Environment and Development, chaired by the Norwegian Prime Minister, Gro Harlem Brundtland. In its report, *Our Common Future*, the Commission defined sustainable development as 'development which meets the needs of the present without compromising the ability of future generations to meet their own needs' (World Commission on Environment and Development, 1987, p. 8). Working on the assumption that the limits to growth are determined by technology and social organization as much as by the carrying capacity of the earth, the report took the view that the key objective of development should be to meet human needs. Thus, while the Commission identified consumption patterns in the richer northern countries as a major issue, it also stressed the reciprocal relationships between poverty and the environment. Specifically, the report suggested that poverty is 'a major cause and effect of global environmental problems' (p. 3).

By broadening the economy versus environment debate to include a social dimension, the Brundtland Report succeeded in bridging the gap between north and south and brought environmental concerns from the fringes of political debate into the mainstream. The concept of sustainable development was to become widely accepted and served as the basis for the consideration of practical policy implications. However, the Commission's approach has also been criticized on a number of counts. In particular, it has been suggested that, while its conception of sustainable development helped to create a consensus about the importance of environmental concerns, the definition put forward in *Our Common Future* is so general that it transcends its own internal contradictions and becomes virtually impossible to oppose (O'Riordan, 1995). The danger with such a definition is that sustainable development becomes almost meaningless as a vast range of conflicting philosophies can take shelter under its banner (Munton, 1997; O'Riordan and Voisey, 1997). Consequently, while the Brundtland definition has been widely used as a starting point for discussions of sustainability, there have been a multitude of attempts at formulating more specific definitions. Unfortunately, the principal outcome of these efforts is that 'there are almost as many definitions of sustainable development as there are writers who contemplate it' (O'Riordan and Voisey, 1997, p. 4).

Despite the range of views that have emerged around the concept of sustainable development, two key principles have generally survived from the Brundtland Report and continue to inform the approach taken in the UK. First, there is general agreement that sustainability involves the adoption of a holistic approach to understanding how social, environmental and economic processes interact. While different interests inevitably place different degrees of stress on the importance of each of these, debate has, in the main, focused on how meeting human needs in the short term can be balanced with longer-term social and ecological concerns. That this view of sustainability has gained widespread acceptance is shown in a recent government report which posits that 'sustainable development is about ensuring a better quality of life for everyone, now and for generations to come. It encompasses environmental, social and economic goals' (DETR, Local Government Association and Local Government Management Board, 1998, para. 3.1).

Second, it is also widely accepted that the key implication of sustainable development for government is that an integrated approach to policy making is required, in which sustainability becomes a central element of all areas of public policy. The Brundtland Report pointed clearly to the limitations of environmental protection policies that operate in isolation from the broader thrust of what government does. Again, this approach has been recognised by the British government, if only implicitly, in a recent consultation document that stresses the importance of policy areas such as transport, education, health, employment and regeneration in contributing to sustainable development (DETR, 1998h). Moreover, while there has, as yet, been little indication of a wholesale shift in public policy in light of the sustainable development agenda, there are at least tentative signs that this is beginning to happen in some policy areas, such as urban regeneration (Bennett and Patel, 1995).

However, despite this formulation, tensions inevitably remain. While it is possible to identify projects or initiatives that simultaneously promote social, economic and environmental well-being, these are frequently rather small-scale and are dwarfed by the more zero-sum choices presented to decision-makers.

Local Government and Environmental Policy

Environmental policies in the UK have substantially followed this shift from the concept of environmental regulation and 'end of the pipe' solutions to sustainable development. Perhaps surprisingly, the UK was something of a pioneer in relation to early environmental policy. In 1956 the Conservative government passed a Clean Air Act and this was added to by a subsequent Act passed by the Labour government in 1968. In 1970, the UK became the first country to create an environment department represented in Cabinet (McCormick, 1994). Yet, although British governments in the post-war period had introduced a variety of measures concerned with 'the regulation of human activities which have an impact on our physical surroundings' (Blowers, 1987, p. 278), it was not until a 1990 White Paper that a clear statement of environmental policy could be identified (Gray and Flynn, 1994). Yet, although the White Paper, 'This common inheritance' (DOE, 1990) was able to list over 350 environmental measures that were already in place, it made only limited proposals for new policy initiatives. Instead, the White Paper stressed a preference for market-based solutions, a position that was confirmed by the publication of 'Sustainable development: the UK strategy' (DOE, 1994). Thus, the only significant piece of legislation to arise from the White Paper was the 1990 Environmental Protection Act, which sought to establish tighter controls on pollution and introduced the 'polluter pays' principle.

Until recently, the environmental policy role of local authorities mirrored developments at a national level. Thus, local authorities had long assumed the task of enforcing national public health regulation. For instance, local councils were empowered to take action against emitters of black smoke under the Public Health Act of 1875 and against companies discharging mining or industrial waste into rivers under the Rivers and Pollution Prevention Act of 1876. As the government began to introduce stricter environmental regulations in the 1970s, it was logical to place the responsibility for enforcement with local authorities. However, there was considerable variation in the extent to which they took this responsibility seriously (McCormick, 1994). In the main it appears that 'local authorities were much more interested in promoting economic growth in their own areas and were reluctant to constrain industry with pollution control requirements' (Booth, 1998, p. 119). As a result, until very recently environmental issues lacked any real degree of prominence on local political agendas. Five of the most recent and most widely used texts on UK local government (Hampton, 1991; Stoker, 1991; Cochrane,

1993; Wilson and Game, 1994; Stewart and Stoker, 1995c) make little or no mention of local environmental policies.

However, from the late 1980s, as environmental issues became a significant issue in UK politics, it was local authorities, often working alongside environmental interest groups, that were to prove the major source of policy innovation (Munton, 1997). The burgeoning membership and increased activism of environmental pressure groups, growing international-level attention to environmental issues and the Green Party's success in gaining 15 per cent of the votes cast in the UK at the 1989 European elections were prominent indicators of this 'second wave' of environmental consciousness. However, just as significant, if less newsworthy, were the steps being taken by local authorities to promote greater environmental awareness through measures such as environmental charters, action plans and audits (Ward, 1993). A survey of 453 local authorities carried out in 1992 found that 61 per cent had some form of environmental charter and 45 per cent had environmental action plans (Wilson and Raemaekers, 1992). In addition, a LGMB survey of UK local authorities carried out in the early 1990s pointed to local councils expanding their environmental policy remit (Mills, 1994). Mills reported that 72 per cent of local authority chief executives either agreed or agreed strongly with the statement that 'the environment is a key policy issue in this authority'. Moreover, a total of 70 per cent disagreed or disagreed strongly with the view that 'global environmental issues are not relevant to this authority' (p. 4).

There is little evidence that these developments were a result of the Conservative government's somewhat sudden conversion to environmental issues. As Mills (1994, p. 4) notes, much of the activity being pursued by local authorities 'including the production of environmental strategies, audits, state of the environment reports . . . is non-statutory'. Indeed, as with other aspects of local government policy making discussed in this volume, it was arguably the government's attempts to centralize decision making that prompted local authorities to take up environmental concerns. The growth of interest in sustainable development from the late 1980s can therefore be seen as stemming from 'the desire of local authorities to reassert and develop their role in an area where many responsibilities have been removed from local government control to quangos and agencies or privatised' (Voisey et al., 1996, p. 45). In particular, given the heightened public concern about environmental issues at that time, embracing sustainable development offered local authorities an opportunity to regain popular support (Ward, 1993). As a result, environmental policy was seen as a means of 'creating new political space for local authorities, through the concept of local guardians of the environment and equally a way of defending their traditional service role' (p. 466).

Aside from the desire among local authorities to reassert their role as initiators of policy, three other important factors have prompted councils to take up the sustainable development agenda. First, there is little doubt that one key stimulus for local authority action came from the burgeoning UK environmental movement, which, following a philosophy of 'think globally, act locally', had come to pay increasing attention to lobbying local authorities (Ward, 1993). The publication of an Environmental Charter for Local Government by Friends of the Earth (1989) was a particularly important development. This document listed 193 steps that local authorities could take to promote environmental protection. Ward (1993) suggests that the charter served to fill an information gap in local government, as officers who had been asked to draw up environmental plans were struggling to find working models on which to base them. As a result, the 3,000 copies which made up the charter's original print run were 'sold out instantly' and 'most key officers connected to environmental plan documents have read a copy' (p. 472).

Second, the European Union gained a remit to develop environmental policy initiatives following the signing of the Single European Act in 1986. It has since issued some 200 or more directives concerned with environmental regulation, and the responsibility for their implementation has frequently rested with local authorities (Taylor, 1998). The EU's Fifth Environmental Action Programme, issued in 1992, signalled a shift towards more integrated policy measures designed to bring about sustainable development, some 40 per cent of which depended on local authority involvement for their implementation (Local Government Management Board, 1993a). The significance of these developments for UK environmental policy in the early 1990s was substantial. Writing in 1991, Milton argued that 'the most striking feature of the government's policy on pollution is the extent to which it is dictated by EU directives' (p. 6). Significantly, the growth of European environmental regulation has also led to increased pressure on local authorities from environmental pressure groups, which have not only monitored progress in implementing EU directives, but also successfully brought cases of non-compliance to the European Court of Justice (Ward, Buller and Lowe, 1996).

The third, and perhaps most significant, factor has been the Agenda 21 initiative, agreed by the United Nations in 1992. This furnished local authorities in the UK, and across the globe, with a significant environmental policy role, again with the emphasis placed on the achievement of sustainable development. Agenda 21 reinforced two significant features of developments in environmental policy in the 1980s. First, it confirmed the shift that was taking place in the role of local government away from enforcing national-level environmental regulations towards developing locally based policies to promote sustainable development. Second, it clearly demonstrated that the growing importance of international governance in establishing sustainable development frameworks had its counterpart in a greater role for local government in implementing them in practice. Since 1993, Agenda 21 has become the key dynamic behind environmental policy developments in UK local authorities and has increasingly embraced the kinds of activity initiated by councils in the earlier part of the decade. Given the importance of the Agenda 21 initiative, we now turn to examine in depth its implementation by UK local authorities.

Agenda 21

At the UNCED summit held in Rio de Janeiro in 1992, an agreement was made between more than 150 states to implement Agenda 21, a 600-page action plan aimed at introducing sustainable development. The purpose of Agenda 21 was to assign clear responsibility for the task of bringing about sustainable development to various tiers of government. Consequently, the document makes specific reference to the roles that international, national and local authorities will be expected to play in putting sustainable development into practice. Significantly, the Agenda 21 agreement assigns a key role to local authorities. This role is discussed in detail in chapter 28 of the plan, which suggests that if Agenda 21 is to be successful, 'the participation and co-operation of local authorities will be a determining factor in fulfilling its objectives'. To underline the importance accorded to local government, the agreement stipulates that all local authorities should develop a Local Agenda 21 by 1996.

The central role accorded to local authorities is a reflection of two key principles that underpin the Agenda 21 initiative. First, in keeping with the approach advocated by *Our Common Future*, Agenda 21 advocates that sustainable development can be achieved only through a holistic approach to policy making. Importantly, it suggests that the development of a holistic policy agenda which integrates local economic and social policies with transport, land-use planning and other spheres to achieve a comprehensive approach to sustainable development is best achieved 'at the level of governance closest to the people' (chapter 28). Thus, local authorities are seen to be essential to Agenda 21: 'agreements and policies have to lead to tangible processes which almost always start at the local level' (Aydin, 1995, p. 13). Second, Agenda 21 is premised on a

191

view that the pursuit of sustainable development must be founded on the involvement of a wide range of local interests, through which local authorities 'learn from citizens and from local, civic, community, business and industrial organisations and acquire the information needed for formulating the best strategies' (chapter 28). This approach, which has much in common with a more general trend towards partnership working in public policy, is justified by a concern to ensure that sustainable development is underpinned by a broad societal consensus regarding its benefits and that sustainability is synonymous with empowerment. It also suggests a key role for local authorities, since they 'are closer and more accessible to the communities they serve than are national governments and international organisations' (Aydin, 1995, p. 12).

The UK local government community was quick to respond to the Agenda 21 initiative. While the reference to local government in chapter 28 was unambiguous in assigning a key role to local authorities, this was not the only part of the document relevant to local government. Indeed, because of the wide-ranging policy competences of UK local authorities, it was estimated that, in a British context, the implementation of about two-thirds of the proposals would require local authority input (Local Government Management Board, 1993b). Thus, following the Rio Summit the lead role in developing Local Agenda 21 was delegated by the local government associations to the LGMB. Through a series of publications, seminars, briefings and other activities, the LGMB set about promoting Local Agenda 21 to the wider local government community as well as providing individual authorities with support in taking the initiative forward.

At the time of these early efforts to promote the take-up of Local Agenda 21 in the UK, a number of observers suggested that the attitude of central government meant there would be little scope for local authorities to develop a meaningful role in initiating sustainable development. Some suggested that the national government response to the Rio Summit, 'This common inheritance', had established a policy framework that would do little to help, and would most probably hinder, local authorities' efforts to draw up Local Agenda 21s (Gordon, 1994). Others pointed to the weakness of local government in the UK, particularly in the context of tightening resource constraints, the growing pressures of responding to CCT legislation and the uncertainty created by the Local Government Review (Bosworth, 1993). In such circumstances, it seemed all too likely that a non-statutory concern such as Local Agenda 21 would drop off the agenda of many local authorities (Wilks and Hall, 1995).

Yet, despite these often pessimistic prognoses, available evidence suggests that most UK local authorities have attempted to embrace the sustainable development agenda and, as a result, 'have helped lead the way internationally in promoting Local Agenda 21' (DETR, Local Government Association and Local Government Management Board, 1998, para. 1.1). It has been suggested that, within the EU, 'the UK has the most explicit response to Agenda 21 of any member state' (O'Riordan and Voisey, 1997, p. 2). Moreover, the same authors, whose conclusions are based on a programme of research carried out for DG XII of the European Commission, point to significant local institutional change associated with Agenda 21, suggesting that 'by far the most vibrant institutional innovations were taking place at this level, most notably in the UK' (p. 19). There is also evidence that British local authorities have made more progress in implementing Agenda 21 than their counterparts elsewhere in Europe. For example, whereas more than forty UK local authorities had prepared a Local Agenda 21 strategy by 1996 (IDeA, 1999), none had done so in Germany, a country widely associated with progressive environmental policies (Bundesministerium für Raumordnung, Bauwesen und Städtebau, 1996).

These forty or so local authorities which pioneered the adoption of Local Agenda 21 have been critical to the initiative's subsequent development in the UK. In particular, the early efforts made by authorities such as Woking, Kirklees and Leicester have informed the subsequent spread of the initiative to other local authorities through the dissemination of good practice. Thus, in 1995 the LGMB brought together the lessons of the first three years' experience of Agenda 21 in UK local authorities to establish thirteen goals for the creation of a sustainable community (Local Government Management Board, 1995). Similarly, recent DETR guidance on Local Agenda 21 draws heavily on the experience of local authorities that have made most progress in implementing the initiative (DETR, Local Government Association and Local Government Management Board, 1998).

Though few local authorities in the UK achieved the goal established at the Rio Summit that Local Agenda 21 strategies should be in place by 1996, the level of commitment among British local councils has been confirmed by the results of numerous surveys. A survey commissioned by the LGMB in 1996 found that 91 per cent of respondent authorities had committed themselves to engaging in the Local Agenda 21 process and that 40 per cent were aiming to produce a strategic document by the end of that year (Tuxworth and Carpenter, 1996). A subsequent survey found that three-quarters of UK authorities were in the process of producing an Agenda 21 strategy (Local Government Management

Board, 1997). These results were confirmed by a further survey carried out in autumn 1998, which found that 36 per cent of respondents had already produced a Local Agenda 21 strategy and that a further 45 per cent were committed to producing one by December 2000 (IDeA, 1999). In total, the IDeA survey identifies 130 UK local authorities that had adopted a Local Agenda 21 strategy by the end of 1998.

However, it would be presumptuous to assume from these survey data that UK local authorities have undergone a genuine conversion to the theory and practice of sustainable development as a result of Local Agenda 21. The IDeA survey also appears to reveal significant variation in the comprehensiveness of the strategies that have been produced, in their linkages to the authorities' wider activities and in the extent to which mechanisms are in place to assess success and failure. The survey suggests that relatively few authorities have been able to ensure that Local Agenda 21 makes sustainable development an integral element in all key policy areas. For example, only 37 per cent of respondents said they had procedures in place for all council committees to consider their impact on sustainable development. Moreover, of those authorities that had agreed an Agenda 21 action plan, 42 per cent stated that these were not linked to other statutory or non-statutory plans and strategies. The survey also suggests that there is a widespread lack of attention to developing measures to assess the impact of Local Agenda 21: of the 146 respondents replying to the questions on evaluation, 60 per cent said that they had not developed indicators to evaluate progress.

The extent of this variation can also be illustrated through an analysis of two distinctive Local Agenda 21 strategy documents produced by Oxfordshire County Council and the London borough of Brent. The first of these, Oxfordshire Agenda 21, was published in April 1997. The strategy demonstrates clear links with the Oxfordshire Structure Plan and establishes a complementarity of objectives between them. It also establishes a clear objective to integrate Local Agenda 21 with anti-poverty strategies at both the county and district levels. Moreover, Oxfordshire Agenda 21 shows evidence of an attempt to approach sustainability comprehensively. Thus, it identifies the key policy areas and issues that need to embrace elements of sustainability, including education, health, energy, waste, the built environment, transport, farming and wildlife, and considers the factors that influence these in Oxfordshire, such as national trends and policy frameworks. Within this context, the strategy establishes what can be done at a local level and lists clear aims and objectives for local action. In addition, the document establishes a baseline position in relation to eight key areas: community; health; energy and buildings; resources and waste; transport and access; open space and wildlife; sustainable land use, food and agriculture; work and economy.

These baseline positions were then used as the basis for an assessment of the extent of progress two years later, in April 1999.

The London borough of Brent's document was produced in May 1997 and subsequently updated in 1999. While Brent's Local Agenda 21 also identifies a number of key areas central to the achievement of sustainability, the approach taken contrasts sharply to that in Oxfordshire. Rather than analysing the local context, discussing the elements of sustainability and identifying objectives and targets, the document summarizes 175 separate projects under eleven headings. While each project description defines expected outputs and assesses what progress has been made in meeting these, the contribution that each is intended to make towards promoting sustainable development is rarely made explicit. Moreover, many of the individual projects listed were established in the context of other programmes, such as City Challenge, or are Objective 2 funded initiatives. While this approach could, on the one hand, be interpreted as an attempt to ensure that sustainable development concerns are present in all projects undertaken with council involvement, it can also be argued that Brent's strategy represents little more than a pragmatic compilation of initiatives, most of which would have been in existence without Local Agenda 21.

The variation in local authority responses to Local Agenda 21 demonstrates that, while producing a local sustainable development strategy is one thing, ensuring that it induces policy change within the local authority, securing its acceptance by key partners and putting it into practice are quite different matters. Grafting a strategy on to an existing local authority structure or merely securing its endorsement by existing partnership bodies is unlikely to lead to integrated policy approaches. Rather, the Local Agenda 21 must itself become a significant catalyst for local institutional change. While such changes are observable in a small number of localities, there is scant evidence that Local Agenda 21 is helping to initiate a widespread process of institutional reform. Rather, most observers have suggested that the dominant tendency remains one of bolting sustainability on to existing agendas and policies, with the consequence that it tends to remain a relatively marginal environmental policy concern (O'Riordan and Voisey, 1997; Littlewood and While, 1997).

Moreover, to some extent, the pragmatic 'add-on' approach has been legitimated by a joint recommendation by the DETR, LGA and LGMB that local authorities focus on a more incremental, small-scale approach to Local Agenda 21 (DETR, Local Government Association and Local Government Management Board, 1998). This advice is motivated by two main concerns. First, it is a recognition of the problems that have been experienced in bringing about a comprehensive, strategic approach to

195

Local Agenda 21 based on the idea of sustainability as a meta-concept that should inform the way in which local governance operates. Thus, in line with the approach taken by authorities such as Brent, it is recommended that 'rebadging existing programmes taking credit for current achievements can demystify the strategy' (p. 1). Second, the advice represents an attempt to move the sustainability agenda away from a pure focus on environmental issues towards a clearer integration of environmental, economic and social objectives. As a result, Agenda 21 is primarily portrayed as a means of ensuring a better quality of life and it is stressed that 'sustainable development is not about self-sacrifice' (p. 5). However, while the painless pragmatism of this approach is likely to be welcomed by many, it is difficult to see how it will result in anything more than a series of projects that operate at the fringes of local governance. Indeed, there is little prospect of such pragmatic approaches rising to the challenge of bringing about an integrative approach to local policy making which ensures that meeting human needs does not serve to diminish 'irreplaceable' resources (Munton, 1997).

Barriers to Local Agenda 21

Despite the early enthusiasm among local authorities for Local Agenda 21, commentators have increasingly echoed the more pessimistic prognoses voiced immediately after the Rio Summit. As efforts to implement the initiative have progressed, a number of barriers to achieving sustainable development locally have become increasingly evident. Four main barriers have been pointed to. First, it has been suggested that a lack of commitment from central government to the promotion of sustainable development has undermined the capacity of local authorities to achieve it at a local level. Second, the fragmented nature of local governance, itself a product of central government's failure to ensure policy integration, is said to have undermined the capacity to local authorities to bring together the range of policy areas relevant to sustainable development. Third, there is considerable evidence of the continued priority given in many localities to economic growth over and above environmental concerns. Fourth, the internal culture of local authorities is seen as hindering the progress of Local Agenda 21 in a number of important ways.

Central government

That local authorities should have responded so enthusiastically to the Local Agenda 21 initiative, particularly in comparison to their counterparts elsewhere in Europe, appears to have little to do with the efforts of UK national government. Although some attempts have been made to develop a more comprehensive national-level approach to sustainable development, a strategic vacuum remains at the level of central government. The national sustainable development strategy, published in 1994, made a strong case for policy integration, but 'like the 1990 white paper, it lacked concrete proposals to bring this about' (Taylor, 1998, p. 143). Likewise, while the Labour government's decision to combine environment, transport and regional policy in a single government department has created the potential for the kind of integrated policy approaches that sustainable development requires, there are, as yet, few indicators that such integration is occurring.

There are signs that the Labour government is beginning to develop the centre's role in relation to sustainable development, and commitments have been made at the highest level to supporting the Agenda 21 process (see below). Yet, as Bennett (1999) notes, in comparison to initiatives such as Best Value, the political profile of Agenda 21 remains relatively modest and, given the far-reaching reform agenda envisaged for local government, it is unlikely to be prioritized by local authorities faced with a requirement to introduce a series of statutory changes.

Local governance and the problem of fragmentation

The fragmentation of local governance in the UK presents an additional hurdle to bringing about the policy integration that is a prerequisite for the achievement of sustainable development (Littlewood and While, 1997). Although UK local authorities are multi-functional, the last two decades have been characterized by a progressive erosion of local government functions and the growing use of single-purpose agencies to implement government policy (see chapter 3). Paradoxically, this tendency to farm out policy responsibilities to separate organizations has occurred despite a growing realization that many of the most important policy challenges require a cross-sectoral approach. A governance problem has thus emerged in relation to a number of policy issues, the nature of which is put succinctly by Davis and Stewart:

> The fragmentation of the government of cities, towns and rural areas between different organisations and institutions is reducing the capacity of the system to deal with issues that require different functions or institutions to work together. Yet so many of the emerging issues in our society require just such a capacity for integration. The environmental issues and the aspiration to sustainable development, the growth of crime and the aspiration to safer communities, racial discrimination and the aspiration

to equal opportunities, are all issues which require different organisations and institutions to work together. They cannot be solved on a functional basis. (1994, p. 30)

Littlewood and While (1997) suggest that achieving such policy integration would best be approached through the agreement of a community contract. In doing so, they echo the concept of community governance and the notion of the community plan advocated in the Labour government's White Paper, 'Modernising local government'. The relationship of Local Agenda 21 to the community planning process is discussed below.

The growth imperative

That difficulties have been experienced in bringing Local Agenda 21 to the centre of the local policy process is not altogether surprising. Many local authorities are under intense pressure to find solutions to local social and economic problems, the causes of which invariably stem from sources external to the locality and certainly beyond the control of local government. In such circumstances, there is often a tendency to look for quick fixes rather than long-term solutions – a tendency which is exacerbated by the growth of public–private partnerships in local economic policy. Although such partnerships have developed precisely because of the dwindling capacity of local government to steer the local economy independently, the need to secure consensus in such fora often leads, by default, to a focus on short-term development objectives. Consequently, it may be argued that while the emergence of local governance has led to the growth of a more strategic approach to local decision making, partnership arrangements have generally been characterized by ways of working that 'focus on immediate action rather than long-term policy formulation, and are likely to favour short-term development or growth agendas' (Littlewood and While, 1997, p. 115).

This prioritization of short-term economic development is by no means universal. Indeed, in many parts of the south-east of England and along the M4 corridor there have been growing attempts to find ways of easing development pressures while maintaining high levels of employment and enhancing the quality of life. Consequently, the extent to which there is perceived to be an inherent tension between immediate economic development and longer-term sustainable development varies significantly between localities (Wilks and Hall, 1995). It is perhaps no surprise that many of the most progressive approaches to Local Agenda 21 have therefore tended to emerge in local authorities in London and the south-east of England, such as Merton, Sutton, Woking, Wycombe and

Oxfordshire. This geographical variation in the extent to which local authorities have brought Local Agenda 21 to fruition is also illustrated by IDeA's most recent list of authorities that have produced Local Agenda 21 strategies. These authorities include eighteen of the thirty-two London boroughs (56 per cent), but just three of the fifteen authorities that make up the Merseyside–Greater Manchester conurbation (20 per cent). Major cities that have not yet produced a Local Agenda 21 strategy include Liverpool, Manchester, Leeds, Sheffield and Glasgow.

The internal culture of local government

Research carried out by CAG consultants in 1998 and 1999 considered the main barriers faced by local authority officers responsible for Agenda 21 (CAG Consultants, 1999). The authors point to a number of factors that have restricted the development of Local Agenda 21s, some of them external, but most of them internal to the local authorities themselves. Among the principal barriers listed were a lack of resources; the low political priority given to the initiative, both nationally and locally; political opposition within the local authority; and problems created by departmentalism and bureaucratic inertia within the council. The picture that emerges from the report is one of committed individual officers ploughing a lonely furrow and operating with severely restricted resources and limited political or management support. Moreover, in such circumstances, their task is a daunting one of having to convince reluctant members and chief officers of the benefits of undertaking a non-statutory task which, potentially, could involve significant organizational and policy implications for the authority as a whole. Given the constant requirement of local authorities to adjust to legislative change and embrace new statutory duties, Agenda 21 frequently finds itself towards the end of the list of chief officers' and members' priorities.

Those authorities that have been at the forefront of implementing Local Agenda 21 are frequently also those that have pioneered new organizational arrangements and taken the greatest steps towards constructing multi-agency partnerships that enable more effective policy integration. Among the local authorities that had produced Local Agenda 21 strategies by 1999, a number are also widely cited as examples of how to achieve community governance, including Norwich, Cambridge and Milton Keynes. Nine authorities that have adopted a Local Agenda 21 strategy, such as Cumbria, Middlesbrough and Suffolk, are among the twenty-two pathfinder authorities in the LGA's New Commitment to Regeneration (NCR) initiative, which is also concerned with the promotion of cross-sectoral, multi-agency working. Moreover, other

NCR pathfinders, such as Barnsley, Kirklees and North Tyneside, are also seen to be leading the way in the adoption of new political arrangements, such as the introduction of cabinets in local government.

Labour and Local Agenda 21

Since Labour came to power in May 1997, increased efforts have been made by national government to both encourage and support local authorities in the development of Local Agenda 21. At the United Nations Special Assembly Session on the Environment held in New York in June 1997, Blair announced that he wanted 'all local authorities in the UK to adopt Local Agenda 21 strategies by the year 2000'. To progress towards this goal, the DETR published a report in February 1998, produced jointly with the LGA and the LGMB and aimed at encouraging the take-up of Agenda 21 among local authorities (DETR, Local Government Association and Local Government Management Board, 1998). Entitled *Sustainable Local Communities for the 21st Century: why and how to prepare an effective Local Agenda 21 strategy*, the document reviews examples of good practice among UK local authorities and provides practical advice as to how a Local Agenda 21 strategy can be achieved. At the same time, the DETR also published a consultation paper on the development of a revised UK strategy for sustainable development, thus recognizing, at least in principle, the importance of national government's role in underpinning attempts to implement Agenda 21 locally.

However, it is arguably the government's wider agenda for local government that has the most significant implication for the future development of Agenda 21. The key issue raised by the CAG Consultants' report on Local Agenda 21 was the question of the relationship between Local Agenda 21 and the government's modernizing local government agenda. The Labour government's agenda for local authorities, which is discussed in detail in chapter 12, has given rise to a series of new policies. Chief among these are the replacement of CCT with Best Value and the requirement placed on local authorities to produce a community plan. The latter, in particular, is seen to raise a number of dilemmas in relation to Local Agenda 21. Although at the time of writing the requirement to produce a community plan had not been made statutory, a White Paper had signalled their introduction. The White Paper states that community plans will 'place on councils a duty to promote the economic, social and environmental well-being of their areas' (DETR, 1998d, p. 80). As with Local Agenda 21, the community plan is to be drawn up following extensive consultation with local residents. Most significantly of all:

> It will put sustainable development at the heart of council decision-making and will provide an overall framework within which councils must perform all their existing functions. So, in taking decisions, affecting their area or its people, councils will have to weigh up the likely effects of a decision against the three objectives – economic, social and environmental – and if necessary strike a balance to ensure that the overall well-being of their area is achieved. (p. 80)

Defining community plans in this way is important to future development for two main reasons. First, there is considerable overlap between the two initiatives. There are likely to be a number of ways of reconciling this overlap, ranging from a decision to produce a community plan that is also the Local Agenda 21 through to a variety of means of linking the two as parallel, but distinctive, strategies. Quite how the relationship between the two initiatives will develop in future is difficult to judge at the time of writing. However, given that it is probable that community plans will eventually be a statutory requirement, it is likely that many of the authorities that have been slow to develop a Local Agenda 21 will now take the pragmatic step of combining the two. Second, the community plan defines sustainable development in a relatively weak sense and does not place any degree of primacy on environmental protection. By defining the policy challenge as one of promoting the 'well-being' of the locality, the White Paper suggests that social and, in particular, economic objectives will dominate the conception of sustainable development. As such, the spirit of the community plan is evidently different to that of Agenda 21 and is likely to shift the sustainable development agenda further away from environmental issues.

Conclusion

The enthusiasm with which many British local authorities have embraced the sustainable development agenda is indicative of the broader trend outlined in this book of local government seeking to redefine its role. Local authorities have been placed under few, if any, requirements by central government to introduce such policies. Indeed, it appears that, at least initially, local authorities greeted Agenda 21 with enthusiasm precisely because it was a policy initiative in which central government has limited interest and over which it has no significant control. This view is confirmed by O'Riordan and Voisey (1997, p. 46), who suggest that a key reason why the sustainability agenda has been taken up by a large number of UK local authorities is 'the desire of local authorities to re-assert and develop their role in an area when many responsibilities have been removed from local government control'.

That there should be variation in the extent to which UK local authorities have seen sustainable development initiatives such as Agenda 21 as an opportunity worth pursuing is not surprising. As we have noted, the extent to which environmental concerns are present on local political agendas and the degree to which the internal culture of local authorities recognizes and values the approach to policy making signified by Local Agenda 21 varies significantly. What is perhaps more significant is the fact that a relatively large number of local authorities have made considerable progress in tackling the barriers presented by the lack of a strong central government role in promoting sustainable development and by the fragmented nature of local governance, which are experienced more or less equally by all local authorities.

Thus, while the extent to which local authorities have wished to pursue activities in this particular policy sphere varies enormously, the evidence from the development of local environmental policies offers some confirmation of the creative autonomy thesis. Although Local Agenda 21 has not led to fundamental changes in the *majority* of local authorities, this should not detract us from the conclusion that it has acted as an important catalyst for change in at least a minority of local authorities. This is of particular significance, since the involvement of local authorities in sustainable development is only likely to grow in the future. However, the extent to which it will be Local Agenda 21 that leads to further local institutional change now depends primarily on how local authorities regard its status in relation to their community plans. Should local authorities accept the 'weak' definition of sustainable development that currently appears to characterize the government's notion of community planning, the recent drive towards councils acting as stewards of the local environment may begin to take a back seat in favour of economic and social objectives. At the same time, however, it is equally likely that many of those councils that have pioneered the Local Agenda 21 approach will seek to interpret community planning as an opportunity to bolster their role in environmental protection. What is clear is that sustainable development is now at the heart of wider attempts to recast the role of local government.

10

The Europeanization of British Local Government?

Introduction

Since the mid-1980s, when the decision to create a single market provided a powerful catalyst for a new phase of European integration, European issues have become a progressively important concern for local authorities. Indeed, although the European policy process may often appear remote and opaque, there is no UK local authority that has not been affected by it in some way. At a very minimum, individual councils have found themselves responsible for ensuring the implementation of a substantial proportion of European legislation while, for a number of local authorities, the European Union (EU) has also become a significant provider of funding through the structural funds. Moreover, because of the growing importance of the emerging European polity, local authorities throughout the member states have sought to find ways of influencing European institutions, both individually, in the form of direct lobbying, and collectively, through the formation of Europe-wide networks. It is in the context of these developments that a number of observers have pointed to a 'Europeanization' of British local government (Goldsmith, 1993; John, 1994).

In this chapter we examine the extent to which European integration has impacted upon local authorities and seek to assess the wider significance of these developments. In the first part of the chapter, we outline the principal ways in which a local authority's work may take on a European dimension and, underlining the fact that the majority of these are opportunities rather than obligations, we note how individual authorities are likely to vary in the importance that they give to such activities.

We then turn to consider four key aspects of the EU–local authority relationship in some depth, assessing the extent to which each provides evidence of a Europeanization of UK local government. Through this analysis we demonstrate that, while the extent of Europeanization varies significantly, there is evidence to suggest that a number of British local authorities have been particularly active in pursuing the European agenda. In the final section of the chapter, we consider the relevance of claims of multi-level governance and of the 'hollowing out' of the nation-state and assess the extent to which there is evidence to support these claims. We conclude that viewing the Europeanization of local authorities as part of a wider search for creative autonomy may provide the most suitable interpretation of recent developments.

The EU and Local Government

European integration impacts upon local government in a number of ways and it is useful to distinguish between the most direct implications for local authorities of the EU's expanding role, such as EU legislation and the structural funds, and the more indirect outcomes associated with European lobbying and networking activities. It is also important to note that local authorities can engage with the EU policy process on a number of levels. In a review of the implications of European development for local authorities, John (1994, pp. 3–4) suggests that the European function within a local authority can consist of up to ten separate tasks. He presents these as a continuum ranging from mandatory implementation tasks through to more ambitious activities associated with European policy development (see figure 10.1).

Since there is only a formal requirement on local authorities to undertake the first of these ten tasks, the extent to which an individual local authority has become 'Europeanized' therefore depends on the degree to which it has attempted to move beyond this basic minimum. John suggests that his continuum can be used to characterize four distinctive ways of defining the 'European function' within local authorities. First, there are a group of authorities that may be termed 'EU minimal' as they do nothing more than undertake the first three tasks listed in the diagram. A second group comprises 'EU financially orientated' authorities, since they have supplemented the three core activities with those of securing European funding, usually in the context of wider economic development strategies. The third local authority type is described as 'EU networking', as it has not only formed local partnerships around European issues but also become involved in cross-national projects and interna-

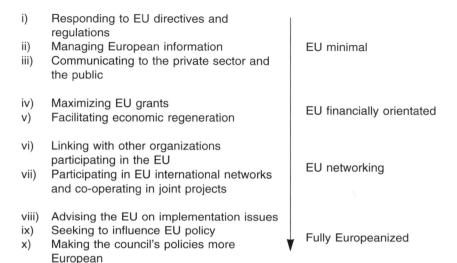

i)   Responding to EU directives and
        regulations
ii)   Managing European information   EU minimal
iii)   Communicating to the private sector and
        the public

iv)   Maximizing EU grants
v)   Facilitating economic regeneration   EU financially orientated

vi)   Linking with other organizations
        participating in the EU
vii)   Participating in EU international networks   EU networking
        and co-operating in joint projects

viii)   Advising the EU on implementation issues
ix)   Seeking to influence EU policy
x)   Making the council's policies more   Fully Europeanized
        European

Figure 10.1 The European function in local authorities
Source: Adapted from John (1994a).

tional networks. Finally, there is the 'fully Europeanized' authority, which embraces all ten elements of the EU function, including the task of assessing ways in which all of the council's policies could relate to the European project.

This typology indicates that individual local authorities have a considerable degree of choice regarding the extent to which they wish to 'Europeanize'. Of the ten elements of the European function, only the first could be described as obligatory, while the remainder offer local authorities a series of opportunities to access funds, build links with other organizations and influence the European policy debate. Because of the opportunities open to them, there is therefore likely to be an inherent dynamic pushing councils progressively towards greater Europeanization. Thus, John suggests that, while relatively few councils are likely to reach the level of involvement implied by the fully Europeanized authority, most will be seeking to expand the range of activities encompassed by their European portfolio.

The extent to which a local authority is Europeanized will generally be reflected in the decisions it has made about where to locate and how to integrate the European function into its broader organizational structure. For example, a local authority that has adopted a strong financial orientation towards the EU as part of its economic development activities may well regard the economic development unit as the natural place for a European officer, as has been the case with several northern metropolitan authorities that have succeeded in gaining significant European Regional Development Fund (ERDF) resources. Conversely, where the authority defines the European function in terms approaching full Europeanization, it is likely that the full range of European tasks will be co-ordinated from the chief executive's department, since this will enable the relevant officer(s) to 'be more involved with networking, supporting other departments and helping the authority influence policy' (John, 1994a, p. 10).

There is clear evidence of the progressive Europeanization of local authorities during the 1990s, along the lines postulated by John. A report compiled by the Audit Commission (HMSO, 1991) pointed to considerable variation in the extent to which local authorities had taken action in respect to European integration. The report suggested that less than a third of local authorities had reviewed what implications the European agenda might have for them. Similarly, a survey carried out by the LGMB in 1993 found that just 20 per cent of local authorities had adopted an authority-wide strategy for European issues (Local Government Management Board, 1993d). Yet, by 1996, 80 per cent of local authorities surveyed by Martin (1998) reported that they were confident of their ability to respond to EU legislation, suggesting a significant increase in the numbers that had undertaken such exercises.

A similar trend is evident in relation to the employment of staff dedicated to European issues. The LGMB survey found that 43 per cent of English and Welsh local authorities had European officers in 1992, whereas a survey carried out by Goldsmith (1993) one year later estimated that 60 per cent of UK local authorities had such staff. Drawing on survey data from 1996, Martin (1998) found that the proportion of local authorities with officers specifically dedicated to European matters had risen to 75 per cent. The growth of local authority offices in Brussels shows a similar picture. Whereas there were only five offices in Brussels representing UK sub-national authorities in 1989 (John, 1994a), by 1996 a third of authorities surveyed by Martin (1998) had some form of representation in the city. Finally, there is also evidence to suggest that UK local authorities have invested significantly in developing linkages with their counterparts in other European countries. Thus, while the LGMB survey found that a quarter of local authorities in England and Wales were involved in European networks in 1992, Martin (1998) suggests that this had increased to a half by 1996.

The surveys carried out in the early 1990s revealed significant variation in the level of Europeanization between different types of local authority. The survey by the Audit Commission (1991) found that 70 per cent of London boroughs and metropolitan councils and 63 per cent of shire counties had reviewed what impact the EU would have on their authority, whereas only 19 per cent of shire districts had done so. The LGMB survey found that around 25 per cent of respondents were involved in transnational networking activities in 1992, but that this figure rose to 65 per cent among county councils. Likewise, the proportion of county councils and metropolitan councils with European officers was 87 per cent and 89 per cent respectively in 1992, compared to the local authority average of 43 per cent.

A number of observers have noted that, despite the extent of government centralization in the UK and the antipathy that national governments have shown for the European project, British local authorities have generally responded to the EU more enthusiastically and effectively than many of their European counterparts (Goldsmith, 1993; John, 1996b). British local authorities were particularly effective in responding to the new opportunities offered by the gathering pace of European integration in the late 1980s and the early 1990s. There are many other signs of British local government leading the way. For instance, UK local authorities have emerged as some of the most effective networking and lobbying agencies among sub-national actors in Europe and, as a result, have often been allowed by other European local government associations to take the lead in joint lobbying campaigns (John and McAteer, 1998). Finally, as table 10.1 shows, by 1995 the UK had more sub-national bodies with offices in Brussels than any other member state. Moreover, the twenty-three UK sub-national offices represented a quarter of all those established by local and regional authorities in the twelve member states.

Local authorities and the implementation of EU legislation

The role that local authorities play in implementing EU policies is particularly significant in a British context because of the wide range of responsibilities that they have for the implementation of domestic policies (John, 1996b). Thus, writing in 1993, Terry estimated that local authorities were responsible for the implementation of 101 directives relating to food, environment, and health and safety alone, and the number is only likely to have grown since then. Two distinctive responsibilities are placed on local authorities by EU legislation: the need to ensure local authority compliance with EU directives and regulations, and the role that local authorities are given in enforcing such legislation (cf. Terry, 1992). In terms of compliance, local authorities are required to meet regulations on matters as diverse as public works, supplies con-

Table 10.1 Numbers of sub-national offices in Brussels, 1995

Member states	No. of offices
UK	23
France	19
Germany	18
Spain	13
Belgium	8
Denmark	8
Netherlands	3
Italy	0
Ireland	1
Greece	1
Portugal	1
Luxembourg	0
Total	95

Source: John (1995).

tracts, employment, environmental health, vocational education, consumer protection and competition policy. In relation to enforcement, local authorities have a key role in ensuring that others meet regulations in a range of areas, such as the composition, safety and labelling of foodstuffs.

European legislation therefore furnishes UK local government with an important implementation role which, it has been suggested, will lead to growing contact between local authorities and the European Commission (Bongers, 1992). However, the extent and the significance of such developments should not be over-stated. National governments, rather than local authorities, retain responsibility for enforcing EU directives, and communication over such issues generally takes place between the Commission and central government. Moreover, there has been only limited growth of EU competence in policy areas such as education and social services, which remain the major spending functions of UK local authorities, and it is difficult to imagine such developments occurring in the immediate future (John, 1996b). It should also be noted that there is nothing in EU law which dictates that specific aspects of EU legislation must be implemented by local authorities (John, 1996b).

The structural funds

European structural policy is characterized by its fair share of jargon – a problem that is exacerbated by the tendency for frequent reforms to bolt on new principles and programmes and, hence, new terminology. Some basic explanation is therefore required for the uninitiated. The origins of the structural funds are in the European Regional Development Fund (ERDF), which was launched in 1975 as a means of compensating member states for the EEC's wish to set limits to the level of state aid to industry. Independently from the ERDF, a European Social Fund (ESF) was also established in the 1970s to fund employment training and retraining initiatives. Although the size of both these two programmes grew steadily, it was not until the Single European Act of 1986 brought the issue of cohesion on to the agenda that they received any significant level of funding.

The Single European Act had two further important implications for European regional development and social policy measures. First, the ERDF and the ESF were brought together with the European Agriculture Guarantee and Guidance Fund (EAGGF) and became collectively known as the structural funds (to which the Financial Instruments of Fisheries Guidance was added in 1993). Second, structural policies became a central element of the wider development of cohesion policy, which also includes a separate Cohesion Fund, established in 1993 (the Cohesion Fund provides assistance for infrastructure projects in the poorest member states and operates independently from structural policy agreements). During the course of the 1990s, cohesion policy became an increasingly central element of EU policy and expenditure has grown accordingly. In 1985 the EC's structural fund consisted of ECU 3.7 billion and made up 17 per cent of the total EC budget. By 1999, expenditure had risen almost tenfold, to ECU 33 billion, representing 37 per cent of EU expenditure (Bachtler, 1998). The ERDF remains the largest and most important single element of EU cohesion policy.

Since 1989 the operation of the EU's structural policies has been determined by specific objectives that are mapped on to the uneven levels of economic development within the EU territory, thus ensuring both thematic and geographic concentration. In the period from 1988 to 1999, seven different objectives were established. Objective 1, the largest part of the fund, provided assistance to regions deemed to be lagging behind (defined as having a GDP per head less than 75 per cent of the EU average). Support for areas suffering from industrial decline was provided by Objective 2. Objectives 3 and 4, which were not explicitly geographically targeted, had the respective aims of supporting programmes aimed at combating long-term and youth unemployment, and providing funding for schemes helping workers to adapt to industrial change and new production methods. Finally, Objective 5a and Objective 5b were concerned with structural adjustment in rural areas, while Objective 6 offered assistance for development and structural readjustment in regions with extremely low population densities.

A review of the structural funds was instigated in the period after 1997 as part of the EU's Agenda 2000 programme, and an agreement for their reform was reached in 1999. Under the new arrangements there has been a considerable streamlining, achieved largely through an amalgamation of the previous objectives. As a result, there are now three objectives:

- Objective 1: support for regions that are lagging behind (the former Objective 1 plus the relatively small Objective 6);
- Objective 2: support for other regions experiencing structural economic change (previously Objectives 2 and 5b);
- Objective 3: support for the development of human resources (formerly Objectives 3 and 4).

The structural funds were relatively unimportant to UK local authorities before the late 1980s. While a few large councils, such as Birmingham and Strathclyde, had accessed money from the funds, European funding opportunities were unknown to the majority of local authorities. Since the late 1980s this picture has changed considerably. During this time, the UK has benefited significantly from growing EU expenditure on cohesion policies, receiving some £14 billion in the ten-year period from 1989 to 1999 (Martin, 1998). This injection of funding is largely accounted for by the increase in the UK's direct allocation from the structural funds following the 1988, 1994 and 1999 reforms. Particularly significant injections of funds followed from the Commission's decision to grant Objective 1 status to three areas of the UK in 1994 (Merseyside, Northern Ireland and the Highlands and Islands of Scotland). In 1999, as these three programmes came to an end, Objective 1 status was granted to South Yorkshire, Cornwall and West Wales, together with a further five years of Objective 1 funding for Merseyside.

Despite the complexity of EU programmes, there is evidence of a high degree of awareness among British local authorities of what funding opportunities are available and of a relatively high degree of success in securing financial assistance. According to Martin (1998), 75 per cent of local authorities in the mainland UK have bid for EU assistance. Moreover, authorities had received funding from more than sixty different EU programmes and initiatives, suggesting broad-ranging knowledge of what is available to them (p. 242). Moreover, the scale of the resources available to UK local authorities has made the EU a key player in local economic development and regeneration policies. Almost half of the authorities surveyed by Martin (1998) cited EU policies as having 'a major effect' on their regeneration policies. Moreover, three-quarters 'reported that EU programmes were a vital source of finance for regeneration and many felt that, without EU assistance, they would have been forced to abandon their regeneration programmes' (p. 241). The growing importance of the EU to local regeneration initiatives has also been reinforced by trends in UK policy during the 1990s. At the same time as large areas of the UK were being given Objective 1, 2 or 5b status in the mid-1990s, the single regeneration budget and other forms of domestic funding assistance, such as the National Lottery, were becoming available to areas of the country that had previously been ineligible for additional regeneration funding (Martin, 1998). This has enabled more local authorities to raise the matching funding required to access EU programmes.

However, in more recent years the significance to local authorities of European funding may have declined slightly. In common with other initiatives, European programmes have increasingly required local authorities to enter into a partnership role. UK central government pushed hard for local partnerships to have a significant business element and resisted the Commission's insistence that a broad range of social partners should have a place on the monitoring committees (Martin, 1998). As public–private partnership also become a precondition of most of the discretionary domestic funding programmes that could be used to raise matching funding, local authorities were increasingly forced to share EU resources with other actors. Thus, whereas local authorities had received 70 per cent of the ERDF resources allocated to their areas from 1989 to 1993, by 1996 the proportion had fallen to less than 50 per cent (Martin, 1998).

Local authority lobbying

Since the late 1980s, UK local authorities have become increasingly involved in European lobbying. As a result, whereas the number of UK local authorities with offices in Brussels could be counted on one hand in 1988, in the period from 1989 to 1994 a further eighteen offices were opened in Brussels by UK sub-national bodies (John, 1995). Since many of these offices were established by consortia of local authorities, the total number of authorities represented is considerably higher. At the same time, the UK local government associations also strengthened their European lobbying function in the early 1990s, resulting in the Local

Government International Bureau (LGIB) setting up an office in Brussels in 1992. This growth in lobbying activity during the 1990s has been prompted, in part, by the growth in the EU's regulatory powers, the implications of which have led to a growing concern among local authorities to lobby national government and, increasingly, the Commission on policy issues. However, it was undoubtedly the growing significance of the structural funds that prompted the bulk of this increased investment in lobbying activities.

It is inevitably difficult to assess what results such lobbying has yielded, since causal relationships are virtually impossible to demonstrate. It is certainly the case that UK local authorities have been able to achieve a much greater presence in European policy debates, and their lobbying activities may have influenced the Commission on the designation of Objective 1 and Objective 2 areas. The efforts of London local authorities in advocating that an urban dimension be added to the structural funds as part of the 1994 reform may have helped to ensure the introduction of the URBAN programme. Likewise, the lead role played by UK local authorities in a number of pan-European lobbies may have helped secure funding for particular areas of the UK. For instance, John (1996b) points to the prominent part played by English county councils in the lobby for the KONVER programme, which provided aid for localities suffering from the decline of the defence industry.

However, to conclude from such superficial evidence that local authorities have been successful in their lobbying activities would clearly be inappropriate. Just because UK councils have lobbied for policies that the EU has introduced does not necessarily mean that they have been influential in the policy process. The presence of a lobbyist in a decision-making process is not necessarily an indicator of influence, since even an apparent 'insider' may have been invited to add weight to a predetermined policy position (Christiansen and Dowding, 1994). As John (1996a) notes, apparent lobbying successes need to be seen in the context of power struggles within the European institutions. Citing the example of the UK-led Florence Group, which lobbied for a continuation of Objective 2 status at the time of the 1993 reforms, John argues that the EU's decision to retain the existing system was due in large part to divisions within the Commission. Indeed, the impetus for the formation of the lobby was a product of the split between those within the Commission advocating 'no change' and those supporting wholesale reforms. It was as a result of these divisions that the Commission invited all Objective 2 authorities to a meeting in Florence in July 1991, at which the Florence Group was formed (John, 1996a). In this instance, 'lobby success *reflected* rather than affected bureaucratic faction-fighting within the Commission' (John and McAteer, 1998, p. 108, original emphasis).

Moreover, several case studies of the European lobbying efforts of UK sub-national government suggest there is limited evidence of their success (John and McAteer, 1998; McAteer and Mitchell, 1996). Using a case study of the lobbying campaign of UK local authorities in the Intergovernmental Conference that led to the Amsterdam Treaty of June 1997, John and McAteer play down the grander claims about sub-national policy influence. Led by the LGIB and the Convention of Scottish Local Authorities, the British local government community lobbied for the treaty to include measures that would strengthen the position of local authorities in the emerging European polity. These proposed measures included a clear definition of the principle of subsidiarity, the creation of a legal basis for the principle of local government and a revision of the EU's powers in a number of specified areas to ensure a guaranteed role for local and regional government. John and McAteer argue that these were relatively cautious objectives, pursued pragmatically through a well-organized campaign. Moreover, they suggest that the campaign showed that UK local authorities demonstrate a high degree of Europeanization compared to many of their continental counterparts, as evidenced by the energy and resources they devote to European matters and the access they have to Commission officials. Yet, despite its numerous strengths, the authors are forced to conclude that 'overall the results of the lobby were not productive' (p. 121).

In part, the failure of the local government lobby to influence the outcome of the intergovernmental commission (IGC) stemmed from its failure to target national policy-makers to a sufficient degree. Although they were relatively successful in gaining access to key players in the Commission and the European Parliament, the lobbyists failed to gain access to the British ministers responsible for the IGC negotiations (John and McAteer, 1998). This conclusion is confirmed by Bomberg and Peterson (1998), who suggest that intergovernmentalism continues to dominate the EU decision-making process and that, as a result, sub-national authorities also need to target national government if their lobbying strategies are to prove effective.

Local authority networking

The 1990s also witnessed a significant growth in the number and significance of Europe-wide networks of sub-national authorities. Although several Europe-wide networks were established in the 1980s, it was in the first half of the 1990s that significant numbers emerged. There have been several important factors driving this mushrooming of networks. The growth of EU policy competences, and in particular the structural funds, have provided localities with a direct interest in the European policy process. First, as we have noted, the gathering pace of integration thus provided a spur for sub-national authorities to mobilize collectively around particular issues. Second, there was growing evidence by the late 1980s that 'the EU would respond more positively to European-wide cross-national initiative rather than to separate national or regional lobbies' (Benington and Harvey, 1998, p. 154). Third, the creation of the Single Market created concerns in many quarters about the possible negative consequences of intensified competition between cities and regions. It was felt that networks promoting co-operation between localities could help to mitigate the harmful and potentially zero-sum consequences of intensified competition (Dawson, 1991). Finally, the availability of EU financial support in the early 1990s, provided for by the establishment of the RECITE (Regions and Cities in the New Europe) programme under Article 10 of the ERDF, enabled hitherto loose associations of actors to develop into fully fledged networks. In the period 1990–1 alone, ECU 49 million were spent under the RECITE programme to support thirty-seven networks between cities and regions (Commission of the European Communities, 1992).

That the European Commission should wish to fund organizations intent on scrutinizing its activities and lobbying it for further resources may, at first sight, seem paradoxical. However, there is a powerful logic underpinning the Commission's approach. In part, it shared the concern of the cities and regions establishing the networks that the Single Market might give rise not only to widening inter-regional and inter-urban disparities, but also to increased political tensions between sub-national governments as a result of increased economic competition. When, in 1991, ECU 18 million were made available to support twelve networks under the RECITE programme, the rationale put forward by Commissioner Bruce Millan was that such networks 'would contribute to the overall aim of economic and social cohesion in Europe by promoting a sense of solidarity and identity of purpose between regions and cities across the whole community' (cited in Dawson, 1991, p. 2). However, there is undoubtedly an important sub-text to the Commission's encouragement of Europe-wide networks: the attempt to boost support for the European project among sub-national governments (Goldsmith, 1993).

In general, European networks of sub-national authorities have defined their purpose as a dual one. First and foremost, all are intended to promote exchange between their members, leading to the transfer of knowledge and best practice. Second, such networks also seek to lobby and influence the European policy process. However, there is some evidence that UK local authorities have looked upon such networks in a slightly more opportunistic manner. Martin (1998) suggests that local authorities have joined such networks primarily to enhance funding opportunities, rather than to influence policy. Based on his survey data, he finds that 'very few authorities believed that these networks provided them with a means of influencing EU policies' (p. 241). Thus, while Martin finds that 50 per cent of local authorities in the UK have established links with their counterparts in other European countries, the most commonly cited reasons for such linkages were to access EU funds available for pilot projects and to exchange experience.

A report by the Local Government International Bureau (1992) pointed to British involvement in twenty-three Europe-wide networks. Local authorities participate in a vast array of European networks, which following Benington and Harvey (1998) may be divided into three broad categories. First, there are a number of sectoral networks. These focus on the local and regional impact of restructuring in key industrial sectors. Examples are EURACOM (European Action for Mining Communities), CAR (Co-operation between Automobile Regions) and MILAN (Motor Industry Local Authority Network). Second, spatial or territorial networks have been formed by towns, cities, regions and other distinctive geographical units to enhance communication and co-operation across national boundaries. EUROCITIES and the Atlantic Arc are prominent examples. The third group, thematic networks, are concerned with particular policy issues, many focusing on aspects of social policy. Networks such as Quartiers en Crise, which is concerned with concentrations of poverty in European cities, and EuroLink Age, which focuses on ageing and on the elderly, are representative of this type of network.

It is impossible to provide a comprehensive overview of the full range of European networks in which UK local authorities have become active. Examples of networks involving UK local authorities are as follows:

- *EURACOM* Established in 1988, this network was significantly inspired by the Coalfield Communities Campaign (CCC), which had mobilized local authorities in the UK around issues concerned with pit closures in the mid-1980s. The CCC provided a blueprint for the formation of similar networks in other EU member states, resulting in the formation of a further six associations with some 450 local authority members which, together with the CCC, formed EURACOM (Benington and Harvey, 1998). With EURACOM representing a substantial number of localities facing serious social and economic problems resulting from the decline of the coal industry, there is evidence that its lobbying was an important factor in the Commission's decision to establish RECHAR, an initiative aimed at the regeneration of coal-mining and former coal-mining areas (Benington and Harvey, 1998).

- *EUROCITIES* A network representing large, mainly non-capital cities with a population of 250,000 or more, EUROCITIES was founded in 1986. Its principal objectives are to facilitate co-operation between its members, to promote the exchange of best practice and to lobby the EU on relevant policy matters. It has been particularly involved in advocating a European urban policy and in lobbying for the inclusion of clear recognition of the role of local authorities in the European treaties. Its founding members included Birmingham and some 20 per cent of the network's members are British local authorities.

- *Quartiers en Crise* Launched as 'a network of 25 European towns and cities which share problems of serious urban decline', Quartiers en Crise had its origins in an exchange programme between ten European towns. With Manchester, Belfast and Paisley among its members, the network has placed particular emphasis on the pro-motion of bilateral co-operation and the transfer of knowledge between towns and cities facing similar challenges.

- *POLIS* This was established as a network to look into issues con-cerned with mobility management in urban areas, particularly in light of the anticipated increase in mobility arising from the creation of the Single European Market. Again, the network has placed special stress on facilitating technical co-operation and exchange between its members, aiming particularly 'to strengthen institutional and technical capabilities in the effective management of transport'. UK members include Bristol, Liverpool, Glasgow and Southampton.

How Significant is Europeanization? Competing Interpretations

These trends towards the Europeanization of local government have been interpreted in a variety of ways. Two interpretations that have received particular attention are the concept of multi-level governance and the notion of the hollowing-out of the nation-state. The two interpretations are closely related, since both assume that the process of European inte-gration is leading to an enhanced role for sub-national government, at the expense of national government. Moreover, both are closely related to the notions of a 'Europe of the Regions' and of subsidiarity, which have found considerable expression in EU policy debate. In the remain-der of the chapter, we outline the nature of these competing interpreta-tions and assess what evidence may be available in a UK context to support or refute them.

The notion that the European policy process represents a system of multi-level governance is particularly associated with Marks, who has developed his analysis in a series of papers (Marks, 1992; Marks, 1993; Marks, Hooghe and Blank, 1996). Following Marks, multi-level governance may be defined as 'a system of continuous negotiation among nested governments at several territorial tiers – supranational, national, regional and local' (Marks, 1993, p. 392). Marks argues that the dominant accounts of the EU policy process, which have been informed by assumptions drawn from intergovernmentalism and neo-functionalism, place too much stress on the importance of national governments. This bias, he suggests, has ignored the fact that regional and local actors are increasingly important in influencing European policy and that the Commission has made growing efforts to build relationships with sub-national interests. Moreover, Marks argues that 'European integration is a polity creating process in which authority and policy-making are shared across multiple levels of government,' (Marks, Hooghe and Blank, 1996, p. 342). To substantiate these claims, the policy process surrounding the ERDF, particularly since the reform of the structural funds in 1988, is suggested to represent the archetypal case of such multi-level governance (Marks, 1993).

Marks argues that the 1988 reform of the structural funds strengthened the role of the Commission over national governments and created direct links between the Commission and individual regions (Marks, 1992; 1993). The new arrangements, which resulted from the initiative of the European Commission and which were accepted by the Council of Ministers with minor amendment, established that the structural funds would be administered as a partnership between the Commission, central and sub-national government and other relevant agencies. According to Marks, this change was an attempt by the Commission to strengthen the role played by regional and local institutions – a strategy that he also sees the Commission employing in subsequent amendments to the structural funds. Moreover, he also suggests that sub-national actors exert an important influence on member states' positions in the Council of Ministers and at intergovernmental conferences. As a result, Marks argues that there is a vital process of institutional formation that goes on 'beyond the areas that are transparently dominated by member states' (Marks, 1993, p. 105).

Some observers have taken the multi-level governance thesis a stage further and have suggested that the Europeanization of local government represents part of the process of the 'hollowing out of the nation-state'. The logic behind this development is similar to that cited in relation to multi-level governance. It is argued that, since it is committed to realizing subsidiarity and to the notion of a Europe of the Regions, the

European Commission has had strong incentives to deal with local authorities. This logic applies particularly in the UK, where national government has invariably appeared intent on blocking moves towards such concepts. At the same time, local authorities have had similarly powerful motives for entering into direct contact with the Commission. These motivations have not merely been financial. Thus, Rhodes (1997) notes that UK local authorities have become increasingly enthusiastic about the EU and suggests that this enthusiasm resulted particularly from local government frustration with central government – 'the receptiveness of the European Commission fuelled the enthusiasm of sub-national authorities, its behaviour contrasting sharply with that of the UK central government' (p. 144).

There is a degree of plausibility in both accounts. To begin with, there are good reasons why the Commission has sought to build direct relationships with local and regional authorities. Goldsmith (1993) suggests that there are clear reasons for the European Commission seeking to deal directly with sub-national government. The first of these is the Commission's need for alternative sources of information which will counterbalance the subjective intelligence that it receives from national governments. In addition, since local and regional governments are often responsible for putting EU policy into practice, working with sub-national government may assist the Commission's efforts at regulation and serve to bring about better implementation of its policies. Goldsmith adds that since many of the Commission's programmes are clientelistic in nature, in that they are designed to encourage support among key interests for its work, the Commission is also likely to seek to promote the role played by sub-national governments, since this may help to break down the more nationalisitic assumptions that often act as a barrier to further integration.

In addition, both theses suggest that European integration is serving to strengthen the position of sub-national government. Two frequently cited examples suggest that the EU has strengthened the standing of sub-national authorities in the UK. The first of these is provided by the conflict that occurred between UK central government and local authorities over the former's interpretation of the additionality principle in European programmes. The reform of the structural funds had established that EU support should not be used to substitute for domestic expenditure and that grants would therefore be given only where projects could show evidence of match-funding. However, the UK government, which had significantly cut regional policy expenditure since the late 1980s, was to prove persistently vague about how it was meeting the additionality principle. This dispute reached a head over the EU's RECHAR programme, which had been set up to provide funds for the restructuring of declining coalfield areas. The Commissioner for Regional Policy, Bruce Millan, refused to release the UK allocation of £100 million because of the failure to show evidence of match-funding (Bache, 1999). In the resultant stand-off, British local authorities supported Millan, eventually resulting in the UK government agreeing to ensure that matching funding would be supplied.

The second example is the possible impact that the EU's structural funds have had on the process of institution building in the English regions. It has been suggested that during the 1990s, the Commission acted as a catalyst for the development of regional governance from above and from below (Stewart, 1994). By placing increasing stress on the importance of regional structures to structural fund allocations and by encouraging local authorities and other sub-national actors to form regional associations, the Commission is seen to have had a direct hand in the government's decision to create the Government Offices for the Regions (Stewart, 1994). While causality is very difficult to prove in relation to the government's decision to create regional offices, what is clearly documented is the way in which the European Commission prompted the growth of a regional consciousness from the bottom up. McCarthy and Burch (1994, p. 31) suggest that in the early 1990s it became evident that 'the message from Brussels was for regions to take regional strategies into their own hands'. The same authors show that views expressed by Graham Meadows, the Commission's director of Objective 2 programmes, were a significant impetus behind the formation of the North West Regional Association and its decision to draw up a regional economic strategy. (Meadows told delegates to a conference at Manchester Airport that the Commission intended in future to use evidence of regional consciousness as a criterion in making decisions about the designation of Objective 2 areas.)

However, there are numerous problems with both the multi-level governance and the hollowing-out theses. First, beyond the examples referred to above, there is relatively limited evidence that Europeanization is strengthening the influence that local authorities have over policy. As John and McAteer (1998) suggest, for the multi-level governance thesis to be sustainable, it must demonstrate that the input of sub-national actors goes beyond their right to be consulted. Thus, multi-level governance 'would involve continual influence from all levels of government on policy and on the development of the institutional framework of the EU' (p. 106). Yet less than a quarter of local authorities in the UK feel that they have been able to exert any influence whatsoever on EU policies (Martin, 1998, p. 241). Moreover, there is very little evidence of sub-national actors engaging directly with the European Commission: only 14 per cent of British local authorities claim to have regular contact with Commission officials. As a result, Martin (1998, p. 241) is led to conclude that 'to a large extent, the road to Brussels still runs through Whitehall and Westminster'. Consequently, John and McAteer (1998) suggest that the multi-level governance literature often adopts a relatively naive view of the role played by sub-national actors, in which it is assumed that their presence automatically translates into influence over policy. Thus, to the extent that there is multi-level governance in the EU, it consists of a top-down policy implementation process rather than a bottom-up approach to policy formulation (John and McAteer, 1998).

Second, the scope for the European Commission to shape central–local relations in the UK is limited. Rhodes (1997) suggests that policy networks involved are relatively weak and the sums of money, although significant in the regions where they are most heavily concentrated, are a small proportion of UK central government grants to local authorities. Particular limitations are imposed by central government's ability to maintain its gatekeeping role. At the centre of Marks's thesis is the claim that the 1988 reforms to the structural funds strengthened the role of the Commission *vis-à-vis* national governments. However, there is no evidence that this has been the case. It is certainly true that, prior to 1988, EU regional policies in the UK were subject to extensive central government control (Rhodes, 1997). The Department of Industry operated as the focal point for the administration of the ERDF and local authorities were not required to play any formal part in the process. This analysis is confirmed by Anderson (1990), who argued, on the basis of fieldwork carried out in the 1980s, that sub-national actors applying for the structural funds were dependent on central government. In a British context, Anderson pointed particularly to the regional offices of the Department of the Environment, which he saw as a mechanism through which national government played a 'gatekeeper' role.

However, whether this picture has significantly changed because of the Commission's stress on the need for local partnerships is not clear in a British context. Throughout the EU, national governments continue to retain a powerful position in relation to the structural funds, deciding on which programmes they recommend to the Commission and retaining control over capital approvals. As John (1996b) notes, the extent to which nation-states permit European policy to bring about a major shift of power and resources within its own territory therefore depends 'on the willingness of national governments to transfer functions to sub-central governments, to allow locally elected institutions to apply for the structural funds, and to give them matching funding when they apply for community initiatives' (p. 132). Although local partnerships have been strengthened, UK civil servants dominate the monitoring committees as they appoint participants, chair meetings and set the agendas (John, 1996b). Rhodes (1997) also sees UK central government as retaining tight control over the operation of the structural funds in a number of ways, including the establishment of regional offices, by disputing the additionality criteria, and by keeping a high profile in the domestic policy network. In this way it is suggested that 'the UK government can uphold its "gatekeeper role" in the face of pressure for regionalisation from the EU' (p. 159).

A third and related point is that the continued significance of central government's gatekeeping role appears to have limited the influence afforded to local actors. This is seen to be reflected in the fact that the Single Programming Documents (SPDs) produced by the UK government have been remarkably similar (Lloyd and Meegan, 1996; Boland, 1999). In a study of the Merseyside Objective 1 process, Boland (1999, p. 25) argues that the five drivers on which the Merseyside SPD are based 'could quite conceivably be transposed to any other recipient region'. It is also evident that European programmes have been shaped by the priorities and philosophies of UK central government, which has stipulated additional criteria for the composition of local partnerships and even 'top-sliced' European programmes to provide for competitive bidding to the Regional Challenge fund (Martin, 1998). Central government's tight control of the purse strings and its sceptical attitude towards the provision of matching funding have also limited the capacity of local authorities to engage with the European policy agenda. Thus, the lack of availability of matching funding is seen by two-thirds of local authorities to be a major problem when attempting to access EU funding, with a quarter of authorities suggesting that it is a problem to which they have not yet found a solution (Martin, 1998).

Consequently, it has been argued that the operation of the structural funds in the UK tends to be characterized not by multi-level governance but by 'contested governance' (Lloyd and Meegan, 1996; Bachtler and Turok, 1997; Boland, 1999). These authors suggest that while multi-level relationships are evident, they are characterized by conflict between the different tiers of government over policy and resources. Thus, in a case study of the Objective 1 process in Merseyside, it has been argued that the preparation of the SPD for the period 1994–9 was characterized by 'a series of often protracted and mortant wranglings between UK Government representatives, EC officials and the Government Office for Merseyside' (Boland, 1999, p. 25). According to Boland, political and ideological differences between the EC and the UK government dominated the process of drawing up the SPD, which allowed little or no scope for input from the local business and voluntary sectors, from trade unions and other social partners. The result was 'a compromise that lacks innovation' and which 'fails to design specific policies for the specific problems in the regional economy' (p. 25). Under such conditions, there is clearly limited scope for local authorities to use EU policy programmes to exercise autonomous influence over policy. Rather, 'the SPD was denied any real local input from which innovative locally-specific policy ideas could, and more importantly should, have emerged' (p. 26).

In reality, it remains unclear what intergovernmental relationships will actually emerge as a result of European integration. John (1996a) suggests that the increasing importance of a triadic relationship between European, national and sub-national levels of government could lead to a number of possible outcomes. These outcomes may be portrayed as a continuum. At one end of this continuum is the notion of a 'Europe of the Regions', brought about by a process of European integration driven by an alliance of European and sub-national governmental actors, in which power is progressively transferred to the supra-national and sub-national levels, leading to a hollowing-out of the nation-state. At the other end of the continuum is the scenario that European integration proceeds on the basis of national governments transferring some powers and functions to the supra-national level in return for them retaining direct control over the implementation of European policies within their own territory. Thus, both decentralization and centralization are possible outcomes of the EU's increased importance in intergovernmental relations.

It would also seem plausible that both of these scenarios could occur simultaneously. As John (1996b) suggests, there are fifteen different possible forms of multi-level governance in Europe, since the pattern of relations will be different in each member state. Moreover, it is also feasible that elements of decentralization will be observable even where the central state attempts to retain its role as gatekeeper. Despite the centre's (largely successful) attempts to exercise a significant degree of control over the domestic operation of the structural funds, there are a number of channels through which British local authorities engage directly with the European Commission and the wider European policy agenda. Although cases of bypassing central government departments to deal directly with Brussels do appear to be rare, a variety of horizontal relations between local authorities in Europe operate outside of any form of central control.

Conclusion: Europeanization as Creative Autonomy?

In many ways there is something of a paradox evident in the trends we have described here. While the UK government was opting out of key sections of the Maastricht Treaty and tightening the already substantial financial control it had over local government, UK local authorities were busily developing stronger relationships with the European Commission. Yet there are good reasons why UK local authorities have been at the forefront of European initiatives over the past ten years or more. Put simply, they have been spurred on by the frustrating domestic context in which they have had to operate and have seen the EU as an opportunity rather than a threat.

> Some UK local authorities regard the EU function as a potential remedy for constraints on resources and loss of functions in the 1980s; they consider the EU's regional policy and its intervention in the local economy are policies they would like central government to introduce; the EU appears to be more responsive and accessible than central government, recognising local government's role as an independent policy-maker apparently denied in the domestic context. (John, 1996b, p. 297)

Thus, while European integration does not yet appear to be leading to a renaissance of city and regional government prompted by a hollowing-out of the nation-state, the significant steps that UK local authorities have taken towards Europeanization do appear to add weight to the creative autonomy thesis. The EU has opened up a number of opportunities that UK local authorities have seen as a means of offsetting some of the constraints imposed on them by central government. In some cases, the results of such activities have been dramatic. Both Birmingham and Glasgow have financed large-scale regeneration programmes by accessing European funds over a number of years, thereby helping 'to transform their image from rundown UK industrial areas into new cultural capitals of Europe' (Benington and Harvey, 1994, p. 25). Moreover, engagement with the European political process has served to bring a number of UK local authorities and individual local politicians to the heart of European policy debates, with Birmingham and Glasgow again constituting prominent examples.

Admittedly, it is important not to overstate these developments. There is an inherent danger involved in generalizing from the experience of a relatively small number of large local authorities that have invested significantly in developing their European profile. Clearly, the overall picture appears to be somewhat different when we consider the developments in British local government as a whole (Martin, 1998). There are also important limitations in the extent to which local government is able to respond to and influence the changing European agenda. Indeed, it has been suggested that, following a rush of enthusiasm about the prospects of direct EU–local relationships, the mid-1990s saw a considerable slow-down in such developments, which is a reflection of 'cycles of influence and institutional development' in the process of European integration (John, 1996a, p. 139). Thus, while several pioneering UK local authorities may have found that the 1980s and 1990s saw Europe open up a number of avenues for the pursuit of creative autonomy, such opportunities are unlikely to reappear, at least for a while.

Part IV
Sub-national Government under New Labour

11

Towards Regional Government?

The Introduction of Regional Offices, the Moves towards Devolution and the Notion of Regionalism

Introduction

Traditionally, the UK has been described as a unitary political system. In contrast to European Union member states such as Germany and Spain, where the state governments (or *Länder*) and regions respectively enjoy a significant degree of autonomy, there was until recently no system of elected regional government in the UK. Despite a well-established system of local government, the locus of power was firmly centred on Westminster and Whitehall. While Scotland and Wales were administered by the Scottish and Welsh Offices, they were still subject to a considerable degree of central political control. The 1707 Act of Union between England and Scotland placed sovereign political control of Scottish affairs in Parliament at Westminster.

Although the centralized nature of the British system has been contrasted to the more devolved systems of Germany and Spain, the whole concept of devolution, as we will see later in this chapter, is highly problematic. However, we can define devolution as an arrangement whereby certain legislative and executive powers are granted to its constituent parts by the central government of a unitary state. The central government retains ultimate sovereignty and can in theory revoke any devolved powers. However, political pressures may render such a course of events unlikely (Burrows and Denton, 1980, p. 91). In Germany, the 15 *Länder* have their own devolved parliaments and specified legislative competences (Atkinson and Wilks-Heeg, 1999). In Spain, the system of devolution is more asymmetrical with some regions, in particular the Basque Country, Catalonia and Galicia, enjoying greater power than other regions (Coates, 1998).

However, the election of the new Labour government in 1997 has led to important changes in the dynamic of the regional space in the UK. In particular, the elections for a devolved Scottish Parliament and a devolved Welsh Assembly in May 1999 represent a significant shift in the nature of the British political system. Northern Ireland is moving, if somewhat tortuously, towards a revived system of political devolution whose previous incarnation ended in 1972 when its parliament, Stormont, was prorogued and direct rule from London introduced. In England important changes are taking place with the introduction of regional chambers and regional development agencies. Elected regional assemblies, in some regions at least, remain a possibility for the future. Such developments in territorial politics create a number of potential challenges and opportunities for the British political system. Will devolution, as some of its opponents have argued, lead to the break-up of the UK, creating political confusion? Or will it lead to a stronger UK in which diversity is recognized and policies are shaped to meet the needs of different groups of people? What will be the impact on local government? The purpose of this chapter is to analyse the development of the regional space in the UK and to draw some conclusions, even if they are somewhat tentative, about the impact of recent changes on politics and the policy process in the UK.

Administrative Devolution

While there was a general absence of elected regional government in the UK until the elections for the Scottish Parliament and Welsh Assembly in May 1999 (Northern Ireland, it was noted above, did have a devolved Parliament from 1921 to 1972), there has nonetheless been a well-established middle tier of regional administration in the UK. This includes the Scottish Office, the Welsh Office, the Northern Ireland Office and the Government Offices for the Regions in England (GORs). This has been characterized as a disjointed meso-level (Sharpe, 1993). It broadly devolves a degree of administrative control to the regional level while retaining overall political control at the centre.

The Scottish and Welsh Offices

A broad range of services including agriculture, economic development, education, health, social welfare and tourism have been administered by devolved offices in Scotland and Wales. The Welsh Office, based in Cardiff, was established in 1965. The Scottish Office in Edinburgh has a more established pedigree, dating back to the nineteenth century. Indeed, the distinctiveness of Scotland is reflected in the fact that, even before the setting-up of its own parliament, it had its own separate education and legal system. This, it could be argued, conflicts to some extent with the traditional definition of the UK as a unitary political system.

These offices (or departments) were politically accountable not to an elected regional parliament or assembly, but to the Secretaries of State for Scotland and Wales, both holding seats in the British cabinet. In formal terms at least, they took their cue from Westminster, which set out the broad parameters of policy. In reality the situation was more fluid. The Scottish Office, due in part to its longer history, had a tendency to be both more independent and more pro-active than its Welsh counterpart (Wilson and Game, 1994, p. 20). On the other hand, it has been argued that, particularly during the Thatcher period, Scotland has been used as a guinea pig to test out new policy ideas. The introduction of the poll tax (or community charge) is often cited as the prime example. While not all commentators agree with this thesis (Butler, Adonis and Travers, 1994), such a perception helped fuel the nationalism of the 1980s and 1990s, which was in turn to act as a catalyst for devolution.

The Northern Ireland Office

Since the devolved Northern Ireland Parliament, Stormont, was prorogued in 1972, Northern Ireland has been governed under arrangements described as 'direct rule'. Executive and legislative power was transferred from the Northern Ireland government and Parliament to the Secretary of State for Northern Ireland, and the UK Parliament. The Northern Ireland Office was created as a Department of State. The Northern Ireland Office deals in particular with political and constitutional matters as they affect Northern Ireland, in addition to such matters as policing, security, criminal justice policy and community relations. Within the Office, there are a number of agencies, such as the Northern Ireland Prison Service.

Separate from the Northern Ireland Office are six Northern Ireland Departments, which are responsible for a number of functions in the economic and social fields. They are subject to the political direction of the Secretary of State, who is a member of the United Kingdom Cabinet.

Political Devolution in Scotland

Demands for political devolution for Scotland came strongly on to the political agenda in the 1990s. Opinion polls and elections in Scotland demonstrated consistent support for change to the existing constitutional arrangements, whether it be in the form of devolution (with a Scottish Parliament being granted specified powers) or full independence for Scotland as the Scottish National Party (SNP) has demanded. Such support for change was fuelled in no small part by resentment among a large section of the Scottish electorate which saw Conservative governments returned to office three times in the 1980s and early 1990s, despite a large anti-Conservative majority in Scotland.

However, the debate concerning political devolution in Scotland is not a new one. In 1968, the Conservative Party leader, Edward Heath, delivered the so-called Declaration of Perth at the Scottish Party Conference, in which he spoke of an elected Scottish Assembly. At the time this apparent Conservative support for devolution was contrasted to the Labour Party's position which, under the leadership of Harold Wilson, appeared indifferent to the whole issue (Heald, 1980, p. 123). The mid-1970s, however, saw further developments. Against a background of rising nationalism and increasing electoral support for the SNP, the Labour government of 1974–9 spent a considerable amount of time and energy on the issue. In fact, the catalyst to this was the findings of the Royal Commission on the Constitution (more commonly known as the Kilbrandon Commission), which was set up by the Labour government in 1969 to look into the question of devolution. The ultimate outcome of this whole process was the 1978 Scotland Act. The Act devolved certain defined legislative powers to a directly elected Assembly together with certain defined executive powers to a Scottish executive. However, there were a number of areas in which the centre was reluctant to lessen its grip (Bulpitt 1983, p. 189). For example, the Secretary of State was still to have considerable supervisory powers over the new Assembly. Most crucially, the absence of any devolved powers of taxation was a matter for serious criticism (Heald, 1980). The Labour government's proposals were strongly opposed by the Conservative Party, which argued that they would have dangerous implications for the territorial integrity of the UK. The government also faced significant opposition from its own side with forty-three Labour back-benchers either voting against or abstaining on various aspects of the Scottish Bill. One of the most trenchant critics, the Scottish Labour MP Tam Dalyell, claimed the proposals would 'burden the country with an impractical and expensive additional layer of government' (Dalyell, 1977). Despite such opposition, the bill passed into law.

230

However, before devolution to Scotland could become a reality, one more hurdle had to be jumped, the 1979 referendum. Despite receiving the support of the majority of those who voted, the devolution proposals were lost. Crucially, the proposals had failed to secure the support of 40 per cent of the total electorate. Such a condition had been added as an amendment to the bill by those opposed to devolution.

The whole experience proved to be a chastening one for the Labour government. It was to have an important psychological effect on the Labour Party and to provide it with key lessons – lessons that were to prove invaluable as it grappled with the issue of devolution mark two in the 1990s.

In developing new devolution proposals for Scotland almost two decades later, the Labour Party sought to achieve a broad consensus. This was reached through the workings of the Scottish Constitutional Convention, whose origins date back to 1988. Its membership was wide ranging and encompassed the churches, business interests and trade unions, as well as the political parties. The SNP, however, after contributing to some preparatory work, did not join the Convention's deliberation. Its preferred solution was not political devolution, but a fully independent Scotland in the European Union. The Conservative Party in Scotland, strongly opposed to the aims of the Convention, refused to participate from the outset. The Conservatives argued that creating a separate Parliament for Scotland would lead to the break-up of the UK, thus weakening its component parts. Indeed, this argument was a central theme of John Major's 1992 general election campaign.

The essence of the case for a directly elected Parliament for Scotland, as set out by the Constitutional Convention, is based on the democratic legitimacy of the policy decisions of the central Conservative government and their effect on Scotland. As alluded to above, in three successive general elections, in 1983, 1987 and 1992, the Conservative government was returned to office. In Scotland, however, party politics was somewhat different. For example, in 1992 the Conservatives won only ten of the seventy-two seats in Scotland, winning just 26 per cent of the vote, although this was a marginal improvement on their 1987 performance. As the Convention itself stated, 'Scotland has consistently declared through the ballot box the wish for an approach to public policy which accords more closely with its collective and community traditions' (Scottish Constitutional Convention, 1995, p. 7).

The Labour Party went into the 1997 general election with a clear manifesto commitment to create a Scottish Parliament with devolved legislative powers in a range of policy areas. In contrast to the 1978 Scottish Act, proposals for the Scottish Parliament also included tax-varying powers of plus or minus three pence in the pound. The introduction of these tax-varying powers was a direct response to criticisms of the inadequacies of the 1978 proposals and was potentially significant. However, 1996 saw some important changes to the Labour Party's Scottish policy. While the commitment to a Parliament with tax-varying powers remained, the whole matter was to be put to a referendum of the Scottish people. Under the previous policy, the only requirement for the creation of a Scottish Parliament was the election of a Labour government. Indeed, John Smith, the Labour leader until his sudden death in 1994, had declared devolution to be 'the settled will of the Scottish people' (Scottish Constitutional Convention, 1995, p. 8). The introduction of an additional hurdle for devolution caused considerable ructions within the Scottish Labour Party.

Significantly, the referendum was to consist of two questions: one on the question of creating a Scottish Parliament itself, and one on its tax-varying powers. Why this shift in policy? The answer is to be found in the wider realm of British party politics. The Labour Party was, and still remains, sensitive on the question of income tax. Its defeat in the 1992 general election was in part attributed to its tax-raising policies, modest though they were. A central tenet of New Labour under the leadership of Tony Blair was a move away from what were perceived as the tax and spend policies of Old Labour. The change of tack was due, in no small part, to the jibes of the Secretary of State for Scotland, Michael Forsyth, that such devolved tax powers constituted a 'tartan tax'. By introducing the referendum question on tax, Labour hoped to avoid any hostages to fortune. A yes vote in a referendum on tax-varying powers would give the policy greater legitimacy.

With Labour's landslide victory in May 1997, the Conservatives failed to gain a seat in Scotland, polling less than 18 per cent of the vote. In July 1997, the Labour government set out its proposals for Scotland in a White Paper, 'The Scottish Parliament'. The stage was now set for the referendum in September 1998. With the main political parties, except the Conservatives, calling for a yes vote, the result was a clear majority in favour of both propositions, 74.3 per cent for the creation of a Scottish Parliament, and a smaller majority, 63.5 per cent, in favour of tax-varying powers. The turnout was just over 60 per cent. The Scottish Act passed into law in 1998, setting up a Parliament and an executive.

The Scottish Parliament election, May 1998

The elections for the Scottish Parliament were significant for two reasons. First, they would put in place a Parliament in Scotland for the first time in 300 years. Second, the elections were to be fought on a system of pro-

Table 11.1 Share of the vote in the Scottish Parliament elections, 1999

Party	First vote	Second vote
Labour	38.8	33.8
SNP	28.7	27.0
Conservative	15.6	15.4
Liberal Democrats	14.2	12.5
Other	2.7	11.4

portional representation, departing from the pattern of FPTP for all previous mainland British elections. There would be 129 Members of the Scottish Parliament (MSPs). The electors had two votes, one for seventy-three constituency members based on current Westminster boundaries elected by FPTP, and one for a candidate from a regional party list of additional members, thus giving the element of proportionality. The Labour Party emerged as the largest party, but without a majority – a consequence of proportional representation (see table 11.1 and figure 11.1). The ultimate outcome of the election was a coalition government, not witnessed in mainland Britain since the end of the Second World War, between the Labour Party and the Liberal Democrats, despite the latter only finishing fourth with just 14 per cent of first votes. Donald Dewar of the Labour Party was elected as First Minister.

Does this development presage the start of a 'new', more consensual approach to politics? It is too early at this stage to come to firm conclusions about this. The fact that a coalition government has been established is significant in itself. Yet there remain a number of pitfalls in areas

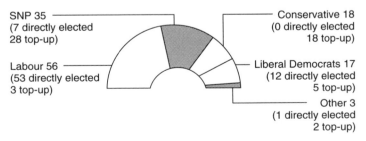

SNP 35
(7 directly elected
28 top-up)

Labour 56
(53 directly elected
3 top-up)

Conservative 18
(0 directly elected
18 top-up)

Liberal Democrats 17
(12 directly elected
5 top-up)

Other 3
(1 directly elected
2 top-up)

Figure 11.1 Distribution of seats in the Scottish Parliament, 1999

such as the Private Finance Initiative and university tuition fees. We will return to these shortly.

Powers and responsibilities of the Scottish Parliament

The Scottish Parliament now has democratic control over many areas that were previously the responsibility of the Scottish Office and other Scottish Departments. All matters that are not specifically reserved have been devolved. The devolved policy areas include:

- health;
- education and training;
- local government, social work and housing;
- economic development and transport (though responsibility for mainline rail services is limited);
- law and home affairs;
- environment;
- agriculture, forestry and fisheries;
- sport and the arts;
- the power to vary income tax by three pence in the pound.

However, in introducing its proposals the government argued that there were many matters that could be handled more effectively on a UK-wide basis. Consequently, a number of important powers have been reserved and are outside the purview of the Scottish Parliament. These include:

- the constitution of the United Kingdom (including matters relating to the civil service, the UK Parliament and electoral law);
- UK foreign policy (including the ability to conclude European Union agreements);
- UK defence and national security;
- the protection of borders (including immigration and nationality, extradition, maritime borders and fishing limits, and responsibility for drugs of misuse);
- fiscal and monetary policy (excepting the three pence in the pound tax-varying power for the Scottish Parliament);
- employment legislation;
- social security policy;
- transport safety and regulation.

There are also a number of shared powers. These relate to previous Acts of Parliament in areas such as transport, science and technology, and mineral exploitation.

Issues arising

A number of issues arise from these various devolved and reserved powers both in relation to the 'new politics' of coalition in Scotland and the general issue of relations between the Scottish Parliament and Westminster.

In relation to domestic politics in Scotland, it should first be noted that the Labour Party has pledged itself not to use the tax-varying powers. There is a potential here for tension within the Labour/Liberal Democrat coalition government, with the Liberal Democrats in the past having called for income tax increases to fund public services. Labour rejects this approach and has instead opted to pump private finance via the PFI, introduced by the previous Conservative government, into public services such as NHS hospitals. The Liberal Democrats have opposed the use of PFIs in this way. Second, there is the question of the Labour Party policy of university tuition fees, which the Liberal Democrats strongly opposed during the election campaign. It proved a major stumbling block during the coalition negotiations and was resolved only after a series of difficult and complex negotiations and the publication of the results of a commission of inquiry (the Cubie Report). A compromise was eventually reached through which university tuition fees will remain, but will be charged as a loan, to be paid back once graduates achieve a specified level of income (the figure of £25,000 suggested in the Cubie Report was subsequently reduced to £10,000 by the Scottish executive). This development has created the first high-profile policy difference between Scotland and the rest of the UK.

There are also a number of potential problems and pitfalls in the relationship between the Scottish Parliament and Westminster. First, relations with the EU remain the responsibility of the United Kingdom Parliament (Scottish Office, 1997, para. 5-1). However, the Scottish Parliament will have an important role in those aspects of EU business that affect devolved areas (para. 5-1). There is clearly a potential here for disputes. In addition, there is the question of how to represent Scottish interests to the EU. The Scottish Parliament and executive have recently established their own office in Brussels, Scotland House. However, the issue of how to represent Scotland in the institutions of the EU, such as the Council of Ministers, is a potential area of disagreement. The 1997 White Paper on Scottish devolution did talk about the ministers of the Scottish executive having a role in relevant Council of Minister meetings. Yet the Scotland Bill did not entrench this as a statutory right. Scottish ministers may form part of British delegations to Europe, but may have to hold to a British policy line. This could well conflict with Scottish priorities in relation to, for example, fishing quotas. Second, exploration and exploitation of oil and gas supplies remain the responsibility of Westminster. This could antagonize the SNP and others who claim that these fields are Scottish. Third, there is the possibility of a different policy regime emerging in Scotland – a logical consequence of devolution. For example, there are current moves to ban fox hunting in Scotland. This move stands every chance of success as a majority of MSPs support such a ban (*Guardian*, 2 September, 1999). Finally, finance is an area of potential conflict. For the past twenty years, Scotland has been funded by a block grant known as the Barnet formula. This is approximately proportionate to its percentage population of the United Kingdom. In 1978 English Labour MPs on the Treasury select committee argued that the formula gave Scotland a 19 per cent higher share than the English average. However, the way the statistics are calculated is highly problematic. An SNP spokesperson, Andrew Wilson, claimed that official Treasury figures showed that between 1979 and 1995 Scotland contributed £27 billion more to London than it received (quoted in the *Herald*, 19 December 1997).

Constitutional implications of devolution

The creation of a Scottish Parliament with devolved legislative powers raises a number of key constitutional questions, and has significant implications for the rest of the UK. In presenting its case for Scottish devolution, the government argued that it is important to have a United Kingdom of which all feel a part. Meeting the aspirations of Scotland and, for that matter, Northern Ireland, Wales and the English regions would enhance and safeguard the Union (Scottish Office, 1997, para. 3-1). However, Scottish devolution has given rise to a number of questions. A particular issue is the so-called West Lothian question. In its current formulation, it asks why Scottish Members of Parliament at Westminster have the right to vote on all matters affecting England, while Members of Parliament with English constituencies will have no say on those matters devolved to the Scottish Parliament. It is argued that there is a clear constitutional imbalance, or asymmetry, with a potential for resentment in England (Bogdanor, 1999, p. 189). Indeed, the situation does at first sight appear somewhat lopsided, but the United Kingdom is entering waters that to a degree are uncharted and there will doubtless be a process of learning. There are, however, some precedents. For example, Northern Ireland Members of Parliament have, by convention, in the past tended not to vote on some matters that are not applicable to Northern Ireland. The same precedent could be followed in the case of Scotland. Indeed, some commentators play down the West Lothian question. For example, Bogdanor notes the difficulty in understanding 'why the question has been thought to constitute a conclusive objection to asymmetrical devolution' (p. 189). He is right to point out that English MPs have shown little interest in domestic Scottish affairs. Scottish legislation has been largely the concern of Scottish MPs. Brown (1998) concedes that the constitutional position as regards Scottish MPs may be somewhat paradoxical, but argues that it is 'nothing like as odd as many other features of the British polity'. He gives the example of the hereditary principle in the House of Lords (p. 217). He does concede that the arrangements will not be very symmetrical or 'very neat', but states that 'symmetry should be left to the mathematicians' (p. 217). Indeed, he is right to argue that symmetry and neatness have little to do with politics. Politics is complex and multi-faceted. The devolution process reflects this.

There are plans to reduce the number of Scottish MPs at Westminster (they currently stand at seventy-two). This will not take place before the next general election. However, any reduction in the number of Scottish MPs presents the Labour Party with a potential electoral dilemma. Only on three occasions, in 1945, in 1966 and most notably in May 1997, has Labour had a majority of seats in England. It has tended to rely on its strong support in Scotland (and Wales for that matter). While Labour continues to enjoy high levels of support in 'middle England', the situation is not so acute. If that support fades, the situation may become entirely different.

In relation to the government's argument that devolution would enhance the Union, we have noted above the position of the previous Conservative leader, John Major, that it would lead to the break-up of the United Kingdom. Various commentators have taken issue with this. Paterson (1998, p. 53), for example, has argued that 'such alarm at the prospect of divergence is misplaced'. With the Scottish Parliament now a reality, the Conservatives under William Hague have now dropped their opposition, arguing that it must be made to work.

Part of the hidden agenda for New Labour's devolution strategy was to undercut support for the SNP, which argues for an independent Scotland within the EU. How effective this will be is a matter for debate. If we look at table 11.1, we can see that the SNP recorded just under 29 per cent of first votes for the Scottish Parliament, up nearly 7 per cent on its general election performance. However, opinion polls tend to put SNP support at a higher level for the Scottish Parliament than for a British general election.

The role of the Secretary of State

There remains an important role for the Secretary of State under the new constitutional arrangements. The office holder will represent Scotland in those matters reserved to the UK Parliament. Moreover, the Secretary of State will be responsible for developing communication between the Scottish Parliament and executive and the UK Parliament and government on matters of mutual interest (Scottish Office, 1997, para. 4-12). He or she will meet with the Scottish executive where appropriate to discuss particular issues, or to discuss relations (para. 4-14).

Scottish devolution and local government

The Scottish Parliament has general responsibility for legislation and policy making concerning local government. It sets the framework within which local government operates and has the power to make changes to the powers, boundaries and functions of local councils. The Scottish executive is responsible for the system of local taxation, the support of local authority current expenditure, and the control and allocation of capital allowances to local councils (Scottish Office, 1997, para. 6-5). Furthermore, it is for the Parliament and the executive to decide on the details of their relationship with local councils (para. 6-6). This opens up interesting possibilities for Scottish local government. The report of the Constitutional Convention, which the Labour Party signed up to, contained a commitment 'to secure and maintain a strong and effective system of local government', which 'will embody the principle of subsidiarity so as to guarantee the important role of local government in service delivery (Scottish Constitutional Convention, 1995, p. 17). The Convention also argued that the Scottish Parliament should embody the principles outlined in the European Charter of Local Self Government, in particular Article 4, which states that 'local authorities shall, within the limits of the law, have full discretion to exercise their initiative with regard to any matter which is not excluded from their competence nor assigned to any other authority' (European Charter of Local Self Government, cited in Scottish Constitutional Convention, 1995, p. 17). If adopted, this would imply a move away from the traditional *ultra vires* model that has governed central–local relations in the UK. Indeed, in the summer of 1999 the McIntosh Commission on Scottish local government recommended that Scottish local authorities should have a power of general competence. Other recommendations include a review of local government finance, the introduction of proportional representation for local elections, and the consideration of the transfer of various quango functions to local authorities (quoted in *Local Government Chronicle*, 16 July 1999).

Thus, a different pattern of central–local relations is a distinct possibility in Scotland. This could have wider implications, acting as a catalyst for change in local government in England and Wales, with local government leaders anxious not to be left behind.

Political Devolution in Wales

Nationalist sentiments, though by no means marginal, did not have the same resonance in Wales as in Scotland. Support for the Welsh Nationalist Party, Plaid Cymru, stood at around 10 per cent at the general election of 1997. Despite this, however, proposals for a degree of political devolution to Wales were put in place. Following on from the recommendations of the Kilbrandon Commission, the 1978 Wales Act laid the basis for a Welsh Assembly. Bulpitt (1983, p. 189) has argued that in constitutional terms 'the Welsh Assembly was meant to be little more that an enlarged county council'. Indeed, the powers of the Welsh Assembly were to be considerably less than those of its Scottish counterpart. In particular, it was to have no devolved primary legislative powers.

Despite the limited powers proposed for the Assembly, there was, as in the case of Scotland, significant opposition to the proposal. The Conservatives, echoing a debate that would resurface two decades later, argued that if devolution proposals for Wales and Scotland were implemented, they would lead to the break-up of the United Kingdom. There was also intense opposition from a number of leading Welsh Labour MPs, most notably the future leader of the Labour Party, Neil Kinnock. This internal opposition had a particularly debilitating impact on the pro-devolution case, the March 1979 referendum producing a four to one vote against devolution. For Barry-Jones and Wilford (1979, p. 6), 'the ultimate victory of the No-Assembly campaigners was attributable in large part to their success in injecting the virus of doubt into the public mind'.

However, the election of the Labour government in May 1997 brought the question of an Assembly for Wales back on to the political agenda. The Labour Party set out its proposals in a 1995 policy paper: *Shaping the Vision: a report on the powers and structure of the Welsh Assembly*. It proposed an elected Assembly for Wales. The rationale behind the proposals was that 'in a modern democracy decisions should be made as close to the people as possible, devolved to nations, regions, and local

Table 11.2 Share of the vote in the Welsh
Assembly elections, 1999

Party	First vote	Second vote
Labour	37.6	35.4
Plaid Cymru	28.4	30.5
Conservative	15.9	16.5
Liberal Democrats	13.4	12.6
Other	4.7	5.1

communities within Britain, in order to give people more control over
their own lives' (Welsh Labour Party, 1995, para. 2).

In July 1997, the government published its White Paper 'A voice for
Wales', outlining its plans for Welsh devolution. As in Scotland, the
proposition was put to a referendum. However, support for devolution
was a great deal less than in Scotland, with the yes vote securing just
over 50 per cent of the vote. The Government of Wales Act subsequently
passed into law in 1998 establishing a National Assembly for Wales. The
Assembly comprises some sixty Assembly Members (AMs). It is headed
by a First Secretary together with a number of Assistant Secretaries who
are responsible for various policy areas such as health and education.
They form the Assembly Executive Committee, which is formally
answerable to the Assembly itself.

Elections for the Welsh Assembly took place in May 1999. Forty seats
were elected by FPTP and the rest distributed proportionally after aggre-
gating each party's vote in the five existing European constituencies in
Wales. Labour emerged as the largest party, but was short of a clear
majority. There was a strong showing from Plaid Cymru (see table 11.2
and figure 11.2). Alan Michael, the Labour leader, was elected as First
Minister, but at the head of a minority administration.

The powers of the Welsh Assembly

Unlike the Scottish Parliament, the Welsh Assembly does not have any
primary legislative or tax-varying powers. However, it does have powers
to develop and implement policy in a range of areas. These include:

- agriculture;
- culture;

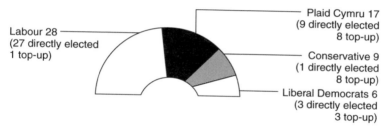

Labour 28
(27 directly elected
1 top-up)

Plaid Cymru 17
(9 directly elected
8 top-up)

Conservative 9
(1 directly elected
8 top-up)

Liberal Democrats 6
(3 directly elected
3 top-up)

Figure 11.2 Distribution of seats in the Welsh Assembly, 1999

- economic development;
- education and training;
- the environment;
- health;
- local government;
- housing;
- social services;
- arts, sport and recreation;
- transport and roads;
- the Welsh language.

Despite its lack of primary legislative powers, the Assembly has the potential to influence policy. It has now assumed the powers of the Secretary of State in relation to secondary legislation, known as statutory instruments. Previously, Secretaries of State for Wales had to deal with some 500 such instruments. The Assembly now has the power, within the framework of the law as set out in various Acts of Parliament, to decide on such matters as the designation of environmentally sensitive areas or the detail of the school curriculum. In addition to its role in secondary legislation, the Assembly has inherited the Secretary of State's power to issue directions and guidance. This could include, for example, laying down requirements for local authority child care provision. The Assembly also performs the role of democratic oversight and strategic co-ordination of the various non-elected public bodies in Wales. There are approximately eighty such bodies with an annual budget of some £2 billion a year.

Issues arising

A number of issues arise from the setting-up of the Assembly. It has been argued that the Labour Party in opposition committed itself to devolution but did not consider the practicalities. While it may be over-stating the case to say that the 'whole structure of Wales's new government was designed from scratch in scarcely two years' (*The Economist*, 3 July 1999), the fact that the previous Conservative government, opposed to devolution, banned civil servants from discussing it militated against effective planning. This has created a number of potential problems and clashes.

First, negotiations with the EU remain the responsibility of Westminster and Whitehall. However, there may be issues, devolved to the Assembly, which British ministers will have to negotiate about in Brussels. What if the policy of the Assembly differs from that of the British government? Second, although previous powers of the Welsh Secretary in relation to health and education have been devolved to the Assembly, responsibility for public health and teacher training will remain at Westminster. Third, there is also the question of policy divergence between Wales and Westminster. Take the question of school funding. In his 2000 budget, the Chancellor of the Exchequer, Gordon Brown, announced details of specific new funds for schools in England and Wales. The original proposal was for such funds to go directly to schools in both England and Wales. However, in Wales the Assembly has agreed that they should be channelled through local authorities. This is a pointer to the new kind of politics that may develop in the post-devolution period. Finally, for some, the process of devolution in Wales is a developing one. Ron Davies, the former Welsh Secretary, has described it as not an event but a process, whereby the powers of the Assembly may develop over time. Some commentators have raised concern over this (see Bradbury, 1998, p. 135). Time alone will tell if such a process will develop.

The role of the Secretary of State

The Secretary of State for Wales retains an important role in the new constitutional arrangements for Wales. First, he or she will continue to make the case for the interests of Wales when policy is being formulated by the UK government. Second, the Secretary of State represents Wales as a member of the Joint Ministerial Committee of the UK government and devolved administrations. Third, he or she has the responsibility for guiding primary legislation that affects Wales through the Westminster Parliament. In addition, the Secretary of State has the power to transfer the Welsh budget from the Treasury to the Assembly. The office holder is obliged to consult with the Assembly on the UK's legislative programme as it affects Wales, and can also participate, but not vote, in Assembly debates.

The role of local government

As mentioned above, the Assembly has taken on those powers in con-
nection with local government that were previously exercised by the Secretary of State for Wales. The Assembly also has the final say on whether
to use reserve powers to cap the budget of particular local authorities.
The Welsh Local Government Association has welcomed the considerable scope for secondary legislation in relation to local government
(*Local Government Chronicle*, 4 December 1998). There is potential for
different modes of working in Welsh local government. Secondary legislation could be used to bolster local government, and the Assembly
is more likely to pursue such a course than the Secretary of State for
Wales. Furthermore, any additional powers granted to Scottish local
government may well fuel demands for more powers for Welsh local
government.

Political Devolution in Northern Ireland

Political devolution in Northern Ireland remains highly controversial and
contingent on a number of factors. As previously mentioned, political
devolution to Northern Ireland effectively ended when its Parliament,
Stormont, was prorogued in 1972. However, the Belfast Agreement of
1997 laid the basis for the return of some self-government to Northern
Ireland (Meehan, 1999). It consists of three strands. Strand one deals
with internal arrangements for Northern Ireland. This includes the
setting-up of an Assembly with a number of executive and legislative
powers currently the responsibility of government departments and non-
departmental public bodies. These powers include agriculture, economic
development, education, environment, health, housing and social services. However, the implementation of the agreement has been fraught
with difficulties. The reasons are complex. This is the product of mis-
trust and political division, a culmination of many years of conflict in
Northern Ireland.

English Regionalism

In contrast to devolution to Scotland, and to a lesser extent Wales, the
question of English regionalism has been subject to relatively little debate
and has been described as the dog that never barked (Harvie, 1991).
More recently, however, the question of English regionalism has enjoyed

more prominence. It has been argued that 'English regional government is the Cinderella of New Labour's constitutional reform plans' (Tomaney, 1999, p. 75). We will return to this shortly. However, the debate around English regionalism is not a new one. The Redcliffe-Maud Commission, which was set up in 1966 to look at the structure of local government in England and Wales, made various proposals for an English regional tier. The Kilbrandon Commission, set up in 1969, although primarily concerned with Scottish and Welsh devolution, did make a number of suggestions on devolution for England. Moreover, despite the lack of an elected regional tier in England, there has still been a regional dimension, which one might characterize as a system of regional governance. For example, from 1964 to 1984 there was a system of regional economic planning by which England was split into eight regions. This system was subsequently abolished by the Thatcher government, to which economic planning was anathema. There has also been a long-established system of regional administration responsible for the work of various central government departments.

The regional dimension was given further impetus in April 1994 with the setting-up of the ten Government Offices for the Regions (GORs). A key role of the GORs was to ensure the effective co-ordination of government departments at the regional level. However, they have been the subject of some criticism. Jacobs, while acknowledging the improved co-ordination between government departments in policy areas such as urban regeneration through the single regeneration budget, claims that their introduction 'represented a missed opportunity because they did not strive to fit EU initiatives into a wider project of regional democratisation' (Jacobs, 1997, p. 47). Their primary focus 'was the achievement of efficiency and rationalisation, not accountable regional government' (Atkinson and Wilks-Heeg, 1999, p. 156).

While attention paid to devolution has understandably focused on the situation in Scotland, Northern Ireland and Wales, there have been some important recent developments in the English regions. Labour's landslide general election victory in May 1997 has put the question of an emerging regional space in England firmly on the political agenda. While in opposition, the Labour Party put forward a number of proposals in relation to the English regions (Labour Party, 1996). These proposals and others are being implemented in government. The central thrust of the proposals is a critique of 'the lack of a democratic accountability within the GORs and their ability to provide the necessary strategic co-ordination for the economic development of the English regions' (Atkinson and Wilks-Heeg, 1999, p. 156). Richard Caborn, a long-standing advocate of a strengthened role for the English regions, was appointed as the Minister for the Regions in May 1997 in the newly

Table 11.3   GDP per capita in the English regions, 1996

	GDP per capita (£)	GDP per capita as % of EU 15 average
North East	15,311	85
North West	16,412	91
Yorkshire and the Humber	16,186	89
East Midlands	17,044	94
West Midlands	16,193	93
Eastern	17,489	97
London	25,422	140
South East	19,334	107
South West	17,122	95

Source: Eurostat, 1998.

created Department of the Environment, Transport and the Regions (DETR). A central element of Caborn's brief as the minister responsible was to formulate a strategy to improve the effectiveness of English regional governance, to help bridge what he describes as the 'economic deficit and democratic deficit' within the English regions (*New Statesman*, 26 June 1998).

What then is the strategy of the Labour government? Richard Caborn has spoken about the poor economic performance of a number of the English regions (Hansard, 14 January 1998). Table 11.3 illustrates this by calculating the regions' GDP per capita as a percentage of the average of the fifteen European Union member states. In only two regions, London and the South East, did the GDP per capita exceed the EU average. In an attempt to tackle this problem, in April 1999 the government set up nine regional development agencies (RDAs) for England. These RDAs will play the key strategic role in economic development. Separate arrangements exist in London where the newly created Greater London Authority (GLA) will have responsibility for economic development. The RDAs have five specific objectives (DETR, 1998f, para. 3.5):

- economic development and social and physical regeneration;
- business support, investment and competitiveness;
- enhancing skills;
- promoting employment;
- sustainable development.

In addition, they have taken over the role of the former regional development organizations (RDOs), which were responsible for inward investment, together with the regional dimension of English Partnerships. They have also take over a number of the functions of the GORs, including the single regeneration budget and the area of European Union structural funds.

The RDAs have a wide remit and will be expected to adopt the best elements of Scottish Enterprise, the Welsh Development Agency and the Northern Ireland Development Agency, 'which have played such an important role in improving the economic prospects of their countries' (DETR, 1998f, para. 3.4). The RDAs will be expected to make things happen. Their role will go beyond the framing and monitoring of a regional strategy. They will be expected 'to pull the levers to ensure that the agreed strategy is implemented' (para. 3.4).

Second, in an attempt to tackle the perceived 'democratic deficit', the regional reforms seek to provide democratic oversight to the current system of regional administration. A two-stage process is involved. In the first stage, so-called regional chambers have been created. They are not directly elected bodies, but instead consist of elected councillors nominated by local authorities, business interests, trade unions, voluntary organizations and other relevant bodies in the region. Elected councillors make up 70 per cent of the membership of the regional chambers. The first regional chambers were set up in the Yorkshire and Humberside and North East regions in early 1998. Regional chambers are now in place in the nine regions outside London. There are separate arrangements in London, where an executive mayor and Greater London Authority have been set up following elections in May 2000. The second stage, envisaged as a longer-term objective, would see the setting-up of directly elected assemblies in those regions where there is demand. We will return to this issue shortly. It should be noted that, unlike the Scottish Parliament, regional assemblies, and for that matter regional chambers, will not have primary legislative or tax-varying powers. The powers of any elected regional assembly will be more akin to those of the Welsh Assembly.

The regional chambers will have responsibility for a number of areas. These include:

- economic development;
- co-ordinating bids for European Union regional funding;
- environmental protection;
- strategic land-use planning;
- transport;

- tourism, arts and leisure;
- scrutiny of health service policy and resource allocation.

To bridge the 'democratic deficit' at the regional level, regional chambers have formal rights of scrutiny and consultation in respect of GORs, the newly created RDAs, regional quangos, next steps agencies and the privatized utilities. As the regional chambers have been in place for only a relatively short period of time, it is difficult to come to any firm conclusions about their effectiveness in bridging the democratic deficit. There are, however, a number of potential problems. The RDAs, it is stated, will be required to take into account the views of regional chambers (DETR, 1998f, para. 1.3). However, this apparent nod to regional accountability is undermined by the fact that the RDAs are non-departmental bodies accountable to ministers (para. 10.1). This would appear to undermine democratic accountability at the regional level, suggesting that there is greater emphasis on bridging the regional 'economic deficit' than the 'democratic deficit'. Furthermore, research has shown that elected local councillors make up less than one-third of each of the RDAs (quoted in *Local Government Chronicle*, 18 December 1998). However, this situation is to some extent counterbalanced by the existence of sub-regional partnerships in which local authorities have combined with the private sector to promote economic development. The RDAs have stated that, rather than deliver policies directly, they will seek to work through these sub-regional partnerships (see chapter 6).

English regionalism and regional identity

Is there public support for creating an elected regional tier? Various commentators cast doubt on this. John and Whitehead (1997, p. 7) argue that the lack of strong English regional identities, together with a long-established, relatively stable system of centralized government, have militated against notions of regionalism in England. Tindale (1995, p. 3) suggests that 'Evidence of strong regional identity is hard to find'. Sharpe develops the point, arguing that the 'overwhelming unitariness of British political culture, especially in the great trunk of England ... works against all forms of territorial politics' (1993, p. 290). Opinion poll evidence from the mid-1990s appears to lend supporting evidence to such views. A 1995 MORI poll found that only 26 per cent of those questioned supported the idea of giving greater powers to the English regions. A large majority, 60 per cent, were opposed. A system three poll in the same year produced similar results. The highest level of support was

42 per cent in the North East region, with the lowest being in the South West.

A number of bodies are actively campaigning for elected regional government. For example, the Campaign for a Northern Assembly has been in existence since 1992. In March 1999, the Campaign for Yorkshire was launched. It seeks a directly elected assembly. The chairman of the campaign, Paul Jagger, argues that Yorkshire is a region 'with a strong sense of its own identity' and deserves a greater say in its own destiny (*Guardian*, 24 May 1999). Moreover, the population of a Yorkshire region, depending on how you measure it, is around 5 million people. This compares with a population in Wales, which now has its own assembly, of 3 million. Whether there is sufficient support for an elected assembly for Yorkshire is debatable. However, a telephone poll conducted by Yorkshire Television in the middle of 1999 recorded 60% support for the idea (*Guardian*, 24 May 1999).

In the south-east, notions of a regional identity are much more problematic. One of the key counties in the region is Kent. As part of a 'EuroRegion' involving Nord Pas de Calais in France and the three Belgian regions, Brussels-Capital, Wallonia and Flanders, its affinity lies not with the South East region but with Europe. As the council leader, Alexander Bruce Lockhart, said in 1997: 'Kent is happy to be seen as a European county. Nobody feels that they are part of a South Eastern region. There is no regional identity, no popular demand' (quoted in the *Independent*, 23 October 1997). Underlying tensions within the South West region were reflected in a debate over where to place the headquarters of its RDA. Exeter was the final choice. The debate reflected tensions between urban areas such as Bristol and the more rural areas in the South West region such as the county of Cornwall. One Cornish bishop's assertion that Bristol is nearer to Manchester than to Truro may lack some geographical accuracy (quoted in *The Economist*, 5 June 1999). However, it is emblematic of divergent identities within the region.

A number of studies have looked at the role of intra-regional networks pursuing structural fund support from the European Union. One case study by Garisse looked at the west of England, more specifically, the counties of Avon (since abolished), Gloucestershire and Wiltshire. She notes that 'The increase in such intra-regional networks and the instances of regional collective action could be interpreted as a nascent form of region building' (Garisse, 1997, p. 1). However, she goes on to argue that such regional networks 'currently remain too narrow in scope to transform themselves from politically instrumental alliances into socially constructed regions' (p. 20). She concludes that such 'networks' do not constitute a sufficient foundation for region building. In a further study, Jacobs looked at what he describes as 'the emergence of complex regional networks and public/private partnerships in European Union regional economic development initiatives in the English West Midlands' (Jacobs, 1997, p. 39). He draws conclusions somewhat similar to Garisse, arguing that while such networks are important, they 'do not signify the establishment of a democratically accountable regional government' (p. 39).

English regionalism and local government

What are the implications of the development of the English regional space for local government? Labour claims, in line with the principle of subsidiarity, that the powers of local government will not be affected, and that the shift in power will be from centre to locality (Labour Party, 1996, p. 11). However, some concern has been expressed at the potential weakening of local government. Commentators such as George Jones argue that regional government will impact on the powers of local government. For him, the most appropriate method for decentralizing power in the UK is to give greater authority to local government (Jones, 1988). Tindale (1995, p. 5) contends that political devolution to the English regions 'might lead to further weakening of local government'. It is interesting to note that the Redcliffe-Maude Commission's proposals in the early 1970s were strongly opposed by the English county councils, concerned with the potential impact on their authority and influence.

It is only possible to draw tentative conclusions about the impact on local government of the first stage of the Labour government's plans for the English regions, the creation of regional chambers and the RDAs. Local government does have a voice in the new regional arrangements. Local councils have significant representation in the regional chambers. Such chambers, it is argued, are not in competition with local councils, but are there to act as their regional voice. However, local councils have already established regional co-ordinating bodies, representing all the regions of England. Will chambers be of additional benefit to local government? Time alone will tell. Local councils also have seats on the RDAs, although, as we noted above, local councils make up only one-third of their representation.

Part of the rationale for Labour's plans for the English regions, as we have seen, is to bring some democratic accountability to the myriad of quangos that operate at the regional level. However, many of these quangos are involved in policy areas that were previously the responsibility of elected local government. These include further and higher education, some aspects of housing management and elements of public transport. The McIntosh Commission on local government in Scotland has recommended that, whenever the role of quangos is reviewed, serious consideration should always be given to transferring their functions to local government. A similar approach could be adopted in England and Wales.

When we move to stage two of Labour's plans for the English regions, namely the creation of directly elected regional assemblies, there are further implications for local government. Before elected regional assemblies come into being, 'a predominantly unitary system of local government' will have to be in place (Labour Party, 1996, p. 12). This means, by implication, the effective end of county councils. This could well lead to a further round of local government reorganization. After the machinations of the Local Government Commission (discussed in chapter 5), it is doubtful if this is what local government needs.

Conclusion

The devolution policy of the Labour government and the creation of the Scottish Parliament and the Welsh Assembly mark a significant shift in the pattern of central–local relations in the UK. We are moving from a unitary system where effective power lay in Westminster and Whitehall towards a system of multi-level governance (Mitchell, 1998, p. 76). Opponents of devolution argue that it will lead to the break-up of the United Kingdom. Its supporters argue that, by recognizing regional differences, the Union will be strengthened. Whatever the relative merits of the two cases, the Scottish Parliament and the Welsh Assembly are now established political institutions. They are not going to go away. The policy switch of the Conservative Party in support of devolution is an explicit recognition of this process.

There are many issues still to be resolved. With plans for a devolved parliament for Northern Ireland now in serious doubt and political devolution to the English regions some way off, arrangements could be said to be rather lopsided. The variation in powers between the Scottish Parliament and the Welsh Assembly adds to this. However, such an asymmetrical system is not unique in Europe. Spain is often held up as a potential model for the UK (Coates, 1998).

There is no doubt that the UK 'faces far-reaching constitutional change with regard to the relationship between its constituent parts' (Coates, 1998, p. 259). There will be challenges and difficulties to overcome. It will be a process of learning. The way is open, however, for new

250

and interesting developments. For example, in Scotland, where powers over local government have been devolved, there is the potential for innovation in areas such as the introduction of proportional representation and moves towards a general competence model of local government. This could have spill-over effects in both England and Wales.

12

Local Government under New Labour

Introduction

From 1979 to 1997, successive Conservative governments sought to restrict the role and powers of local government by various financial restrictions and policy changes. The theme of this book has been that local government was not reduced to a mere agency role, but instead managed to carve out a creative autonomy in a number of areas. It did, nonetheless, see its status considerably reduced. Labour's election victory in May 1997 held up the prospect of change. Under its leader, Tony Blair, Labour laid stress on the need for change, for a new approach to British politics. It is the purpose of this chapter to analyse the initial impact of New Labour on local government and the prospects for local autonomy. While it is inevitably difficult to make a thorough assessment of New Labour's agenda for local government when the proposed legislation is just beginning to enter the statute book, a number of key themes and trends can be identified.

In its May 1997 general election manifesto, the Labour Party grandly spoke of bringing power back to local people by renewing local democracy and revitalizing civic government. All this, one might plausibly assume, suggests a radical departure in central–local relations in the UK and points the way towards a renaissance of local government.

How accurate a view is this? It is certainly true that the rhetoric surrounding the Labour government's policy for local government strikes a more positive tone than that of the Thatcher and Major governments. However, as this chapter will seek to prove, 'there are within the policy a number of uncertainties and contradictions which may undermine New Labour's apparent commitment to revitalise local government' (Atkinson, 1999, p. 133). For example, Tony Blair has talked of creating 'a reborn and energised local government' (quoted in the *Guardian*, 3 November 1997). Yet, writing in a pamphlet for the Institute for Public Policy Research, a left-of-centre think tank, he strikes a less positive tone, stating that central government will be quick to intervene, should local authorities fail to carry out their role effectively (Blair, 1998). The policy of the Labour government to give the Secretary of State for Education the power for the first time to send in inspectors to run LEAs is a good illustration of this. Thus there exists an apparent paradox in New Labour's local government policy, with the language of decentralization and centralization sitting side by side. However, this apparent paradox can to a large degree be explained by the nature of the New Labour project, a central component of which is the drive to modernize (Giddens, 1998). Local government is no exception. Blair has gone on record to state that for local 'councils to get more powers they must modernise and change'. He argues that 'there are too many councils which still do not understand that change is not an option. It is a necessity' (quoted in *Local Government Voice*, July 1998). This modernization strategy consists of a number of components, chief among them democratic renewal, modernizing local decision making and enhancing service quality.

It is important to stress at the outset that New Labour's plans for local government have not developed in a vacuum. New Labour has drawn to a considerable extent on the policy paper produced in 1995 by the Commission for Local Democracy (CLD), entitled *Taking Charge: the rebirth of local democracy*. It has also drawn on the experience of a number of Labour-controlled local councils and has consulted with the local authority organizations on some key aspects of policy. However, the reforms have not been greeted with universal applause; while many of the proposals have been welcomed by the local government community as a whole, sharp criticism has also been voiced by a number of key local Labour figures.

The local government strategy of New Labour will be evaluated under the following themes:

- the legal and constitutional status of local government;
- reforming local government finance;
- restructuring local decision making;
- revitalizing local democracy;
- enhancing service quality.

Constitutional Change and Central–Local Relations

Developing a general competence model?

It is important to understand the constitutional position of local government. Its role and influence are clearly limited. The UK, as we have already noted, has traditionally been described as a unitary political system with effective power residing in the centre at Westminster and Whitehall. This can be contrasted with more decentralized political systems in Europe, such as Germany and Spain. However, the creation of a Scottish Parliament and Welsh Assembly will change the pattern of central–local relations in the UK.

In chapter 1, we noted how local government in the UK operates on the constitutional principle of *ultra vires*. This contrasts with a general competence model of local government. Here local government is broadly free to act in any policy area provided such activity is not restricted by legislation (Chandler, 1996). The CLD, during its deliberations, called for the introduction of such a model for the UK. Were such a proposal to be implemented, it would signal a major change in central–local relations. In opposition, New Labour did appear to signal that it was willing to go some way towards the introduction of the general competence model. In a 1995 policy paper it was critical of existing constitutional arrangements for local government, which it described as too restrictive and leaving little room for innovation (Labour Party, 1995, p. 13). In government, Labour made a number of proposals in a 1998 consultation paper. First, a duty would be placed on local government to promote the social, economic and environmental well-being of the communities it serves. Second, local authorities could be given new powers to meet local priorities (DETR 1998e, chapter 6). These proposals were confirmed in the White Paper issued in July 1998 (DETR, 1998d) and were included in the Local Government Bill published in November 1999.

The introduction of a general competence model would clearly broaden the scope of activity for local councils and limit the 'capacity for central government intervention in local affairs' (Pratchett and Wilson, 1997, p. 19). However, the extent to which New Labour is actually committed to giving new powers to local government is still a matter for debate. Indeed, it concedes that its proposals 'would not extend significantly the scope of what local authorities can do at present' (DETR, 1998e, chapter 6). There have even been signs that New Labour is backtracking on its own limited proposals. For example, the proposal that local councils would have a duty to promote the social, economic, and environmental well-being of the communities they serve was conspicuously absent from a draft Local Government Bill published in 1999. This produced a number of protests from the LGA, after which the government changed tack. Speaking at an LGA seminar in June 1999, the Local Government Minister, Hilary Armstrong, argued that local authorities were 'uniquely placed to provide vision and leadership for the communities they represent'. She then confirmed that the government would 'legislate to give local authorities the powers they need to promote the economic, social, and environmental well being of their areas' (*Local Government Chronicle*, 2 July 1999). Although actual legislation appeared to be some way off, provision for these powers was eventually included in the Local Government Bill issued in late 1999. In addition, the recommendations of the McIntosh Commission for a statutory power of general competence for Scottish local government (see chapter 11) may act as a further spur to English local government.

The British constitution and local government

It has frequently been stated that the institutional underpinnings of local government in the UK are weak (Loughlin, 1997). In the absence of a formal written constitution, the position of local government is not protected within the British political system. As such it can be the subject of fundamental change. The abolition of the Greater London Council and the metropolitan counties in 1986 is a case in point. A scenario such as this would be unimaginable in a political system such as Germany, where local government has certain rights enshrined in the constitution (Peters, 1993).

What is the attitude of New Labour to the constitutional status of local government? Within its first year of office, it signed the European Charter of Local Self-Government. This charter seeks to spell out what should be the relationship between central government and local government. It was drawn up under the auspices of the Council of Europe and as a consequence it has only an advisory status. It does, however, set out some important principles about the position of local government in the wider political system. For example, Article 2 states that 'the powers and responsibilities of local government must be recognised and laid down in the law, or, even better, in the constitution'. Even if we view the charter in symbolic terms, it could still provide a focus for debate on the future of local government and be a catalyst for a strengthened and revitalized local government system.

It has been argued, quite correctly, that local democracy cannot be revived in the absence of change in the wider political institutions of the

UK (Pratchett and Wilson, 1997, p. 25; Loughlin, 1997, p. 33). House of Lords reform could play a key role in this. One possibility would be to give a major representative role to local government in a revised upper house. Potential models can be found on the European continent. In France, for example, the upper house, the Senate, has a strong local government presence. In Germany, the state governments (or *Länder*) are represented in the Bundesrat, the upper house of the federal parliament.

A reformed upper house with strong local government representation would be an important step forward in entrenching and developing the role of local government in British politics. It would provide an important indicator of the extent of the current government's commitment to a revitalized local government.

Local Government Finance

The Labour government elected to office in May 1997 reaffirmed its commitment to keep within the previous Conservative government's spending plans for its first two years in office. In addition to this, the Chancellor, Gordon Brown, has stressed the importance of keeping a tight rein on public expenditure. This is all part of an effort to break with the alleged 'tax and spend' of 'Old Labour' and establish a reputation for financial rectitude. The implications of such a strategy seem to be that strict controls on the spending of local councils are set to continue.

The future of capping

The attitude of New Labour to the question of capping is somewhat ambiguous. Although it made a commitment in its general election manifesto that it would 'abolish crude council tax capping', it went on to state that it would retain 'reserve powers for use in extreme cases'. In announcing the financial settlement for local government for 1998/9, Deputy Prime Minister John Prescott indicated that there would be a slight easing of the capping restrictions. However, the broad capping regime remained in place. In April 1999, Prescott announced that there would be no capping for the financial year 1999/2000. Despite this, the twelve local authorities with the largest increases in both budgets and council tax were called to the DETR and given a warning about their future financial plans (DETR press release, 13 April 1999).

The government produced its proposals for local government finance in the Local Government (Best Value and Capping) Bill towards the end of 1998. Hilary Armstrong argued that the bill would strengthen local financial accountability. She did, however, concede that the government would retain the right to regulate the level of council tax through the mechanism of reserve powers (quoted in the *Local Government Chronicle*, 4 December 1998). These reserve powers are expected to be enshrined in legislation for the financial year 2000/1. These powers will allow ministers to look at budget increases over a number of years, and give them the power to cap those local councils that have had large year-on-year budget increases. The government will also have the power to force councils to reduce their budgets below those of previous years and, where they would produce an excessive rise in council tax, below their SSA. The use of these reserve powers has been criticized by Neil Kinghan, finance director of the LGA, who argues that they erode financial autonomy and hence democratic accountability (Kinghan, 1998). Others have welcomed the ending of the crude system of universal capping, but ask whether its replacement is just as questionable (Ian Brooke, *Local Government Chronicle*, 30 April 1999).

In addition, John Prescott announced that for 1999/2000, the government would claw back, on a pro rata basis, council tax benefit (paid to those on low incomes) from those councils deemed to have imposed excessive council tax rises, defined as an increase of more than $4\frac{1}{2}$ per cent. The policy was strongly criticized by Sir Jeremy Beecham, chair of the LGA, who argued that it would not keep council tax levels down, but would make the situation worse (quoted in *Local Government Chronicle*, 4 December 1998).

The business rate (NNDR)

As we noted in chapter 4, control of business rates was taken out of local authority control in 1990 and replaced by the NNDR. In opposition, the Labour Party committed itself to returning the business rate to local control (Labour Party, 1995, p. 19). This suggested a move away from the centralizing tendencies of 1979 onwards, offering the prospect of a greater level of local financial autonomy. However, the government has made it clear that, in the medium term at least, the wholesale reform of local finance is off the agenda. Mark Lambith, director of finance at the DETR, told the environment select committee inquiry into local government finance in late 1998 that he did not believe allowing councils to raise more of their own funds would strengthen local autonomy (quoted in *Local Government Chronicle*, 13 November 1998). The government in its formal response to the select committee rejected a shift in the balance of funding (DETR, 1999d, Introduction, para. 12). This is at odds with one of the key recommendations of the Layfield Committee, which we discussed in chapter 4. It was also contradicted by the environment select committee inquiry, which rejected 'the notion that there is no link between the proportion of finance raised locally and democratic accountability/local autonomy' (DETR Select Committee, 1999, Introduction, para. 95). It seemed to mark a radical departure from previous government thinking. In February of the same year, Hilary Armstrong stated that local authorities 'must raise more of their own finance and be less dependent on central government'. Echoing the sentiments of Layfield, she went on to argue that this was the 'way to real subsidiarity and genuine local autonomy' (*Local Government Chronicle*, 13 November 1998). However, the government has now ruled out the full return of the business rate to local control for the foreseeable future. This again reflects the uncertainties of New Labour towards local government reform. The government's White Paper (DETR, 1998d) did put forward the idea that local councils could raise a supplementary rate of 1 per cent of national business rates, rising to a maximum of 5 per cent over time. The proposals are heavily dependent on consultation with local business. However, the proposal for the supplementary business rate was not included in the bill on local government finance.

Local authorities and financial freedom

Hilary Armstrong has now made it clear that the debate on greater local financial autonomy is effectively closed (*Local Government Chronicle*, 16 July 1999). While this may be the case in terms of public finance, there is still the potential for local authorities to make more use of the financial powers they have. This could involve the development of new forms of joint venture with private business (Kinghan, 1998). We saw in chapter 6 how a number of innovative local authorities have actively sought and developed partnerships with the private sector. This trend is set to continue under the current Labour government. The government has floated the idea that local councils might put their spending plans to referenda of local people (DETR, 1998c). If implemented, it would mark a radical departure with past practice. Indeed, a similar idea was considered by the Thatcher government in the early 1980s. It was, however, rejected. In an interesting pilot, people in a referendum in Milton Keynes on 23 February 1999 voted to approve a council tax increase of some 10 per cent, more than twice the level suggested by central government. The ballot, undertaken by the Electoral Reform Society, produced a turnout of some 45 per cent (*Guardian*, 24 February 1999). This is significantly higher than turnout for recent local elections (see chapter 7). This might suggest that, when there are real issues to decide, people will turn out to vote. This may provide us with some lessons in that a strengthened local government with more effective powers might encourage higher voter turnout.

On a general level, the whole issue of local government finance reveals that, despite some of the rhetoric, New Labour is determined to keep a firm hold on local authority expenditure. There are two principal reasons for this. First, the government is, as we have already noted, very keen to display fiscal rectitude. Second, and perhaps this is the key point, it is sceptical of the capacity of certain sections of local government to behave responsibly. As an illustration of this, the Education Secretary, David Blunkett, published in June 1999 a list of fifty-seven local education authorities which, in his opinion, were failing to pass increases in national schools spending on to local schools (*Guardian*, 24 June 1999). Mr Blunkett stated that he could not rule out removing local councils' spending powers over education budgets (*Independent*, 18 June 1999). Such a move would, if implemented, mark a radical shift in central–local relations.

Reforming Local Decision Making

A key part of the Labour government's modernization strategy for reforming local government is the creation of new political structures, which it argues 'are fundamental to the modernisation process' (DETR, 1998d, para. 3.1). The aim is to introduce 'clearer, more transparent and accountable leadership in local government' (Pratchett, 1999, p. 5). Decision making at the local level has traditionally been made through a series of council committees, comprised of elected councillors, which mirror particular service areas. Unlike central government, there has been no formal separate executive. The Labour government's proposals plan to change this situation. The government argues that traditional committee structures 'lead to inefficient and opaque decision making' (DETR, 1998d, para. 3.4). What is needed are 'new structures which create a clear and well known focus for local leadership' (para. 3.12). It proposes a separation of the executive and backbench roles of local councillors. The executive would take the lead role in policy making with backbench councillors performing a scrutinizing role. This represents a major change in political decision making at the local level (Leach, 1999, p. 77). There is a compulsion element to the proposals, as all local councils in England and Wales will be required to reform their decision-making structures. Three models have been put forward:

- A directly elected executive mayor with a cabinet. The mayor will be directly elected by local people and will appoint a cabinet from among the councillors.
- A cabinet with a leader. The leader will be elected by the council and the cabinet will be made up of councillors either appointed by the leader or elected by the council.
- A directly elected mayor with a council manager. The mayor will be elected by local people, with a full-time manager appointed by the council.

The first and third models share the principle of a directly elected mayor with executive powers. They are significantly different to the current mayoral system in local councils, which is largely ceremonial. The whole issue of directly elected mayors has proved highly controversial. The CLD recommended that each local authority should have a directly elected mayor and a separately elected assembly (Commission for Local Democracy, 1995, para. 4.3).

Supporters of directly elected mayors argue that they will enhance local democracy. For the CLD, they would be 'highly visible and thus highly accountable' (para. 4.15). It is argued that 'the mayor would be a more conspicuous and active executive of the council who would be associated with specific policies and who would be better placed to provide direct leadership to achieve these policies' (Pratchett and Wilson, 1997, p. 20). New York and Barcelona, both with executive mayors, are just two of the cities held up as examples.

Plans have already been put in place for a Greater London Authority (GLA) with a directly elected mayor for London together with a separately elected assembly. We will return to this shortly. There was speculation that the government would legislate to make the introduction of elected mayors compulsory. Tony Blair is known to be a keen supporter of elected mayors. However, this has not happened. Controversially, the New Local Government Network has called for elected mayors to be forced on major cities. This met with a strong response from the LGA (quoted in *Local Government Chronicle*, 18 June 1999). In a consultation document, the government has outlined the possibility of pilot projects for directly elected mayors in other major cities (DETR, 1998e, ch. 5). However, as things stand, London is the only city due to have a directly elected mayor. This is not to rule out further developments. Newcastle City Council is, for example, planning a referendum on reforming its political structures, which will include the option of a directly elected mayor. The Liverpool Democracy Commission, a body made up of representatives from the local authority, local universities and the private sector, has undertaken extensive research on options for democratic renewal in the city. In 1999 the Commission issued a report on its findings recommending, among other things, the establishment of a directly elected mayor for the city (Liverpool Democracy Commission, 1999). However, despite unambiguous support from the Liberal Democrat leader of the council, the report has met with opposition from the majority of local councillors and, at the time of writing, its status remains uncertain.

Such opposition is not confined to Liverpool. The whole issue of directly elected mayors is also highly controversial within local government circles more generally. For example, a survey for the BBC radio programme *Today* found that 75 per cent of local councils did not support such an idea (quoted in *Local Government Chronicle*, 2 July 1999). In Scotland, the McIntosh Commission on local government has ruled out for the present the introduction of directly elected mayors 'because of the complete lack of support for the idea' (quoted in *Local Government Chronicle*, 25 June 1999). Several Labour local government leaders have also expressed reservations. John Harman, the highly respected former leader of Kirklees Council, has warned that the concept of directly elected mayors 'runs against the role and purpose of the elected local representative' (quoted in *New Statesman*, 6 December 1996). On the other hand, Albert Bore, Labour leader of Birmingham City Council, has come out in favour of elected mayors (quoted in *Local Government Chronicle*, 16 July 1999).

Councils that have so far opted to reform their political structures have generally gone for some variant of the second model: that is, a cabinet with a leader. A survey by the LGA found that 81 per cent of local authorities had recently reviewed, or had in progress, plans to consider the creation of a separate executive (Local Government Association, 1999). The London borough of Croydon has, for example, announced plans to move towards a cabinet system. In Cheshire, the county council has agreed in principle to move towards a cabinet system as well. Gwynedd Council in Wales, controlled by Plaid Cymru, has also announced plans to set up a cabinet-style administration. There are, however, legal problems. Cabinet systems in which members of the executive have individual freedom to act, as well as take decisions together with others, are not available under current legislation (Local Government Association, 1998). The introduction of local cabinet government will also present a significant cultural challenge for many local councils (Leach, 1999, p. 92). Whether they can succeed in meeting the challenge, only time will tell.

Renewing Local Democracy

New Labour, in developing its local government strategy, has spoken in grand terms of revitalizing civic government and renewing local democracy (DETR, 1998e, chapter 1). Reforming the local decision-making process is a part of this process. There are, however, a number of other components.

Participation and consultation

Participation and consultation are key expressed aims of the Labour government. It has said that it wishes to see them embedded in the culture of all local authorities (DETR, 1998d, para. 4.6). Specifically, local authorities are, for example, now legally obliged to consult local groups in respect of the Best Value initiative. More generally, the government has put forward a number of proposals as part of its participation strategy. These build on existing developments (see chapter 8) and include citizen juries, community forums open to all interested local organizations and individuals, advisory groups and user panels. It has even gone so far as to produce guidance papers for officers and members on how to encourage participation (DETR, 1998b). Some local authorities already encourage such participation. A survey of all local authorities in England in 1996, for example, found that over 50 per cent of those that responded had consultative fora. Twenty-nine per cent had customer panels. However, only 2 per cent had citizen juries (Sweeting and Cope, 1997, p. 5).

The government is also keen that local authorities should use referenda where appropriate (DETR, 1998d, para. 4.8). We have already seen how this might apply when local councils set their council tax and budgets. It has also suggested that local people could decide in a local referendum to have a directly elected mayor if either 5 per cent of the local electorate request a referendum or the local council proposes one. It has said it will legislate on this when parliamentary time allows (DETR, 1999a, chapter 2).

In putting forward its proposals, the Labour government claims it is not being prescriptive. It argues that arrangements should fit with local circumstances. Indeed, there is merit in local initiatives. We have already seen in chapter 1 how local government can be used as a testing ground to trial new ideas. These can then be shared with other local authorities. In June 1997, the LGA and the LGMB launched the Democracy Network, the purpose of which is to share best practice and encourage innovations in local democracy.

Encouraging citizen involvement appears, at first sight, to be an important first step in achieving New Labour's goal of renewing local democracy. However, various studies have highlighted the problems inherent in encouraging participation. Indeed, there is a great deal of evidence to suggest that 'local people are unwilling and/or unable to participate in the making of decisions affecting them' (Sweeting and Cope, 1997). More specifically, there is a tendency for those best served by them to come from well-organized and existing groups (Burns, Hambleton and Hoggett, 1994; Mackintosh and Wainwright, 1987). The less well organized, a key target where there have been participation strategies at the local level, have done less well.

Reforming the way we vote

A number of proposals have been made in relation to the way we vote in local elections (DETR, 1998d, para. 4.20). New Labour talks of the need to make local councils more accountable. To this end, it proposes to introduce annual elections for all local councils. Its proposals for voting reform are also driven by concerns over the low turnout at local elections, which we discussed in chapter 7. Tony Blair has stated that we cannot 'be satisfied with turnout levels of less than 30 per cent. We must improve people's participation. We must reconnect people with power, at the local level' (*Local Government Voice*, July 1998). A number of possible changes have been put forward. These include:

- electronic voting;
- changing the day or time of voting;
- mobile polling stations;
- voting in places such as local supermarkets;
- universal postal voting.

The government has been discussing these ideas with local government representatives. They could be tested out in local pilot projects. For example, in the 1998 London borough elections, voters in the borough of Croydon cast their vote at their local Tesco supermarket! The government has stressed that an expanding role for local government is dependent on the creation of a functioning local democracy. Increasing voter turnout is part of this process. With the exception of the newly created Greater London Authority (see below) it is not proposing the introduction of proportional representation for local elections in England and Wales. This was something that was strongly advocated by the CLD. The introduction of proportional representation for local elections in Scotland is, as we discussed in chapter 11, under active consideration.

The Greater London Authority (GLA)

The abolition of the GLC in 1986 left London without a system of city-wide elected local government, a situation unique amongst capital cities in Western Europe. The creation of the new GLA, which came into being in May 2000, redresses this imbalance. However, the government has made it clear that its plans for London do not constitute a GLC mark two. New Labour is anxious to distance itself from the 'loony left' image associated with the GLC and a number of other Labour-controlled local authorities in the 1980s (Lansley, Goss and Wolmar, 1989). The old GLC was a large bureaucratic organization with some 25,000 staff. The GLA will have a core staff of around 200. It will be a strategic authority and will have responsibility for a number of functions. These are: transport, planning, economic development, environment, the Metropolitan Police, fire and emergency planning, culture, media and sport, and finally health.

The GLA will, as the government's own White Paper states, be a unique institution in British local politics with an explicit separation of powers between an executive, in the shape of a directly elected mayor, and an assembly (DETR, 1998a, para. 3.10). The mayor will be the first directly elected political executive in the UK. The assembly will be elected using a variant of proportional representation. This will be the first time that local elections on the British mainland have been carried out in this way.

The mayor is assigned five key roles. These are:

- to act as a voice for London;
- to propose the budget;
- to make key appointments;
- to devise strategies and action plans;
- to co-ordinate activity to implement action plans.

The whole concept of directly elected mayors has, as we noted above, not been free from controversy. There has been concern about the lack of accountability of such an office and a drift towards a presidential style of politics (Ken Livingstone MP, quoted in the *Guardian*, 24 October 1997). In a London context, it has been argued by some commentators that no effective limits have been set on the power of the mayor. The assembly is, in effect, powerless (Jones and Stewart, 1999). How true is this? The White Paper states that the assembly is the forum where the mayor's proposals are critically examined. Amendments to these proposals can be made if a majority can be secured in the assembly (DETR, 1998a, para. 3.18). Yet while it is made quite clear that the role of the assembly is to call the mayor to account, 'at the end of the day the key role of the mayor will be to propose strategies and deliver them' (para. 3.19).

The office of mayor would appear to have the potential for great influence and power. He or she will, after all, represent a population of some 6 million people and have responsibility for a budget of some £3 billion. However, the mayor's room for manoeuvre is limited by the fact that 90 per cent of this budget will be provided and controlled by central government. The mayor's position is further weakened by the lack of any significant direct tax-raising powers for the new GLA. However, the introduction of congestion charging and parking levies would produce some extra revenue.

Service Delivery and Quality

The introduction of Best Value

Improving service delivery and quality is a key element in New Labour's local government strategy. It is introducing a new requirement for local authorities to secure what it calls 'best value' for local people. This will be monitored by the Audit Commission.

To start up this system, Hilary Armstrong announced in December 1997 the setting-up of thirty-seven Best Value pilot projects, thirty-five of which are local authorities. The Local Government Act incorporating Best Value passed into law in August 1999. The Best Value duty comes into effect in April 2000: local councils have a duty to secure the best value in the provision of services. National performance indicators for efficiency, cost and quality will be introduced. (DETR, 1998d, summary, para. 18). Local authorities will be required over a five-year period to undertake performance reviews of all their services. A key aspect of the process is consultation with local taxpayers, service users and the wider business community on how services can be improved (para. 19). It has been argued that Best Value 'provides a welcome opportunity to apply quality initiatives to all aspects of the local authority's work and to make the important links with democratic accountability and community leadership' (Ley and Seghal, 1998). Hilary Armstrong has stated that Best Value is more important than strategic reforms such as the introduction of directly elected mayors (quoted in *Local Government Chronicle*, 8 August 1999). However, the policy is currently still in its infancy (Boyne, 1999).

Nonetheless, many local authorities are making plans for Best Value. Barnsley Metropolitan Borough Council, for example, has produced a detailed timetable on the introduction of the Best Value regime (Best

Value for Barnsley, 1998). However, all in the garden is not rosy. In the summer of 1999, for example, Brighton and Hove Council and Lewes District Council pulled out of a high-profile pilot review of revenues and benefit services after doubts were expressed about the legal status of any enterprise established to run the service (*Local Government Chronicle*, 2 July 1999). In addition, a survey of 249 local authorities in England and Wales in late 1998, carried out by the LGA, LGMB and Warwick Business School, found that 10 per cent were 'not all well prepared'. The survey also found that only 50 per cent of chief officers and 20 per cent of senior councillors fully understood Best Value. Front-line staff had little idea (*Local Government Chronicle*, 13 November 1998).

The Best Value approach also sees the abolition of the existing system of CCT. As we discussed in chapter 6, CCT was part of the new-right agenda of the Thatcher and Major governments to introduce market forces into the delivery of local services. This was a radical departure in local government practice. Supporters of this policy claimed the result was more effective and efficient services. Opponents, including the Labour Party, claimed the policy was too restrictive and often led to falling standards. However, while Best Value moves away from the compulsion aspect of CCT, there will still be an important role for the private sector in the provision of local services. Indeed, the government has made it clear that competition in the provision of services remains a key element within the Best Value approach (DETR circular, 16/97).

The move away from the compulsion aspect of CCT would appear on first inspection to signal a move away from the centralization of the Thatcher and Major governments and a renewal of local democracy. The rhetoric of the Labour government towards local government is indeed more positive than previous Conservative governments. However, it has also made it clear that it is willing to intervene directly in local government should the need arise. Speaking at the Labour Party's local government conference in February 1998, Tony Blair emphasized that the Best Value strategy would not be 'a soft option'. He went on to argue that 'If authorities cannot or will not take the load, we will have powers to intervene.' The outcome may well be greater restrictions on local government. Once again the language of decentralization and centralization sit side by side.

Beacon Councils

The Beacon Council scheme is another important aspect of the drive for quality in local government services. The government states that the scheme is 'at the centre of their modernization agenda'. It goes on to argue that the scheme 'will allow the pace of change to be set by the best in local government' (DETR, 1999b, foreword). In the first phase of the scheme, local authorities that seek Beacon Council status 'put themselves forward as examples of best practice and will be scrutinised by other councils. They have a job to do sharing their experiences with others in a practical, open, and informative way' (para. 3.1). By the middle of 1999, more than half the local authorities in England and Wales had applied for Beacon Council status in a range of service areas, including community safety, education, housing and social services. Only forty, however, will be chosen. The government has stated that the second phase of the scheme may include 'new freedoms and flexibilities' for Beacon Councils (para. 4). This might include the setting of business rates. However, no timetable has been set for the second phase.

The private sector and service provision

We noted in chapter 6 the increasing role of the private sector in local government services from the early 1980s. This trend has continued under the current Labour government: for example, in the field of education, described by Tony Blair as the number one priority for his government. Business is set to play a key role in the so-called education action zones, aimed at deprived rural and urban areas. The scheme was launched at the North of England Education Conference in January 1998 by Michael Barber, the government's special adviser on education. Although involving local authorities, the action zones also have representation from parents, schools, community organizations and local business. In his speech Professor Barber sang the praises of the private sector, arguing that 'Successful companies are uniquely able to manage change and innovation.' By the beginning of 2000, there were some seventy-five education action zones.

The role of the private sector in the education action zones has met with a negative reaction from a number of Labour local government leaders. For example, the Labour chair of the LGA argued in a speech to the North of England Education Conference in January 1998 that the policy 'could lead to the destruction of local democracy'. While this may be somewhat of an overstatement, the role played by business in the education action zones might be said to jar somewhat with the commitment to restore local democracy.

The emphasis on the role of business extends to other areas in education. In a speech to the North of England Education Conference in January 1999, the Education Secretary, David Blunkett, announced that the government was to draw up plans for an improved list of businesses and not-for-profit organizations that could run local education services. Implying irritation with the failure of some local education authorities, he stated that failure would be rooted out. In June 1999, the policy took a step forward when a contract was granted to Nord Anglia, a profit-making educational company, to run parts of the education service in the London borough of Hackney. Estelle Morris, the schools standards minister, welcomed the move. She stated that she expected 'the company to adopt new and more rigorous approaches to improvement. I am confident this marks the beginning of a new era' (quoted in *Local Government Chronicle*, 25 June 1999). Similarly, in May 1999, the London borough of Islington was warned that the private sector would be brought in if standards were not improved (*Guardian*, 17 May 1999).

This stress on the role of the private sector in the delivery of local ser-vices marks a continuation, one might even argue an intensification, of the policy of previous Conservative governments. It reflects, in part, an emerging consensus among the major political parties about the impor-tant role to be played by the private sector in the area of public policy. However, it is also symptomatic of the impatience of New Labour with the failure of certain sections of local government to carry forward its modernization agenda.

Conclusion

Some commentators have referred to 'the deeply rooted cultural change which has developed since the early 1980s in local government', arguing that there is no going back to the old patterns of behaviour (Game and Leach, 1996, p. 6). This is reflected in the policy of the current Labour government towards local government. While the overall relationship between local government and central government may be more positive in tone than it was in the 1980s, local government is by no means guaranteed more autonomy under New Labour. A number of the local government policies of previous Conservative governments are set to continue, albeit in a modified form. Financial restrictions remain firmly in place though universal capping has gone. The role of the private sector is set to continue and, in some areas, to expand. However, CCT is to be superseded by the Best Value framework.

The government has made it clear that greater powers for local government are linked to it embracing the modernization agenda. Hence the drive towards new management structures and the development of strategies to encourage the participation of local people in local decision making. But, as we have noted, there are evident tensions running through the government's approach to local government reform. Many of the reforms do hint at a wish to allow local authorities greater autonomy and increased freedom to act. At the same time, however, there is also a strong element of central compulsion, as well as an evident desire to retain central controls, which runs through the entire reform agenda. Much the same tension has been noted in relation to the government's devolution plans and there are signs that it may become the Achilles' heel of New Labour.

It is important to remember, however, that central government does not hold all the cards. New Labour needs the co-operation of local government if it is to deliver its policy pledges in key areas such as reducing class sizes. This reality again reflects the main assumptions of the power-dependency model of central–local relations (see chapter 2). Herein lies an opportunity for local government as well as a number of pitfalls. For instance, during 1999 the LGA launched an initiative called Local Challenge, the intention of which is to foster greater co-operation between central and local government in key policy areas, such as education. Yet, the way in which the language of centralization and decentralization sit side by side in New Labour's attitude to local government reflects a nagging distrust of local government or, more particularly, certain sections of it. There is no doubt 'a clear potential for a renaissance of local government. Realising it will be another matter' (Atkinson, 1999, p. 146).

Conclusion

In this book we have argued that local government, despite its limitations, has played and continues to play a key role in British politics and public policy. It has an important part to play in encouraging participation in the political process, despite the low turnout in recent local elections. In addition, a vibrant local democracy is an essential element in the diffusion of political power in the UK. Local circumstances often require local solutions. Local government, because of its position on the ground, often has the potential to respond in a more effective way than a far away central government.

Indeed, modern local government developed in the nineteenth and twentieth centuries precisely because it was recognized that it had a key role to play in areas such as public health, housing and education. The creation of the welfare state in the period after the Second World War brought about the biggest growth in the role of local government. For three decades, local government continued to expand. There was a broad consensus among all major British political parties about the value of local government. Although cracks had started to appear in this consensus by the mid-1970s, it was the election of the Conservatives in 1979 that posed the biggest threat to local government. They came to power arguing that a bloated public sector was damaging to the British economy and was crowding out the private sector. The state was to be rolled back. Local government was to feel the full force of the new government's strategy.

What has been the impact on the world of local government? Writing in 1982, Alexander gloomily concluded that 'unless conscious efforts are taken to revive it, the end of local government may be in sight' (Alexander, 1982, p. 2). Indeed, local government faced a mighty onslaught from the centre as successive Conservative governments from 1979 to 1997 imposed a series of increasingly restrictive financial and other policy measures. It would clearly be wrong to deny that local government saw its room for manoeuvre curtailed during these eighteen years. However, Alexander's worst fears have not been realized. Local government is still very much alive and well. It has stoutly defended its role and position, and has carved out a creative autonomy in a number of policy areas. Despite the restrictions imposed upon it, local government remains a major service provider.

The introduction of capping and the ending of the local business rate marked an increasingly centralizing trend in central–local relations in the UK. However, central government did not have matters all its own way. We have seen how a number of local authorities used creative mechanisms in an attempt to thwart the efforts of central government to restrict local authority expenditure. Indeed, somewhat ironically, some of these mechanisms, such as the selling of assets to the private sector and then leasing them back, could be viewed as the forerunners of the PFI. The poll tax, designed to curb local government, proved to be an expensive policy disaster for central government, both financially and politically. Opposed by the overwhelming majority of those in local government, the poll tax neatly illustrates the limits of central government power. It can impose policies on local councils, but it cannot guarantee their success.

We have also seen fundamental changes to the local space. The move to the enabling authority and the increasing involvement of a number of other agencies, both voluntary and private sector, means that local authorities no longer enjoy a monopoly in the delivery of local service. We have moved from a world of local government to one of local governance. This might seem to suggest a diminished role for local government. However, as we have argued, local governance implies a complex network of actors. As various strands of neo-pluralist theory suggest, the relationships between such actors are based on mutual dependencies. With its strategic position and professional knowledge base, local government has the potential to develop new initiatives and expand. It has continued to be a source of policy development from the bottom up. The increasing development of local public/private sector partnerships, which are an important feature of the Labour government's local government strategy, are a good example of this process. They also reflect the tendency, pointed to by regime theorists, for local actors across the public and private sectors to seek to co-operate in order to assemble the capacity to intervene more effectively in local affairs.

Local Agenda 21, although it started life as a global initiative, is another example of local authorities responding to the challenge of new opportunities. In addition, a number of local authorities have taken advantage of the possibilities open to them from the EU. In a climate of domestic financial constraints, they have used EU funds to develop large-scale regeneration schemes. The environment and regeneration are two of the policy areas where the creative autonomy of local government is at its strongest. Though they involve relatively small proportions of local government staff and resources, they are areas that have grown, and will continue to grow, in importance. While this growth is due in part to the public policy priority given to these areas, it is also a reflection of the 'hollowing out' of the state and of the emergence of multi-level governance, which we have identified in this book as key tendencies. In this sense, creative autonomy is a natural outcome of a broader redefinition of the role of local government and of the functions that it performs.

In part, this redefinition will mean a continued shift away from the model of local authorities as sole providers of local public services – a trend that is already well under way. Thus, the introduction of compulsory competitive tendering (CCT) has clearly resulted in an increase in the role of the private sector in the delivery of local services. However, the success of the private sector in winning contracts has, as we saw in chapter 6, been limited. Many local authorities have responded to the challenge of CCT and, in competitive bidding, have retained services in-house. CCT, initially viewed as a threat to local government, has presented it with new challenges and opportunities. Local authorities, many for the first time, have had to question their ways of working and the effectiveness of the services they deliver. This has helped improve service quality. The move to Best Value will further underline these principles and is likely foster an increased pluralism of local service provision.

Yet, there is still a long way to go until we approach anything like the 'pure' enabling authority advocated by Nicholas Ridley. Local government still remains a major player in the delivery of a variety of local services. In the field of social services, local authorities still play an important strategic role, despite the increasing involvement of a variety of other agencies. Indeed, the 1990 Community Care Act has actually increased the role of local government in this area. Other areas are simply not amenable to private provision. It has been suggested, for instance, that 'the routine of social work is not a task that can easily be transferred to the private sector' (Chandler, 1996, p. 48). Local authorities, despite the numerous legislative changes of the 1980s and 1990s, still have a major role in the area of public housing, albeit in partnership with other agencies. In a variety of other service areas, ranging from refuse collection, street cleaning and highway maintenance through to recreation and leisure services, local councils retain significant responsibilities. The pattern of service delivery may have changed, but local government remains a key player.

However, while education is still by a long margin the largest local authority service, the legislative changes of the 1980s and 1990s have 'profoundly altered the role of local councils' (Wilson and Game, 1998, p. 91). They have lost control of the former polytechnics, colleges of higher education and further education colleges. The introduction of the national curriculum has also reduced local discretion. Local management of schools has eroded the role of the local authority. Nonetheless, while these changes suggest a reduced role for local authorities in the field of education, they still have an important role to play. The Macpherson Report, which inquired into the circumstances of the murder of the south London teenager Stephen Lawrence, has recommended that local education authorities should be involved in promoting cultural diversity. This points to an expanding role for local government. As we noted in chapter 12, the Labour government has laid great stress on the importance of improving standards in education. It cannot, however, achieve this on its own. It needs, as it has indeed recognized, the support of local education authorities, in the delivery of its education policy. Again, this is suggestive of the power-dependency relationship between local and central government posited by neo-pluralist theorists of local government such as Rhodes (1981; 1988; 1997). Local authorities possess a number of valuable resources, such as professional skills, which are crucial to the achievement of central government objectives. In general terms, while central government can seek to impose its will on local government, it cannot control its day-to-day operations. Local professional autonomy still plays an important role.

Local government, for many years in the political backwaters, became a key focus of British politics in the 1980s and 1990s. That it has survived is a product both of its durability and of its important role in the shaping of public policy. During the last two decades, local government has been subject to great change, but many local authorities have been successful in repositioning themselves in the face of this change and have found a variety of ways of pursuing creative autonomy. In this book we have identified a number of areas where this has taken place and we would suggest that more research is needed to identify the full extent of creative autonomy, in both emerging and traditional policy fields. We have suggested that, contrary to many accounts, local government has maintained a key role as a major provider of public services. Whether local authorities prove able to translate the lessons of creative autonomy into policy areas such as education, housing and social services will be an important test of both our thesis and their resolve.

Conclusion

Labour's general election victory in 1997 has not put an end to the process of change at the local level. In many ways, it has been accelerated. While central–local relations are clearly less heated than under the previous Conservative governments, local government still faces a number of challenges. The current Labour government has made it clear that greater autonomy for local government is dependent on the latter's ability to modernize. At the same time, devolution in the UK presents local government with new opportunities. If our thesis is correct, and past experience and evidence is a guide, local government will respond in a positive and creative way to the challenges that lie ahead.

Notes

Chapter 2   Theories of Local Government and Local Governance

1   These would primarily include the following: elite theory (Hunter, 1953), pluralism (Dahl, 1961), neo-elite theory (Bachratz and Baratz, 1970), neo-Weberian perspectives (Rex and Moore, 1967; Pahl, 1970), a range of Marxist variants (Castells, 1977; Cockburn, 1977; Castells, 1983; Duncan and Goodwin, 1988b), the dual polity model (Bulpitt, 1986; 1989), the dual state model (Cawson and Saunders, 1983; Saunders, 1986), the neo-pluralist power-dependence model (Rhodes, 1981; 1988), public choice theory (Tiebout, 1956; Parks and Oakerson, 1989), the notion of urban growth machines (Logan and Molotch, 1987), urban regime theory (Stone, 1989; 1993) and regulation theory (Stoker, 1989; Painter, 1995).

2   Two accounts postulating the onset of post-Fordist local government did predate Stoker's analysis (Hogget, 1987; Geddes, 1988), but they applied notions of post-Fordism influenced more by management theory and the magazine *Marxism Today* than by the regulationist school.

Chapter 3   British Local Government since 1979

1   A similar view is taken by Gamble (1988), who suggests that governmental centralization was the inevitable outcome of the Thatcher governments' basic objections to strengthen the state and to reduce the extent of state intervention. In order to achieve these objectives, the Thatcher governments increasingly became aware of the need for sub-national government and quangos to consent to the centre's agenda, since a great deal of intervention was carried out in institutions beyond the direct control of the central state. When this consent was not forthcoming, the government sought instead to impose compliance through increased central control and the creation of new, single-purpose agencies.

References

Adonis, A. and Twigg, S. (1997) *The Cross We Bear: electoral reform for local government.* London: Fabian Society.

Alexander, A. (1982) *The Politics of Local Government in the United Kingdom.* London: Longman.

Amin, A. (ed.) (1994) *Post-Fordism: a reader.* Oxford: Blackwell.

Anderson, J. J. (1990) Skeptical reflection on a Europe of regions: Britain, Germany and the ERDF. *Journal of Public Policy*, 10, 417–47.

Arnold, R. (1999) *New political structures – potential problems for hung councils.* Conference paper, Political Association Annual Conference, University of Nottingham, 23–5 March.

Atkinson, H. (1996) *The rise and fall of the London new urban left in London Labour politics 1976–1987.* Doctoral thesis, London: South Bank University.

Atkinson, H. (1999) New Labour, new local government? In G. Taylor (ed.), *The Impact of New Labour*, London: Macmillan.

Atkinson, H. and Wilks-Heeg, S. (1997) *British Local Government Since 1979: the end of an era?* Sheffield: Politics Association Resource Centre/Sheffield Hallam University Press.

Atkinson, H. and Wilks-Heeg, S. (1999) German federalism: a model for English regional government. *Contemporary Politics*, 5(2), 153–69.

Atkinson, M. M. and Coleman, W. D. (1992) Policy networks, policy communities and the problems of governance. *Governance*, 5, 154–80.

Austin-Walker, J. (1984) *The case for not making a rate.* Personal paper.

Aydin, Z. (1995) Local Agenda 21 and the United Nations – how Local Agenda 21 fits into the UN process. *Local Government Policy-Making*, 22(2), 12–15.

Bache, I. (1999) The extended gatekeeper: central government and the implementation of EC regional policy in the UK. *Journal of European Policy*, 6(1), 28–45.

Bachratz, P. and Baratz, M. S. (1963) Decisions and non-decisions: an analytical framework. *American Political Science Review*, 57(3), 632–42.

276

References

Bachratz, P. and Baratz, M. S. (1970) *Power and Poverty*. New York: New York University Press.

Bachtler, J. (1998) Reforming the structural funds: challenges for EU regional policy. *European Planning Studies*, 6(6), 645–64.

Bachtler, J. and Turok, I. (eds) (1997) *The Coherence of EU Regional Policy: contrasting perspectives on the Structural Funds*. London: Jessica Kingsley.

Bacon, R. and Eltis, W. (1978) *Britain's Economic Problem: too few producers*. London: Macmillan.

Bains, M. (chairman) (1972) *The New Local Authorities: management and structure*. London: HMSO.

Baker, K. (1993) *The Turbulent Years*. London: Faber.

Ball, W. and Solomos, J. (1990) *Race and Local Politics*. London: Macmillan.

Barlow, M. (chairman) (1940) *Royal Commission on the Distribution of the Industrial Population, report*, Cmnd 6153. London: HMSO.

Barry-Jones, J. and Wilford, R. (1979) *The Welsh Veto: the politics of the devolution campaign*. Strathclyde: University of Strathclyde.

Bassett, K. (1984) Labour, socialism and local democracy. In M. Boddy and C. Fudge (eds), *Local Socialism*, London: Macmillan.

Batley, R. and Stoker, G. (eds) (1991) *Local Government in Europe: trends and developments*. London: Macmillan.

Benington, J. (1976) *Local Government becomes Big Business*. London: Community Development Project.

Benington, J. and Harvey, J. (1994) Spheres or tiers? The significance of transnational local authority networks. *Local Government Policy Making*, 20(5), 21–9.

Benington, J. and Harvey, J. (1998) Transnational local authority networking within the European Union: passing fashion or new paradigm? In D. Marsh (ed.), *Comparing Policy Networks*, Buckingham: Open University Press.

Bennet, R. (1993) *Local Government in the New Europe*. London: Belhaven Press.

Bennett, J. (1999) Will Best Value bring sustainability in from the cold? *Local Environment*, 4(1), 73–8.

Bennett, J. and Patel, R. (1995) Sustainable regeneration strategies. *Local Economy*, 10(2), 133–48.

Best Value for Barnsley (1998) Barnsley Metropolitan Borough Council.

Blair, T. (1998) *A New Vision for Local Government*. London: IPPR.

Blowers, A. (1987) Tradition or transformation? Environmental policy under Thatcher. *Public Administration*, 65(3), 277–94.

BMRM International (1996) *CCT Non-Bidders*. London: HMSO.

Boddy, M. and Fudge, C. (eds) (1984) *Local Socialism*. London: Macmillan.

Bogdanor, V. (1999) Devolution: decentralisation or disintegration? *Political Quarterly*, 70(2), 185–94.

Boland, P. (1999) Merseyside and Objective 1 status: some lessons on how not to proceed in Wales. *Regions: The Newsletter of Regional Studies Association*, no. 221, June 1999, 22–30.

Bomberg, E. and Peterson, J. (1998) European Union's decision making: the role of sub-national authorities. *Political Studies*, XLVI, 219–35.

References

Bongers, P. (1992) *Local Government in the Single European Market*. Harlow: Longman.

Booth, D. E. (1998) *The Environmental Consequences of Growth: steady-state economics as an alternative to ecological decline*. London, Routledge.

Bosworth, T. (1993) Local authorities and sustainable development. *European Environment*, 3(1), 13–17.

Boyne, G. (1997) Public choice theory and local government structure: an evaluation of reorganisation in Scotland and Wales. *Local Government Studies*, 23(3), 56–71.

Boyne, G. (1999) Processes, performance and Best Value in local government. *Local Government Studies*, 25(2), 1–15.

Boyne, G. and Ashworth, R. (1997) Party competition in English local government: an empirical analysis of English councils, 1974–1994. *Policy and Politics*, 25(2), 129–42.

Bradbury, J. (1998) The devolution debate in Wales: the politics of a developing union state? *Regional and Federal Studies*, 8(1), 120–40.

Brooke, R. (1989) *Managing the Enabling Authority*. Harlow: Longman.

Brown, A. (1998) Asymmetrical devolution: the Scottish case. *Political Quarterly*, 69(3), 215–23.

Bulpitt, J. (1983) *Territory and Power in the United Kingdom*. Manchester: Manchester University Press.

Bulpitt, J. (1986) The discipline of the new democracy: Mrs Thatcher's domestic statecraft. *Political Studies*, XXXIV, 19–39.

Bulpitt, J. (1989) Walking back to happiness? Conservative Party governments and elected local authorities in the 1980s. In C. Crouch and D. Marquand (eds), *The New Centralism: Britain out of step in Europe?* Cambridge: Blackwell.

Bundesministerium für Raumordnung, Bauwesen und Städtebau (1996) *Lokale Agenda 21: Stand und Perspektiven der Umsetzung von Kapitel 28 in Deutschland*. Bonn: Bundesministerium für Raumordnung, Bauwesen und Städtebau.

Burgess, T. and Travers, T. (1980) *Ten Billion Pounds: Whitehall's Takeover of the Town Halls*. London: Grant McIntyre.

Burns, D. (1992) *Poll Tax Rebellion*. Stirling: AK Press.

Burns, D., Hambleton, R. and Hoggett, P. (1994) *The Politics of Decentralisation: revitalising local democracy*. London: Macmillan.

Burrows, B. and Denton, G. (1980) *Devolution or Federalism? Options for a United Kingdom*. London, Macmillan.

Butcher, H., Law, I., Leach, R. and Mullard, M. (1990) *Local Government and Thatcherism*. London: Routledge.

Butler, D., Adonis, A. and Travers, T. (1994) *Failure in British Government: the politics of the poll tax*. Oxford: Oxford University Press.

Byrne, T. (1994) *Local Government in Britain*. London: Penguin.

CAG Consultants (1999) *Barriers to Local Agenda 21: report to the Local Government Management Board*. Luton: Local Government Management Board.

Cairns, D. (1996) Rediscovering democratic purpose in British local government. *Policy and Politics*, 24(1), 17–27.

278

References

Campbell, M. (ed.) (1990) *Local Economic Policy.* London: Cassell.

Carmichael, P. (1994) Analysing political choice in local government: a comparative case study approach. *Public Administration*, 72(2), 241–62.

Castells, M. (1977) *The Urban Question.* London: Edward Arnold.

Castells, M. (1983) *The City and the Grassroots*, Berkeley, CA: University of California Press.

Cawson, A. and Saunders, P. (1983) Corporatism, competitive politics and class struggle. In R. King (ed.), *Capital and Politics*, London: Routledge and Kegan Paul.

Chandler, J. (1996) *Local Government Today.* Manchester: Manchester University Press.

Christiansen, L. and Dowding, K. (1994) Pluralism or state autonomy? The case of Amnesty International (British section): the insider/outside group. *Political Studies*, XLII, 15–24.

Cirell, S. and Bennett, J. (1996) The new game of hardball. *Local Government Chronicle, CCT Update*, 24 May, 2–3.

Clarke, M. and Stewart, J. (1988) *The Enabling Council.* Luton: Local Government Management Board.

Clarke, M. and Stewart, J. (1994) The local authority and the new community governance. *Local Government Studies*, 20(2), 163–76.

Coates, C. (1998) Spanish regionalism and the European Union. *Parliamentary Affairs*, 51(2), 259–71.

Cochrane, A. (1991) The changing state of local government: restructuring for the 1990s. *Public Administration*, 69(3), 281–99.

Cochrane, A. (1992) *From Poll Tax to Council Tax.* London: IRSF.

Cochrane, A. (1993) *Whatever Happened to Local Government?* Buckingham: Open University Press.

Cockburn, C. (1977) *The Local State: management of cities and people.* London: Pluto Press.

Cole, M. and Boyne, G. (1996) Evaluating the structure of local government: the importance of tiers. *Public Policy and Administration*, 11(1), 63–73.

Commission for Local Democracy (CLD) (1995) *Taking Charge: the rebirth of local democracy.* London: Municipal Journal Books.

Commission of the European Communities (1992) *European Co-operation Networks.* Brussels: CEC.

Crosland, A. (1983) *Tony Crosland.* London: Coronet.

Crouch, C. and Marquand, D. (eds) (1989) *The New Centralism: Britain Out of Step in Europe?* Oxford: Blackwell.

Dahl, R. (1961) *Who Governs? Democracy and power in an American city.* New Haven: Yale University Press.

Dalyell, T. (1977) *Devolution: the end of Britain.* London; Jonathan Cape.

Davies, H. (1993) Free market and centralised political power: a British paradox. In R. Bennett (ed.), *Local Government in the New Europe*, London: Belhaven Press.

Davis, H. and Stewart, J. (1994) A new agenda for local governance. *Public Money and Management*, Oct.–Dec., 29–36.

References

Dawson, J. (1991) *Urbanisation and the Function of Cities in the European Community: linkages and networks in urban Europe.* Liverpool: Centre for Urban Studies, University of Liverpool.

Deacon, R. (1997) Identifying the origins of Welsh local government reform. *Journal of Legislative Studies,* 3(3), 104–12.

Dearlove, J. (1979) *The Reorganisation of Local Government: old orthodoxies and a political perspective.* Cambridge: Cambridge University Press.

Department of the Environment for Northern Ireland (1997) *District Council (NI) Rates Statistics Tables 1997/98,* Belfast: DOE.

DETR (Department of the Environment, Transport and the Regions) (1998a) A mayor and assembly for London. London: HMSO.

DETR (Department of the Environment, Transport and the Regions) (1998b) Guidance on enhancing participation in local government. London: HMSO.

DETR (Department of the Environment, Transport and the Regions) (1998c) Modern local government: improving financial accountability. London: HMSO.

DETR (Department of the Environment, Transport and the Regions) (1998d) Modern local government in touch with local people. London: HMSO.

DETR (Department of the Environment, Transport and the Regions) (1998e) Modern local government, local democracy, and community leadership. London: HMSO.

DETR (Department of the Environment, Transport and the Regions) (1998f) Partnerships for prosperity. London: HMSO.

DETR (Department of the Environment, Transport and the Regions) (1998g) Regeneration programmes: the way forward. London: DETR.

DETR (Department of the Environment, Transport and the Regions) (1998h) Sustainable development: opportunities for change. Consultation paper on a revised UK strategy. London: DETR.

DETR (Department of the Environment, Transport and the Regions) (1999a) Local leadership, local choice. London: HMSO.

DETR (Department of the Environment, Transport and the Regions) (1999b) The Beacon Council scheme: excellence in local government. London: HMSO.

DETR (Department of the Environment, Transport and the Regions) (1999c) The government's response to the Environment, Transport, and Regional Affairs Committee's Report – Local Government Finance. London: HMSO.

DETR (Department of the Environment, Transport and the Regions), Local Government Association and Local Government Management Board (LGMB) (1998) *Sustainable Local Communities for the 21st Century: why and how to prepare an effective local Agenda 21 strategy.* Luton: LGMB.

DETR (Department of the Environment, Transport and the Regions) Select Committee (1999) *Local Government Finance.* London: HMSO.

Dobson, F. (1995) *Working Together for Local People: putting public/private partnerships into action.* London: Labour Party.

DOE (Department of the Environment) (1981) Alternatives to domestic rates, Cmnd 8449. London: HMSO.

DOE (Department of the Environment) (1983) Rates, Cmnd 9008. London: HMSO.

References

DOE (Department of the Environment) (1986) Paying for local government, Cmnd 9714. London: HMSO.

DOE (Department of the Environment) (1990) This common inheritance. London: HMSO.

DOE (Department of the Environment) (1991) The internal management of local authorities. London: HMSO.

DOE (Department of the Environment) (1994) Sustainable development: the UK strategy. London: HMSO.

Dowding, K. (1995) Model or metaphor? A critical review of the policy network approach. *Political Studies*, XLIII, 136–58.

Dowding, K., Dunleavy, P., King, D., Margetts, H. and Rydin, Y. (1999) Regime politics in London local government. *Urban Affairs Review*, 34(4), 515–45.

Duncan, S. and Goodwin, M. (1988a) Removing local government autonomy: political centralisation and financial control. *Local Government Studies*, November/December 1988, 49–63.

Duncan, S. and Goodwin, M. (1988b) *The Local State and Uneven Development*. Cambridge: Polity.

Dunleavy, P. (1980) *Urban Political Analysis: The politics of collective consumption*. London: Macmillan.

Dunleavy, P. and O'Leary, B. (1987) *Theories of the State: the politics of liberal democracy*. London: Macmillan.

Dunleavy, P. and Rhodes, R. (1986) Beyond Whitehall. In H. Drucker, P. Dunleavy, A. Gamble and G. Peele, *Developments in British Politics*, London: Macmillan.

Edwards, J. (1997) Urban policy: the victory of form over substance? *Urban Studies*, 34(5/6), 825–43.

Elcock, H. (1982) *Local Government: politicians, professionals and the public in local authorities* (1st edn). London: Methuen.

Elcock, H. (1991) *Local Government: politicians, professionals and the public in local authorities* (2nd edn). London: Methuen.

Elcock, H. (1996) Local government. In D. Farnham and S. Horton (eds), *Managing the New Public Services* (2nd edn), London: Macmillan.

Elkin, S. (1987) *City and Regime in the American Republic*. Chicago, IL: University of Chicago Press.

Fainstein, N. and Fainstein, S. (1986) Regime strategies, communal resistance and economic forces. In S. Fainstein, R. C. Hill, D. Judd and M. Smith (eds), *Restructuring the City: the political economy of urban redevelopment*, New York: Longman.

Farnham, D. and Horton, S. (1996) *Managing the New Public Services* (2nd edn). Basingstoke: Macmillan.

Fenwick, J. and Bailey, M. (1998a) Corporate management in the new unitary councils. *Local Governance*, 24(2), 91–100.

Fenwick, J. and Bailey, M. (1998b) Decentralisation and reorganisation in local government. *Public Policy and Administration*, 13(2), 26–39.

Flynn, N., Leach, S. and Vielba, C. (1985) *Abolition or Reform: The GLC and the Metropolitan County Councils*. London: George Allen and Unwin.

References

Flynn, N. and Strehl, F. (1996) *Public Sector Management in Europe*. Hemel Hempstead: Prentice Hall.

Fordham, G., Evans, R., Fordham, R., Harding, A., Harrison, A. and Parkinson, M. (1998) *Building Partnerships in the English Regions: A Study Report of Regional and Sub-Regional Partnerships in England*. London: DETR.

Foster, C. and Perlman, M. (1980) *Local Government Finance in a Unitary State*. London: Allen and Unwin.

Friends of the Earth (1989) *Environmental Charter for Local Government*. London: Friends of the Earth.

Gamble, A. (1988) *The Free Economy and the Strong State: the politics of Thatcherism* (1st edn). Basingstoke: Macmillan.

Game, C. and Leach, S. (1996) Local government under siege. In L. Pratchett and D. Wilson (eds), *Local Democracy and Local Government*, London: Macmillan.

Garisse, S. (1997) The impact of European regional policy on the development of the regional tier in the UK. *Regional and Federal Studies*, 7(3), 1–24.

Geddes, M. (1988) The capitalist state and the local economy: restructuring for labour and beyond. *Capital and Class*, no. 35, 85–120.

Giddens, A. (1998) *The 3rd Way: The Renewal of Social Democracy*. Cambridge: Polity.

Glennerster, H. (1995) *British Social Policy since 1945*. Oxford: Basil Blackwell.

Goldsmith, M. (1986) *Essays on the Future of Local Government*. Wakefield: West Yorkshire Metropolitan County Council.

Goldsmith, M. (1993) The Europeanisation of local government. *Urban Studies*, 30(4/5), 683–99.

Goldsmith, M. and Newton, K. (1986) Local government abroad. In D. Widdicombe (chairman), *The Conduct of Local Authority Business: Report of the Committee of Enquiry into the Conduct of Local Authority Business*, Cmnd 9797. London: HMSO.

Gordon, J. (1994) Letting the genie out: local government and UNCED. In C. Thomas (ed.), *Rio: unravelling the consequences*, London: Frank Cass.

Gray, A. and Flynn, A. (1994) Environmental policy. In B. Jones, A. Gray, D. Kavanagh, M. Moran, P. Norton and A. Seldon, *Politics UK*, (2nd edn), Hemel Hempstead: Harvester Wheatsheaf.

Gray, C. (1994) *Government Beyond the Centre*. London: Macmillan.

Greer, A. and Hoggett, P. (1996) Quangos and local governance. In L. Pratchett and D. Wilson (eds), *Local Democracy and Local Government*, London: Macmillan.

Hale, R. (1999) More money, more muscle. *Local Government Chronicle*, 6 August, 11.

Hall, S. (1979) The great moving-right show. *Marxism Today*, 23(1).

Hall, S. and Jacques, M. (1983) *The Politics of Thatcherism*. London: Lawrence and Wishart.

Hampton, W. (1991) *Local Government and Urban Politics*. Harlow: Longman.

Harding, A. (1991) The rise of growth coalitions, UK-style? *Environment and Planning C: Government and Policy*, 9(3), 295–317.

References

Harding, A. (1995) Elite theory and growth machines. In D. Judge, G. Stoker and H. Wolman (eds), *Theories of Urban Politics*, London: Sage.

Harding, A. (1999) Regime-formation in Manchester and Edinburgh. In G. Stoker (ed.), *Community, Power and Participation: The changing local government of Britain*, London: Macmillan.

Harvie, C. (1991) English regionalism: the dog that never barked. In B. Crick (ed.), *The Constitution and the United Kingdom*, Oxford: Political Quarterly.

Heald, D. (1980) *Financing Devolution*. Canberra, Australia: The Australian National University.

Hebbert, M. and Travers, T. (eds) (1988) *The London Government Handbook*. London: Cassell.

Hepworth, N. (1976) *The Finance of Local Government*. London: Allen and Unwin.

Herbert, Sir Edwin (chairman) (1960) *Royal Commission on Local Government in London, 1957–1960, Report*. London: HMSO.

HMSO (1945) Local government in England and Wales during the period of reconstruction. Cmnd 6579. London: HMSO.

HMSO (1991) *A Rough Guide to Europe: local authorities and the EC*. London: HMSO.

HM Treasury (1991) *Competing for quality*. Cmnd 1730. London: HMSO.

Hogget, P. (1987) A farewell to mass production? Decentralisation as an emergent private and public sector paradigm. In P. Hoggett and R. Hambleton (eds), *Decentralisation and Democracy*, Bristol: School for Advanced Urban Studies.

Hunter, F. (1953) *Community Power Structure: A Study of Decision Makers*. Chapel Hill: University of North Carolina Press.

IDeA (1999) *Local Agenda 21 Survey: autumn 1998 results*. London: IDeA Sustainable Development Unit.

Imrie, R. and Raco, M. (1999) How new is the new local governance? Lessons from the United Kingdom. *Transactions of the Institute of British Geographers*, 24(1), 45–63.

Jackman, R. (1985) Local government finance. In M. Loughlin and K. Young (eds), *Half a Century of Municipal Decline: 1935 to 1985*, London: Allen and Unwin.

Jacobs, B. (1997) Networks, partnerships and European Union regional economic development initiatives in the West Midlands. *Policy and Politics*, 25(1), 39–49.

Jeffrey, B. (1997) Creating participatory structures in local government. *Local Government Policy-making*, 23(4), 25–31.

Jessop, B. (1990) Regulation theory in retrospect and prospect. *Economy and Society*, 19(2), 153–216.

Jessop, B. (1994) Post-Fordism and the state. In A. Amin (ed.), *Post-Fordism: A Reader*, Oxford: Blackwell.

Jessop, B. (1998) The rise of governance and the risks of failure: the case of economic development. *International Social Science Journal*, 155, 29–45.

John, P. (1994) *The Europeanisation of British Local Government: new management strategies*. London: Local Government Management Board.

References

John, P. (1995) *A Base in Brussels: a good investment for local authorities?* London: Local Government International Bureau.

John, P. (1996a) Centralization, decentralization and the European Union: the dynamics of triadic relationships. *Public Administration*, 74(2), 293–313.

John, P. (1996b) Europeanization in a centralizing state: multi-level governance in the UK, *Journal of Regional & Federal Studies*, 6(3), 131–4.

John, P. (1999) Ideas and interests; agendas and implementation: an evolutionary explanation of policy change in British local government finance. *British Journal of Politics and International Relations*, 1(1), 39–62.

John, P. and McAteer, M. (1998) Sub-national institutions and the new European governance: UK local authority lobbying strategies for the IGC. *Regional & Federal Studies*, 8(3), 104–24.

John, P. and Whitehead, A. (1997) The renaissance of English regionalism in the 1990s. *Policy and Politics*, 25(1), 7–16.

Jones, G. (1988) Against regional government. *Local Government Studies*, 14(5), 1–11.

Jones, G. and Stewart J. (1985) *The Case for Local Government*. London: Allen and Unwin.

Jones, G. and Stewart, J. (1999) Gagging is order of the day. *Local Government Chronicle*, 29 January, 14.

Judge, D. (1995) Pluralism. In D. Judge, G. Stoker and H. Wolman (eds), *Theories of Urban Politics*, London: Sage.

Karn, Valerie (1993) Remodelling a HAT: the implementation of the Housing Action Trust legislation 1987–92. In P. Malpass and R. Mean (eds), *Implementing Housing Policy*, Buckingham: Open University Press.

Kavanagh, D. (1986) *Thatcherism and British Politics: The End of Consensus?* Oxford: Oxford University Press.

Keating, M. (1991) *Comparative Urban Politics: Power and the City in the United States, Canada, Britain and France*. Aldershot: Edward Elgar.

Keil, R. and Lieser, P. (1989) Frankfurt: global city, local politics, *Comparative Urban and Regional Research*, 4, After Modernism: Global Restructuring and the Changing Boundaries of City Life, 39–69.

King, D. (1987) *The New Right: Politics, Markets and Citizenship*. Basingstoke: Macmillan.

King, D. (1993) Government beyond Whitehall. In P. Dunleavy, A. Gamble, I. Holliday and G. Peele (eds), *Developments in British Politics 4*, London: Macmillan.

Kingdom, J. (1991) *Local Government and Politics in Britain*. Deddington: Philip Allan.

Kinghan, N. (1998) If the capping must fit, wear it with great care. *Local Government Chronicle*, 4 December.

Knox, C. (1998) Local government in Northern Ireland: emerging from the bearpit of sectarianism? *Local Government Studies*, 24(3), 1–13.

Kuper, R. (1997) Deliberating waste: the Hertfordshire citizen's jury. *Local Environment*, 2(2), 139–53.

Labour Party (1995) *Renewing Democracy, Rebuilding Local Communities*. London: Labour Party.

284

References

Labour Party (1996) *A New Voice for the English Regions*. London: Labour Party.

Lansley, S., Goss, S. and Wolmar, C. (1989) *Councils in Conflict*. London: Macmillan.

Layfield Committee (1976) *Report of the Committee of Enquiry into Local Government Finance*, Cmnd 6543. London: HMSO.

Leach, S. (1996) The indirectly elected world of local government. *Local Government Studies*, 22(2), 64–76.

Leach, S. (1997) Introduction: the continuing relevance of the Local Government Review. *Local Government Studies*, 23(3), 1–4.

Leach, S. (1999) Introducing cabinets into British local government. *Parliamentary Affairs*, 52(1), 78–93.

Leach, S. and Stewart, J. (1992) *The Politics of Hung Authorities*. London: Macmillan.

Leach, S. and Stewart, J. (1994) The hung authorities – 1993 onwards. *Local Government Studies*, 20(4), 538–46.

Leach, S. and Stoker, G. (1997) Understanding the Local Government Review: a retrospective analysis. *Local Government Studies*, 75(1), 1–20.

Leach, S., Stewart, J. and Walsh, K. (1994) *The Changing Organisation and Management of Local Government*. Basingstoke: Macmillan.

Ley, C. and Seghal, C. (1998) Best Value – moving forward on the new framework. *Local Government Voice*, July, 6–7.

Lindblom, C. E. (1977) *Politics and Markets*. New York: Basic Books.

Littlewood, S. and While, A. (1997) A new agenda for local governance? Agenda 21 and the prospects for holistic local decision making. *Local Government Studies*, 23(4), 111–23.

Liverpool Democracy Commission (1999) *Future: The Leading of Liverpool*. London: New Local Government Network.

Livingstone, K. (1988) *If Voting Changed Anything, They'd Abolish It*. London: Fontana Collins.

Lloyd, P. and Meegan, R. (1996) Contested governance: European exposure in the English regions. In J. Alden and P. Boland (eds), *Regional Development Strategies: a European perspective*, London: Jessica Kingsley.

Local Government Association (1998) *Modernising Political Management Arrangements: options within the existing legislative framework*. London: LGA Publications.

Local Government Association (1999) *Leading the Agenda: case studies of new political management arrangements*. London: LGA Publications.

Local Government Chronicle (1996) CCT Focus 3: themes behind the scenes. *Local Government Chronicle*, 22 November, 14.

Local Government Chronicle (1999) Nine PFI deals win government support. *Local Government Chronicle*, 6 August, 14.

Local Government International Bureau (1992) *International Local Authority Networks Linking to the UK*. London: LGIB.

Local Government Management Board (1993a) *Towards Sustainability: the EC's Fifth Action Programme on the Environment, a guide for local authorities*. Luton: LGMB.

References

Local Government Management Board (1993b) *Agenda 21: A Guide for Local Authorities*. Luton: LGMB.

Local Government Management Board (1993c) *Fitness for Purpose: shaping new patterns of organisation and management*. Luton: LGMB.

Local Government Management Board (1993d) *A Portrait of Change*. Luton: LGMB.

Local Government Management Board (1995) *Indicators for Local Agenda 21: a summary*. Luton: LGMB.

Local Government Management Board (1997) *Local Agenda 21 in the UK: the first 5 years*. Luton: LGMB.

Logan, J. and Molotch, H. (1987) *Urban Fortunes: the political economy of place*. London: University of California Press.

Loughlin, M. (1996) The constitutional status of local government. In L. Pratchett and D. Wilson (eds), *Local Democracy and Local Government*, London: Macmillan.

Loughlin, M. (1997) Ultra vires: hail and farewell. In H. Kitchin (ed.), *A Framework for the Future*, London: Local Government Information Unit.

McAteer, M. and Mitchell, D. (1996) Peripheral lobbying: the territorial dimension of Euro lobbying by Scottish and Welsh sub central government. *Regional and Federal Studies*, 6(3), 1–17.

McCarthy, A. and Burch, M. (1994) European regional development strategies: the response of two northern regions. *Local Government Policy Making*, 20(5), 31–8.

McCormick, J. (1994) Environmental politics. In P. Dunleavy, A. Gamble, I. Holliday and G. Peele (eds), *Developments in British Politics 4*, London: Macmillan.

Mackintosh, M. (1992) Partnership: issues of policy and negotiation. *Local Economy*, 7(3), 210–24.

Mackintosh, M. and Wainwright, H. (1987) *A Taste of Power*. London: Verso.

Macrory, P. (chairman) (1970) *The Report of the Review Body on Local Government in Northern Ireland*. Belfast: HMSO.

Mallaby, H. (chairman) (1967) *Report of the Committee on the Staffing of Local Government*. London: HMSO.

Marks, G. (1992) Structural policy in the European Community. In A. M. Sbragia (ed.), *Euro-politics*, Washington: The Brookings Institute.

Marks, G. (1993) Structural policy and multilevel governance in the EC. In A. Cafruny and G. Rosenthal (eds), *The State of the European Community, Vol. 2, The Maastricht Debates and Beyond*, Boulder, CO: Lynne Rienner.

Marks, G., Hooghe, L. and Blank, K. (1996) European integration from the 1980s: state-centric versus multi-level governance. *Journal of Common Market Studies*, 34(3), 341–78.

Marsh, D. and Rhodes, R. A. W. (eds) (1992) *Implementing Thatcherite Policies: audit of an era*. Buckingham: Open University Press.

Martin, S. (1998) EU Programmes and the evolution of local economic governance in the UK. *European Urban and Regional Studies*, 5(3), 237–48.

Marx, K. and Engels, F. (1983) *Manifesto of the Communist Party*. London: Lawrence and Wishart.

References

Maud, Sir John (chairman) (1967) *Committee on the Management of Local Government, Vol. 1: Report*. London: HMSO.

Meadows, D. H., Meadows, D. L., Randers, J. and Behrens, W. W. (1972) *The Limits to Growth*. London: Pan.

Meehan, E. (1999) The Belfast Agreement and UK devolution. *Parliamentary Affairs*, 52(1), 19–31.

Midwinter, A. and McGarvey, N. (1997) Local government reform in Scotland. *Local Government Studies*, 23(3), 73–89.

Miliband, R. (1973) *The State in Capitalist Society*. London: Quartet.

Mills, L. (1994) Economic development, the environment and Europe: areas of innovation in UK local government. *Local Government Policy Making*, 20(5), 31–8.

Milton, K. (1991) Interpreting environmental policy: a social scientific approach. *Journal of Law and Society*, 18(1), 4–17.

Mitchell, J. (1998) What could a Scottish Parliament do? *Regional and Federal Studies*, 8(1), 68–85.

Mullins, D., Niner, P. and Riseborough, M. (1992) *Evaluating Large Scale Voluntary Transfers of Local Authority Housing*. London: HMSO.

Munton, R. (1997) Engaging sustainable development: some observations on progress in the UK. *Progress in Human Geography*, 21(1), 147–63.

Newton, K. and Karran, T. (1985) *The Politics of Local Expenditure*. London: Macmillan.

Niskanen, W. (1971) *Bureaucracy and Representative Government*. New York: Aldine-Atherton.

Niskanen, W. (1973) *Bureaucracy: servant or master?* London: Institute for Economic Affairs.

Northern Ireland Audit Office (1991) *Economy, Efficiency and Effectiveness: Examination of Certain Matters*. Belfast: HMSO.

Oatley, N. (1998) *Cities, Economic Competition and Urban Policy*. London: Paul Chapman.

O'Connor, J. (1973) *The Fiscal Crisis of the State*. New York: St Martin's Press.

O'Riordan, T. (1995) *Environmental Science for Environmental Management*. Harlow: Longman.

O'Riordan, T. and Voisey, H. (eds) (1997) *Sustainable Development in Western Europe: Coming to Terms with Agenda 21*. London: Frank Cass & Co.

Osborne, D. and Gabler, T. (1992) *Reinventing Government*. Reading, MA: Addison-Wesley.

Pahl, R. (1970) *Whose City?* London: Longman.

Painter, C., Isaac-Henry, K. and Rouse, J. (1997) Local authorities and non-elected agencies: strategic responses and organizational networks. *Public Administration*, 75(2), 225–45.

Painter, J. (1991) Regulation theory and local government. *Local Government Studies*, 17(6), 23–44.

Painter, J. (1995) Regulation theory, post-Fordism and urban politics. In D. Judge, G. Stoker and H. Wolman (eds), *Theories of Urban Politics*, London: Sage.

Parkinson, M. (1985) *Liverpool on the Brink: one city's struggle against government cuts*. Hermitage: Policy Journals.

References

Parkinson, M. (1996) Twenty-five years of urban policy in Britain – partnership, entrepreneurialism or competition? *Public Money and Management*, 60(4), 7–14.

Parkinson, M. and Wilks, S. (1986) The politics of inner city partnerships. In M. Goldsmith (ed.), *New Research in Central–Local Relations*, Aldershot: Gower.

Parks, R. and Oakerson, R. (1989) Metropolitan organisation and governance: a local public economy approach. *Urban Affairs Quarterly*, 25(1), 18–29.

Paterson, L. (chairman) (1973) *The New Scottish Local Authorities: organization and management structures*. Working Group on Scottish Local Authority Management Structures. Edinburgh: HMSO.

Paterson, L. (1998) Scottish home rule: radical break or pragmatic adjustment? *Regional and Federal Studies*, 8(1), 53–68.

Peck, J. (1995) Moving and shaking: business elites, state localism and urban privatism. *Progress in Human Geography*, 19(1), 16–46.

Peck, J. and Tickell, A. (1994) Searching for a new institutional fix: the after-Fordist crisis and the global–local disorder. In A. Amin (ed.), *Post-Fordism: a reader*, Oxford: Blackwell.

Peters, A. (1993) Germany. In J. Chandler (ed.), *Local Government in Liberal Democracies*, London: Routledge.

Pickvance, C. (1991) The difficulty of control and the ease of structural reform: British local government in the 1980s. In C. Pickvance and E. Preteceille (eds), *State Restructuring and Local Power: a comparative perspective*, London: Pinter.

Pickvance, C. (1995) Marxist theories of urban politics. In D. Judge, G. Stoker and H. Wolman (eds), *Theories of Urban Politics*, London: Sage.

Poulantzas, N. (1978) *State, Power, Socialism*. London: New Left Books.

Pratchett, L. (1999) Defining democratic renewal. *Local Government Studies*, 25(4), 1–17.

Pratchett, L. and Wilson, D. (1996) Local government under siege. In L. Pratchett and D. Wilson (eds), *Local Democracy and Local Government*, London: Macmillan.

Pratchett, L. and Wilson, D. (eds) (1996) *Local Democracy and Local Government*. London: Macmillan.

Pratchett, L. and Wilson, D. (1997) The rebirth of local democracy. *Local Government Studies*, 23(1), 15–27.

Pycroft, C. (1995) Restructuring local government. *Public Policy and Administration*, 10(1), 49–62.

Rallings, C. and Thrasher, M. (1991) Local elections: the changing scene. *Social Studies Review*, 5(4), 163–6.

Rallings, C. and Thrasher, M. (1995) Coalitions in Britain: administrative formation in hung councils. *Policy and Politics*, 23(3), 223–32.

Rallings, C. and Thrasher, M. (1999) Pains in the Labour wards. *Local Government Chronicle*, 14 May, 14–15.

Rao, N. (1998) Representation in local politics: a reconsideration and some new evidence. *Political Studies*, 46(1), 19–35.

References

Redcliffe-Maud, Lord (chairman) (1969) *Royal Commission on Local Government in England, Vol. I: Report,* Cmnd 4040. London: HMSO.

Reid, D. (1995) *Sustainable Development: an introductory guide.* London: Earthscan Publications.

Rex, J. and Moore, R. (1967) *Race, Community and Conflict: a study of Sparkbrook.* Oxford: Oxford University Press.

Rhodes, R. A. W. (1981) *Control and Power in Central–Local Relations.* Farnborough, Hants: Gower.

Rhodes, R. A. W. (1988) *Beyond Westminster and Whitehall.* London: Unwin Hyman.

Rhodes, R. A. W. (1997) *Understanding Governance: policy networks, governance, reflexivity and accountability.* Buckingham: Open University Press.

Ridley, N. (1988) *The Local Right: enabling not providing.* London: Centre for Policy Studies.

Roberts, V., Russell, H., Harding, A. and Parkinson, M. (1994) *Public/Private/Voluntary Partnerships in Local Government.* Luton: Local Government Management Board.

Robson, W. A. (1948) *The Development of Local Government.* London: Allen and Unwin.

Ronneberger, K. and Keil, R. (1993) Riding the tiger of modernisation: red-green municipal reform politics in Frankfurt-am-Main. *Capitalism, Nature, Socialism,* 4(2), issue 14, 19–50.

Saunders, P. (1986) Reflections on the dual politics thesis: the argument, its origins and its critics. In M. Goldsmith and S. Villadsen (eds), *Urban Political Theory and the Management of Fiscal Stress,* Aldershot: Gower.

Savage, M. and Warde, A. (1993) *Urban Sociology, Capitalism and Modernity.* Basingstoke: Macmillan.

Scott, R. and Hoye, K. (1996) Local councils' economic development activities. In E. McLaughlin and P. Quirk (eds), *Policy Aspects of Employment Equality in Northern Ireland,* Vol. 2, Belfast: Standing Advisory Commission on Human Rights.

Scottish Constitutional Convention (1995) *Scotland's Parliament, Scotland's Right.* Edinburgh: Scottish Constitutional Convention.

Scottish Office (1997) *Scotland's Parliament.* Edinburgh: HMSO.

Selman, P. and Parker, J. (1999) Tales of local sustainability. *Local Environment,* 4(1), 47–60.

Sharpe, L. (1970) Theories and values of local government. *Political Studies,* 18(2), 153–74.

Sharpe, L. (1993) *The Rise of Meso Government in Europe.* London: Sage.

Shaw, K., Fenwick, J. and Foreman, A. (1994) Compulsory competitive tendering for local government services: the experiences of local authorities in the North of England 1988–1992. *Public Administration,* 72(2), 201–17.

Sinnot, J. (1997) The Local Government Review – an inept process. *Local Government Studies,* 23(3), 90–106.

Smith, G. and Wales, C. (1998) The theory and practice of citizens' juries. *Policy and Politics,* 27(3), 295–308.

References

Smith, M. J. (1993) *Pressure, Power and Policy: state autonomy and policy networks in Britain and the United States.* New York: Harvester Wheatsheaf.

Stewart, J. (1989) A future for local authorities as community government. In J. Stewart and G. Stoker (eds), *The Future of Local Government,* London: Macmillan.

Stewart, J. (1995) A future for local authorities as community government. In J. Stewart and G. Stoker (eds), *Local Government in the 1990s,* London: Macmillan.

Stewart, J. (1996) Reforming the new magistracy. In L. Pratchett and D. Wilson (eds), *Local Democracy and Local Government,* London: Macmillan.

Stewart, J. (1997) Innovation in democratic practice in local government. *Policy and Politics,* 24(1), 29–41.

Stewart, J. and Hams, T. (1992) *Local Government for Sustainable Development.* Luton: Local Government Management Board.

Stewart, J. and Stoker, G. (1988) *From Local Administration to Community Governance.* London: Fabian Society.

Stewart, J. and Stoker, G. (eds) (1989) *The Future of Local Government.* London: Macmillan.

Stewart, J. and Stoker, G. (1995a) Fifteen years of local government restructuring 1979–1994: an evaluation. In J. Stewart and G. Stoker (eds), *Local Government in the 1990s,* London: Macmillan.

Stewart, J. and Stoker, G. (1995b) Introduction. In J. Stewart and G. Stoker (eds), *Local Government in the 1990s,* London: Macmillan.

Stewart, J. and Stoker, G. (eds) (1995c) *Local Government in the 1990s.* London: Macmillan.

Stewart, M. (1994) Between Whitehall and town hall: the realignment of urban regeneration policy in England. *Policy and Politics,* 22(3), 266–77.

Stoker, G. (1989) Creating a local government for a post-Fordist society: the Thatcherite project? In J. Stewart and G. Stoker (eds), *The Future of Local Government,* London: Macmillan.

Stoker, G. (1991) *The Politics of Local Government* (2nd edn). London: Macmillan.

Stoker, G. (1995a) *Intergovernmental relations. Public Administration,* 73(1), 101–22.

Stoker, G. (1995b) Regime theory and urban politics. In D. Judge, G. Stoker and H. Wolman (eds), *Theories of Urban Politics,* London: Sage.

Stoker, G. (1995c) *The struggle to reform local government, 1970–1995.* PAC Annual Conference, September.

Stoker, G. (1998) Governance as theory: five propositions. *International Social Science Journal,* 155, 17–28.

Stoker, G. (ed.) (1999) *The New Management of British Local Government.* London: Macmillan.

Stone, C. (1986) Power and social complexity. In R. Waste (ed.), *Community Power: Directions for Future Research,* Newbury Park, CA: Sage.

Stone, C. (1989) *Regime Politics: Governing Atlanta 1946–1988.* Lawrence: University Press of Kansas.

References

Stone, C. (1993) Urban regimes and the capacity to govern: a political economy approach. *Journal of Urban Affairs*, 15(1), 1–28.

Sweeting, D. and Cope, S. (1997) Modernising local democracy: democratic innovations in local government. *Local Government Policy Making*, 23(5), 3–8.

Taylor, D. (1998) Integrating economic and environmental policy: experience in UK local and regional government. *European Environment*, 8(3), 141–51.

Temple, M. (1993) Policy influence in hung and non-hung councils. *Local Government Policy Making*, 20(1), 18–26.

Terry, F. (1992) The single market and the public sector. In F. Terry and P. Jackson (eds), *Public Domain 1992: the public services year-book*, London: Chatham and Hall.

Thatcher, M. (1993) *The Downing Street Years*. London: HarperCollins.

Tiebout, C. (1956) A pure theory of local expenditures. *Journal of Political Economy*, 64(4), 416–24.

Tindale, S. (1995) *Devolution on Demand: Options for the English Regions*. London: IPPR.

Tomaney, J. (1999) New Labour and the English question. *Political Quarterly*, 70(1), 75–82.

Travers, T. (1986) *The Politics of Local Government Finance*. London: Allen and Unwin.

Travers, T. (1989) The threat to the autonomy of elected local government. In C. Crouch and D. Marquand (eds), *The New Centralism: Britain out of Step in Europe?*, Oxford: Blackwell.

Tuxworth, B. and Carpenter, C. (1996) *Local Agenda 21 Survey 1996*. Luton: Local Government Management Board.

Voisey, H., Bauermann, C., Sverdrup, L. A. and O'Riordan, T. (1996) The political significance of Local Agenda 21: the early stages of some European experience. *Local Environment*, 1(1), 33–50.

Waldegrave, W. (1993) *The Reality of Reform in Today's Public Sector*. CIPFA/PFF Lecture.

Walsh, K. (1989) Competition and service delivery. In J. Stewart and G. Stoker (eds), *The Future of Local Government*, London: Macmillan.

Walsh, K. (1995) Competition and public service delivery. In J. Stewart and G. Stoker (eds), *Local Government in the 1990s*, London: Macmillan.

Ward, N., Buller, H. and Lowe, P. (1996) The Europeanisation of local environmental politics: bathing water pollution in south-west England. *Local Environment*, 1(1), 21–32.

Ward, S. (1993) Thinking global, acting local? British local authorities and their environmental plans. *Environmental Politics*, 2(3), 453–78.

Welsh Labour Party (1995) *Shaping the Vision: a report on the powers and structure of the Welsh Labour Party*. Cardiff: Welsh Labour Party.

Wheatley, Lord (chairman) (1969) *Royal Commission on Local Government in Scotland, Report*, Cmnd 4150. Edinburgh: HMSO.

Widdicombe, D. (1986) *The Conduct of Local Authority Business: Committee of Inquiry into the Conduct of Local Authority Business*, Cmnd 9797-9801. London: HMSO.

References

Wilks, S. (1993) *Talking about Tomorrow: a new radical politics*. London: Pluto Press.

Wilks, S. (1995) Networks of power: theorising the politics of urban policy change. In J. Lovenduski and J. Stanyer (eds), *Contemporary Political Studies*, Belfast: Political Studies Association.

Wilks, S. and Hall, P. (1995) Think globally, act locally: implementing Agenda 21 in Britain. *Policy Studies*, 16(3), 37–44.

Wilks-Heeg, S. (1996) Urban experiments limited revisited: urban policy comes full circle? *Urban Studies*, 33(8), 1263–79.

Wilson, D. and Game, C. (1994) *Local Government in the United Kingdom*. London: Macmillan.

Wilson, D. and Game, C. (1998) *Local Government in the United Kingdom* (2nd edn). London: Macmillan.

Wilson, E. and Raemaekers, J. (1992) Index to local authority green plans (2nd edn). Research paper no. 48, Edinburgh: Edinburgh College of Art/Herriot Watt University.

Wood, A. M., Valler, D. and North, P. (1997) *Local Business Representation and the Private Sector Role in Local Economic Policy in Britain*. University of Sheffield: Department of Town and Regional Planning.

World Commission on Environment and Development (1987) *Our Common Future*. Oxford: Oxford University Press.

Young, K. (1996) Reinventing local government? Some evidence assessed. *Public Administration*, 74(3), 347–67.

Index

accountability 10–11, 112, 119–21, 139–40, 143, 163–5, 170, 179
Agenda 21 *see* Local Agenda 21
aldermen 14
Amsterdam Treaty (1997) 213
Armstrong, Hilary 255–8, 265
Association of County Councils (ACC) 113, 156–7
Association of District Councils (ADC) 156–7
Association of Metropolitan Authorities (AMA) 156–7
Audit Commission 12, 206–7
Austin-Walker, John 94–5
Avon 248–9

Bains Commission (1972) 162, 166–9, 176–8
Baker, Kenneth 62, 103
Banham Commission (1992) *see* Local Government Commission
Barlow Report (1940) 16
Barnsley 200, 265–6
Bates Review (1997) 130
Beacon Councils 266–7
Best Value initiative 5, 124, 129, 141, 197, 200, 256, 262, 265–8, 272
Birmingham 13, 21, 27, 138, 261

Blair, Tony 1, 155, 158–9, 200, 232, 252–3, 260, 263
block grant 92–3, 236
Blunkett, David 259, 267–8
Brent, London borough of 96, 128, 133, 175, 194–5
Bristol 113, 216, 248
Brown, Gordon 242, 256
Brundtland Report 186–7
Business Opportunities on Merseyside (BOOM) 137, 141
business rates 98, 101
    see also National Non-Domestic Rate (NNDR)
Business Services Association 126–7

Caborn, Richard 244–5
CAG Consultants 199–200
Capital Challenge 86
capitalism 57–61
Cardiff 22, 229
centralization 2–6, 11, 32, 35, 55–6, 60–3, 73–81, 163–4, 169–73, 178–81, 207, 222, 265
Chamberlain, Joseph 13, 27
Citizen's Charter 79
City Challenge initiative 74, 78, 195
city technology colleges (CTCs) 69–70

Clarke, Kenneth 130
Clarke, Michael 178
Clean Air Act
    (1956) 188
    (1968) 188
Commission for Local Democracy
    (CLD) 253–4, 260, 263
Community Care Act (1990) 74–5,
    272
community charge *see* poll tax
community governance 5, 176,
    178–81
compulsory competitive tendering
    (CCT) 4, 69, 74, 117, 122–9,
    141–3, 164, 174–5, 179, 181,
    192, 200, 266–8, 272
Conservative Party 1–6, 18, 21, 26,
    55–81, 85–6, 108–14, 118–20,
    123–5, 137–8, 142, 147–61,
    173, 188–9, 230–7, 250, 252,
    256, 266–8, 270–4
Consultative Council on Local
    Government Finance (CCLGF)
    91
Convention of Scottish Local
    Authorities (CoSLA) *see* Scotland
Cornwall 210, 248
corporate management 166–70
council tax 3–4, 86–7, 104–5,
    256–9, 262
creative autonomy 2–6, 24, 33–4,
    56, 75–81, 95–6, 164, 222–4,
    252, 272–3
Croydon, London borough of 12,
    160, 261, 263
Cubie Report 235

decentralization *see* centralization
Department of the Environment
    (DOE) 96–7, 100–3, 220
Department of the Environment,
    Transport and the Regions
    (DETR) 126, 131, 136, 159,
    187, 193–5, 200, 244–5, 256–67
Derbyshire 114, 134
devolution 5, 227–8, 269, 274

see also Northern Ireland;
    Scotland; Wales
DFBO schemes (Design, Build,
    Finance, Operate) 129
direct labour organizations (DLOs)
    65–6, 125
direct service organizations (DSOs)
    125–6, 141
domestic rates 85, 88, 98–102
Doncaster 133, 153
Dorset 114, 132

economic development 24
Edinburgh 22, 229
education 28–9, 64, 66–70, 90–1,
    119, 138, 165, 173–4, 194, 208,
    253, 259, 267–8, 270, 273
Education Act
    (1979) 66
    (1980) 66
Education Reform Act (1988) 69–70,
    173
elected mayors 259–61, 264–5
Electoral Reform Society 258–9
electoral turnout 4, 10, 157–61,
    258–9
elite theory 31, 38–9
enabling authority 4–5, 117–18,
    163–4, 173–5, 178, 271–2
Environmental Protection Act (1990)
    188
EUROCITIES 215–16
European Action for Mining
    Communities (EURACOM)
    215
European Exchange Rate Mechanism
    158
European Regional Development
    Fund (ERDF) 86, 206, 211–14,
    220–1
European Union/Community 3–5,
    24, 54, 136, 183, 190, 203–24,
    227, 231, 237, 246, 272
and the Single Market 214–16
and the structural funds 209–11,
    217–22

'fares fair' policy 18
first past the post (FPTP) 159–60, 233
Fordism 49–52, 81

Germany 179, 193, 227, 254, 256
Glasgow 22, 199, 216
Gloucestershire 114, 248–9
Government Offices for the Regions (GORs) 244–7
Government of Wales Act (1998) 240
grant holdback 93
grant maintained schools (GMS) 70, 119
Grant-Related Expenditure Assessment (GREA) 92–3, 97
grant taper 93
Greater London Authority (GLA) see London
Greater London Council (GLC) see London
Greater Manchester 19, 134
Gummer, John 113–14

Hackney, London borough of 96, 268
Hague, William 237
Harrow, London borough of 133, 151
health care 188, 194, 270
Heath, Edward 21, 59–60, 230
Herbert Commission (1957) 16–18, 25
Heseltine, Michael 73–4, 92, 101–2, 104, 111
hollowing-out 35, 77, 79–81, 217, 222, 272
housing 28–9, 41, 64–70, 137–9, 165, 174, 270, 272
Housing Act
(1980) 65
(1988) 69, 77, 173
Housing Action Trusts (HATs) 119
hung councils 153–5

Inner London Education Authority (ILEA) see London
Intergovernmental Commission (IGC) 213
International Monetary Fund (IMF) 29, 59, 64
Islington, London borough of 96, 171–2, 268

Jenkin, Patrick 94
Joseph, Keith 16

Kent 133, 248
Keynesianism 28–9, 50, 59–60
Kilbrandon Commission (1969) 230, 239, 244
Kingston-upon-Hull 12, 113, 136–8
Kinnock, Neil 239
Kirklees 153, 200

Labour Party 1–6, 19, 27–8, 59, 63–72, 94–103, 108–12, 116–18, 123, 129, 138, 142–3, 147–61, 163, 172, 180, 182, 188, 197–201, 228–69, 271–4
Lambeth, London Borough of 87, 92, 95–6
Lamont, Norman 129–30
Lansbury, George 27
large-scale voluntary transfer 69–70
Lawson, Nigel 102
Layfield Committee 88–90, 99–100, 257–8
Leeds 153, 159, 199
Liberal Party/Liberal Democrats 28, 97, 112, 116, 141, 147–61, 171, 233–5, 261
Liverpool 10, 21, 67–8, 94–6, 123, 140–2, 152, 156, 161, 199, 216, 260–1
Liverpool City Council 123, 140–2, 152, 156
Liverpool Vision 142
Livingstone, Ken 1, 67, 92, 100, 108–11, 264

see also London: Greater London Council
Local Agenda 21 5, 184, 190–202, 271–2
local autonomy 35, 37, 55–6, 62–3, 75–6, 89–90, 93, 123, 151, 182, 268–9, 273
Local Challenge 269
local councillors 26–8, 118–19, 259
  independents 26–8
  role of 163
local democracy 10–11, 252–3, 262–5, 267
Local Democracy Network 12, 262
local education authorities (LEAs) 174, 253
local environmental policy 54, 79, 183–91, 194, 202, 207–8, 254–5
local governance 31–6, 41–54, 116–21, 137
  definition of 117
  and Local Agenda 21 197–8
local government
  effectiveness 11–12
  financing of 85–105, 209–11, 216–24 256–9
  internal culture of 199–200
  internal organization 4, 162–82
  and lobbying 211–13
  and local participation 262–3
  national organization 156–7
  and networking 213–16
  origins of 12–24
  structure and shape of 24–6, 106–21
  two-tier system 18–23, 25, 73, 111–14
  and the voluntary sector 35, 117, 120, 271
  and voting reform 263
Local Government Act
  (1888) 13
  (1889) 14
  (1894) 14
  (1972) 19, 166–8
  (1986) 68
  (1987) 69

  (1988) 124–6, 173–5
  (1992) 73, 124
Local Government Association (LGA) 143, 180, 195, 199, 255, 257, 261–2, 266–9
Local Government (Best Value and Capping) Bill (1998) 256–7
Local Government Bill (1999) 254
Local Government Boundary Commission 15
Local Government Commission (LGC)
  (1958) 17
  (1992–1996) 4, 14–15, 21, 106, 111–15, 120–1, 170, 250
Local Government (Contracts) Act 130–1
Local Government Finance Act
  (1981) 66
  (1982) 93
  (1988) 70–2
Local Government Management Board (LGMB) 12, 126–9, 135, 174, 176–82, 189, 192–6, 206–7, 262, 266
Local Government, Planning and Land Act (1980) 65, 92, 124–5
Local Government Review 177–9, 192
local management of schools 69, 70
local socialism 27, 62, 92–5, 108
London 5, 14, 16–18, 21, 48, 70, 92, 96–7, 104, 119, 127, 130, 138, 149–51, 157, 206–7, 236
Association of London Authorities (ALA) 156–7
Association of London Government (ALG) 157
City of London Corporation 17
East London Partnership 137
Greater London Authority (GLA) 160, 245–6, 260, 263–5
Greater London Council (GLC) 1–4, 17–18, 19, 22–5, 61, 67–8, 92, 95, 100, 106–13, 120, 157, 255, 264

Inner London Education Authority
(ILEA) 17, 69, 95, 110
and Local Agenda 21 198–9
London Boroughs Association
(LBA) 156–7
London County Council (LCC) 14,
17, 25–7, 110
London Fire and Civil Defence
Authority (LFCDA) 110, 119
London Government Act (1963)
17
London Regional Transport (LRT)
119

Maastricht Treaty 233
McIntosh Commission 250, 255, 261
Macrory Report (1970) 23–4
Major, John 2, 63, 73–5, 86, 104–5,
111, 158–9, 231, 237, 252, 266
Mallaby Commission (1967) 166–9
Manchester 21, 67, 96, 132, 199,
216, 248
Marxism 31, 39–41
Maud Commission (1967) 166–9
Merseyside 19, 138, 210, 221
Business Opportunities on
Merseyside (BOOM) 137, 141
Metropolitan County Councils 19,
25, 95, 108–11, 127, 255
Middlesbrough 180, 199
Militant Tendency 67, 140–2
Milton Keynes 12, 199, 258–9
MISC 79 67
monetarism 29, 57–60, 90–1
Municipal Corporations Act (1835)
13, 27, 165

National Health Service (NHS) 16,
22, 27–8, 90–1, 135, 235
National Lottery 211
National Non-Domestic Rate
(NNDR) 88, 97, 101, 104, 160,
257–8
New Commitment to Regeneration
79, 143, 199–200
New Haven 34, 37
new urban left 100, 169

non-elected local government 118–
21
Northern Development Company
(NDC) 139
Northern Ireland 23–4, 210, 228–9,
236
and devolution 243, 250
Norwich 133, 199
Nottingham 113, 132, 136

Oxfordshire 194–5, 198

Patten, Chris 102
Paterson Comission (1973) 166–9
Plaid Cymru 148, 151, 239–42, 261
pluralism 31, 36–8, 273
POLIS 216
poll tax 3–4, 70–3, 85–6, 97–105,
111–14, 229, 271
post-war consensus 28–9
power-dependence model 31, 43–5,
53, 121, 273
Prescott, John 1, 256–7
Private Finance Initiative (PFI) 4, 74,
123–4, 129–34, 234–5, 271
private sector 35, 117, 120, 122–43,
267–9, 271
Project Review Group (PRG) 131
property tax 100
proportional representation 160
Public Health Act (1875) 188
public–private partnerships 4, 117,
131, 135–9, 271
Public Works Loan Board 88

quangos 118–20, 238–9, 250
Quartiers en Crise 215–16

rate capping 67–8, 94–6, 256, 268
Rates Act (1984) 67–8, 92–6
Redcliffe-Maud Commission (1969)
19–22, 25–6, 162, 166–9, 244,
249
regime theory 31, 46–9, 53, 143
regional chambers 246–7
regional development agencies 139,
245–9

regional government 227–50
regionalism, English 243–51
  and local government 249–50
  and regional identity 247–9
regulation theory 31, 49–53
revenue support grant 88, 97
Ridley, Nicholas 163, 173–5, 272
Rivers and Pollution Prevention Act
  (1876) 188

Scotland 5, 14, 22–3, 25, 71,
  97–102, 111–12, 115–18, 126,
  148–50, 156, 160, 168, 210,
  227–9, 255
  Convention of Scottish Local
  Authorities (CoSLA) 156–7, 213
  and devolution 228–39
  and the West Lothian question
  236–7
  see also Scottish Parliament
Scotland Act (1978) 230–2
Scottish National Party (SNP) 148
Scottish Parliament 232–9, 250–1,
  254
  issues arising from 235–6
  powers of 234
  role of the Secretary of State 238
Senior, Derek 21
service delivery and provision 11, 52,
  79, 107, 116–20, 122–9, 163,
  178–81, 265–8, 272–3
Sheffield 67, 96, 134, 151, 153, 156,
  161, 199
Single European Act (1986) 190
Single Programming Documents
  (SPDs) 221–2
single regeneration budget (SRB)
  74–5, 78, 86
single transferrable vote 159–60
Smith, John 232
Southampton 180, 216
South Yorkshire 19, 210
Spain 227–8, 254, 260
standard spending assessments (SSAs)
  71–3, 97
Stewart, John 176, 178

Stormont 24, 228–9
strategic management 174, 176–82
sub-regional partnerships 79
subsidiarity 3, 11, 216–17
sustainable development 183–
  202
Sweden 185–6

Thatcher, Margaret 2, 55–76, 85–6,
  90–1, 98–105, 108–11, 182,
  252, 258, 266
Thatcherism 52, 55–72, 79–81
Tower Hamlets, London Borough of
  171–2
Town and County Planning Act
  (1947) 66
Training and Enterprise Councils
  (TECS) 119, 122, 135

ultra vires 9, 79, 130
unitary authorities 20–1, 25, 112–15,
  170, 180–1
United Nations 183–7, 190–3,
  200
United Nations Conference on
  Environment and Development
  (UNCED) 185, 191
urban development corporations
  (UDCs) 65–6, 118–19, 122,
  137–8

Waldegrave, William 101
Wales 5, 19, 22, 71, 99, 111–12,
  115–16, 118, 148–51, 160, 210,
  227–9
  and devolution 228–9, 239–43
  see also Welsh Assembly
Wales Act (1978) 239
Wandsworth, London Borough of
  128, 175
Water Act (1973) 22, 26
welfare state 3, 10, 14, 28–9, 41, 50,
  58–60, 165, 270
Welsh Assembly 239–243, 250–1,
  254
  issues arising from 241–2

and local government 243
powers of 240–1
role of Secretary of State 242–3
Westminster, London Borough of 128, 132–3

Wheatley Commission (1969) 22, 166–9
Whitelaw, William 67
Widdicombe Report (1986) 10, 27
Wilson, Harold 151, 230
Wiltshire 134, 248–9